the family handyman

BEST
TIPS
& PROJECTS
2018

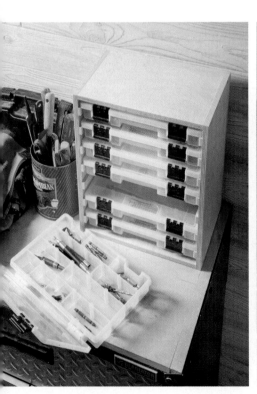

the family handyman

BEST TIPS & PROJECTS 2018

by The Editors of *The Family Handyman* magazine

THE FAMILY HANDYMAN BEST TIPS & PROJECTS 2018
(See page 288 for complete staff listing.)
Editor-in-Chief: Gary Wentz
Project Editor: Mary Flanagan
Contributing Designers: Mariah Cates
Contributing Copy Editors: Donna Bierbach, Peggy Parker
Indexing: Lisa Himes

Vice President, Group Publisher: Russell S. Ellis

Trusted Media Brands, Inc.
President & Chief Executive Officer: Bonnie Kintzer

Warning: *All do-it-yourself activities involve a degree of risk. Skills, materials, tools, and site conditions vary widely. Although the editors have made every effort to ensure accuracy, the reader remains responsible for the selection and use of tools, materials, and methods. Always obey local codes and laws, follow manufacturer's operating instructions, and observe safety precautions.*

ISBN 978-1-62145-397-0

Address any comments about *The Family Handyman Best Tips & Projects 2018* to:
Editor, Best Tips & Projects 2018
2915 Commers Drive, Suite 700
Eagan, MN 55121

To order additional copies of *The Family Handyman Best Tips & Projects 2018,* call 1-800-344-2560.

For more Trusted Media Brands products and information, visit our Web site at tmbi.com.
For more about *The Family Handyman* magazine, visit familyhandyman.com.

Printed in the United States of America.
1 3 5 7 9 10 8 6 4 2

SAFETY FIRST–ALWAYS!

Tackling home improvement projects and repairs can be endlessly rewarding. But as most of us know, with the rewards come risks. DIYers use chain saws, climb ladders and tear into walls that can contain big and hazardous surprises.

The good news is, armed with the right knowledge, tools and procedures, homeowners can minimize risk. As you go about your projects and repairs, stay alert for these hazards:

Aluminum wiring

Aluminum wiring, installed in about 7 million homes between 1965 and 1973, requires special techniques and materials to make safe connections. This wiring is dull gray, not the dull orange characteristic of copper. Hire a licensed electrician certified to work with it. For more information go to cpsc.gov and search for "aluminum wiring."

Spontaneous combustion

Rags saturated with oil finishes like Danish oil and linseed oil, and oil-based paints and stains can spontaneously combust if left bunched up. Always dry them outdoors, spread out loosely. When the oil has thoroughly dried, you can safely throw them in the trash.

Vision and hearing protection

Safety glasses or goggles should be worn whenever you're working on DIY projects that involve chemicals, dust and anything that could shatter or chip off and hit your eye. Sounds louder than 80 decibels (dB) are considered potentially dangerous. Sound levels from a lawn mower can be 90 dB, and shop tools and chain saws can be 90 to 100 dB.

Lead paint

If your home was built before 1979, it may contain lead paint, which is a serious health hazard, especially for children six and under. Take precautions when you scrape or remove it. Contact your public health department for detailed safety information or call (800) 424-LEAD (5323) to receive an information pamphlet. Or visit epa.gov/lead.

Buried utilities

A few days before you dig in your yard, have your underground water, gas and electrical lines marked. Just call 811 or go to call811.com.

Smoke and carbon monoxide (CO) alarms

The risk of dying in reported home structure fires is cut in half in homes with working smoke alarms. Test your smoke alarms every month, replace batteries as necessary and replace units that are more than 10 years old. As you make your home more energy-efficient and airtight, existing ducts and chimneys can't always successfully vent combustion gases, including potentially deadly carbon monoxide (CO). Install a UL-listed CO detector, and test your CO and smoke alarms at the same time.

Five-gallon buckets and window covering cords

Anywhere from 10 to 40 children a year drown in 5-gallon buckets, according to the U.S. Consumer Products Safety Commission. Always store them upside down and store ones containing liquid with the covers securely snapped.

According to Parents for Window Blind Safety, 599 children have been seriously injured or killed in the United States since 1986 after becoming entangled in looped window treatment cords. For more information, visit pfwbs.org or cpsc.gov.

Working up high

If you have to get up on your roof to do a repair or installation, always install roof brackets and wear a roof harness.

Asbestos

Texture sprayed on ceilings before 1978, adhesives and tiles for vinyl and asphalt floors before 1980, and vermiculite insulation (with gray granules) all may contain asbestos. Other building materials, made between 1940 and 1980, could also contain asbestos. If you suspect that materials you're removing or working around contain asbestos, contact your health department or visit epa.gov/asbestos for information.

For additional information about home safety, visit mysafehome.org. This site offers helpful information about dozens of home safety issues.

Contents

1 INTERIOR PROJECTS, REPAIRS & REMODELING

Home Care & Repair 10
Finishing Trim 17
Rustic Barn Door 21
Master the Art of Subway Tile 28
Under-Cabinet Drawer 35
Choosing Drywall &
    Taping Materials 39
DIY Radon Reduction 44
The Simplest Cure for
    Wet Basements 50

Success with Melamine 53
Handy Hints 58
All About Euro Hinges 63
Textured Ceilings 69
Avoid Framing Mistakes 77
Working with
    Self-Leveling Underlayment 82
Great Goofs 87

Special Section: PAINT LIKE A PRO 88

2 ELECTRICAL & HIGH-TECH

Home Care & Repair 100
Protect Against Electrical Surges 107
Bluetooth Wireless Speakers 110

Avoid Freeze-Up Disaster 112
Super-Easy USB Outlet 114
Great Goofs 117

Special Section: SECRET HIDING PLACES 118

3 PLUMBING, HVAC & APPLIANCES

Home Care & Repair 130
Handy Hints 138
Great Goofs 139

Special Section: 10 CLEVER TOOL HACKS 140

WOODWORKING & WORKSHOP PROJECTS & TIPS

Wood 101 146
Simple Timber Bench......................... 152
Perfect Patio Chairs 158
Foolproof Dadoes & Rabbets 164
Custom Picture Ledges 168

Super-Capacity Tool Cart................... 173
How To Buy Rough-Sawn Lumber ... 180
Hot Glue–A Wood Shop Staple! 185
Ultimate Workshop Storage.............. 189
Handy Hints... 196

Special Section: QUICK & SIMPLE GIFT PROJECTS...................................... 198

EXTERIOR REPAIRS & IMPROVEMENTS

Home Care & Repair 210
Build a Long-Lasting
    Retaining Wall 213
Better Than Wood!............................. 218

5 Solutions for a Shabby Deck.......... 223
Working with Bagged Concrete 228
Pour a Perfect Slab............................. 232
Handy Hints... 237

Special Section: STORAGE HODGEPODGE... 238

OUTDOOR STRUCTURES, LANDSCAPING & GARDENING

Home Care & Repair 246
Fabulous Fire Table............................ 248
Double-Duty Pub Shed...................... 257

Patio Planter....................................... 266
Handy Hints... 272

Special Section: DREAM GARAGE STORAGE... 274

Index 284

Acknowledgments... 288

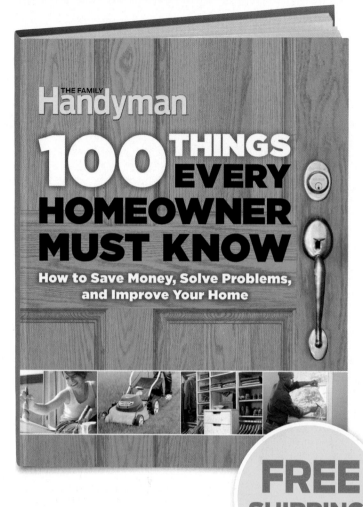

1 Interior Projects, Repairs & Remodeling

IN THIS CHAPTER

Home Care & Repair **10**
   *Adjust a sticking patio door, get rid
   of carpenter ants and more*

Finishing Trim **17**

Rustic Barn Door **21**

Master of the Art of Subway Tile **28**

Under-Cabinet Drawer **35**

Choosing Drywall & Taping Materials......**39**

DIY Radon Reduction **44**

The Simplest Cure for Wet Basements....**50**

Success with Melamine............................**53**

Handy Hints **58**
   Tape-tearing tip and more

All About Euro Hinges **63**

Textured Ceilings......................................**69**

Avoid Framing Mistakes..........................**77**

**Working with
   Self-Leveling Underlayment** **82**

Great Goofs..**87**
   Ask before you borrow

ADJUST A **STICKING** **PATIO SCREEN DOOR**

5 MINUTE FIX

ADJUSTMENT SCREW

ADJUSTMENT SCREW

DOOR FRAME

ROLLER   TRACK

Badly aligned rollers inside the bottom of a patio screen door will cause the door to bind or stick when opening or closing. This stresses the corners of the door, and if the corner joints become loose, the door will eventually fall apart. But you can adjust the door to glide smoothly with just a screwdriver. You'll find two adjustment screws at the bottom of the door, one at each end, that raise or lower separate rollers. Adjust them as shown here.

1 Lower the door. Turn the adjustment screw counter-clockwise and lower the door until it rests on the track. Do the same at the other end of the door.

2 Then raise it. Raise one roller until it lifts the door about 1/4 in. off the track. Slowly raise the other roller until there's an even gap between the door and the track.

GOT CARPENTER ANTS?

Carpenter ants can damage your home, but they can also warn you of serious trouble. They're attracted to damp, rotting wood. So if you see them, there's a good chance that moisture is entering your walls or ceilings, causing structural damage that could cost thousands to repair. For some help identifying carpenter ants, see the website listed below.

Find the nest

To get rid of the ants, you have to find the nest. "Worker" carpenter ants are black or red and black. Look for them when they're most active–generally between sunset and midnight during the spring and summer months. Try setting out honey or tuna packed in water to attract them, then follow them back to their nest. Use a flashlight with red Mylar film over the lens (they can't see red light) so you can see them in the dark—you can buy Mylar film at art supply stores. Small piles of coarse sawdust are a sign that an active nest is nearby.

Once you locate the nest, figure out why the wood is getting wet and fix the problem. For more information, go to familyhandyman.com and search for "water leak."

Kill the ants

After you fix the water leak, it's time to fix the ant problem. Spray an aerosol insecticide into the nest. Reduce the risk of future infestations by not leaving food or sweet drinks out in the open, and by keeping pet food in a tightly sealed container. Also trim any bushes or tree branches that contact the house, and never store firewood against the building. Call an exterminator if none of these strategies work.

The University of Minnesota Extension has lots more great information about carpenter ants at extension. umn.edu/garden/insects/find/ carpenter-ants/

MYLAR

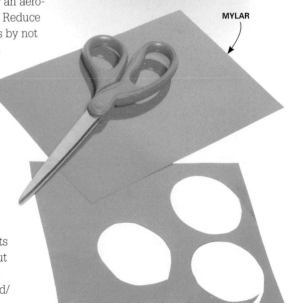

HomeCare&Repair

REPLACE BASEBOARD HEATER COVERS

Got old, rusty "hydronic" (hot water heat) baseboards? You could replace them in their entirety, but that's expensive and time consuming. You could also sand and paint them, but that's a lot of work.

The easiest option is to replace just the front covers and end caps with aftermarket ones made of plastic or metal, which are available at home centers and online. Supplyhouse.com (formerly pexsupply.com) sells several styles of replacement covers, called "baseboarders," for about $16 to $27 per foot. End caps cost about $16 to $28 apiece. The company's website has easy-to-follow installation videos.

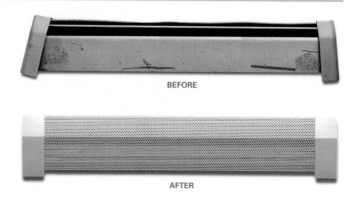

BEFORE

AFTER

SCREW EXTRACTOR

Backing out a screw with a stripped head can be tough. That's why it's a good idea to keep a set of different-size screw extractors on hand. The one shown here is made by Grabit. You just chuck the appropriate-size extractor in your drill, burnish the screw head, flip the extractor end for end and then back out the screw. You'll wonder how you ever got along without them!

DON'T LIVE WITH A BROKEN DEAD BOLT

A dead bolt is the key component of door security. The doorknob latch is no substitute. So if your dead bolt no longer works, replace it now. It's a surprisingly easy job. Just remove two screws in the thumb latch, then remove two screws to remove the plate and bolt. Install the new dead bolt the same way. Try to find a new dead bolt with a bolt plate of the same size. Otherwise, you'll have to either enlarge the recess in the door or live with an ugly gap around the plate.

BOLT

THUMB LATCH

BOLT PLATE

A WOODEN BASEMENT?
ARE YOU KIDDING ME?

A reader wrote us asking about using pressure-treated wood instead of concrete for a basement or crawl space. Senior Editor Travis Larson built homes with wood foundations for many years and had this to say:

"I live in a house that I built 35 years ago with a wood foundation and in my days as a contractor have built dozens of them for customers, and I've never heard a single complaint. They're fast and easy to build, energy efficient and easy to finish, and adding windows or doors is a snap. There is no downside. In fact, it has always puzzled me that wood foundations aren't the choice for all new homes." You'll find lots more information about wood foundations online at southernpine.com/applications/permanent-wood-foundations/

ANGLE BRACKET

JOIST HANGER

12" TREATED BACKFILL BOARD

2x8 FOUNDATION-GRADE TREATED STUDS AT 16" O.C.

5/8" FOUNDATION-GRADE PLYWOOD

WATERPROOFING MEMBRANE

1/2" GRAVEL DRAINAGE FILL

CONCRETE FLOOR

RIGID FOAM INSULATION

2x10 FOOTING PLATE

GRAVEL FOOTING

8"

20"

SUMP PUMP

SUMP BASKET

Sheathing fastened with 8d stainless steel nails; framing with double-dipped 16d nails

SAVE MONEY WITH MDF TRIM

Whether you're making your own trim or buying off the shelf, medium-density fiberboard (MDF) is a great choice for painted interior trim. MDF is basically sawdust and glue compressed into sheets. Less expensive than solid wood, it's also more stable, and it cuts and shapes beautifully with carbide-tipped saw blades and router bits. In fact, with just a few different types of router bits, you can make miles of interior trim and moldings for about one-fifth the price of store-bought moldings made from real wood.

MDF is dusty stuff, though, so wear a dust mask when working with it. You can also buy preprimed moldings made from MDF in dozens of profiles. The main downside to MDF is that water destroys it, so avoid using it outdoors or in damp locations inside the house (like for base trim in a mudroom). Also, don't use it for window stools if your windows sweat a lot because of condensation.

CHIRPING SMOKE DETECTORS

Ever been driven crazy in the middle of the night by a chirping smoke detector? One of your detectors has a dying battery, but determining which detector is chirping is surprisingly tough.

Instead of trying to figure out which smoke detector has the dying battery, just replace the batteries in all the smoke detectors at the same time to eliminate the guesswork. Also be sure to replace any smoke detectors that are older than 10 years because they're no longer reliable.

If there's no manufacture date on any of your smoke detectors, just replace them to be safe. Some newer ones have 10-year batteries in them that you never have to replace; you just replace the smoke detector.

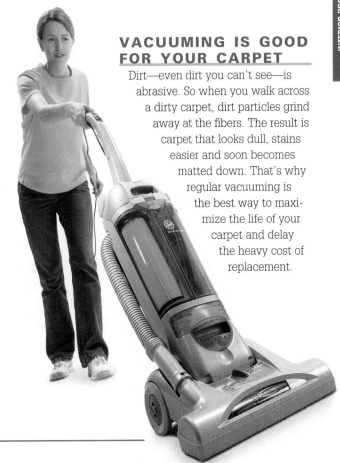

VACUUMING IS GOOD FOR YOUR CARPET

Dirt—even dirt you can't see—is abrasive. So when you walk across a dirty carpet, dirt particles grind away at the fibers. The result is carpet that looks dull, stains easier and soon becomes matted down. That's why regular vacuuming is the best way to maximize the life of your carpet and delay the heavy cost of replacement.

ADJUST A SELF-CLOSING SPRING HINGE

If the self-closing door to your garage isn't closing hard enough to latch properly or the door slams shut, you can adjust the spring tension with a hex wrench and pliers. Start by removing the locking pin (**Photo 1**). Then add or release tension until you get the proper close rate (**Photo 2**).

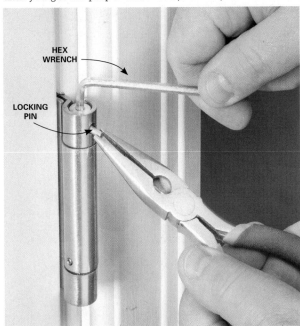

1 Remove the locking pin. Place the hex wrench into the socket at the top of the hinge and turn in either direction to release tension on the pin. Remove the pin with pliers.

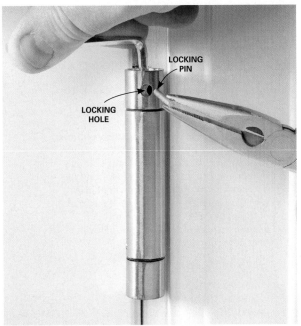

2 Tighten or loosen in small steps. Rotate the wrench until the next hole comes into view and install the pin. Test the door close rate. Repeat until the door closes and latches without slamming.

HOW TO DRIVE DRYWALL SCREWS
LIKE A PRO

These tools make it easy to do the job right

1 Self-feeding drywall screw gun. If you're covering an entire garage or basement in drywall, it's worth getting a self-feeding drywall screw gun. The screws are collated, and the driver presents a screw every time you need one. The least expensive models are corded. **($100 to $200)**

2 Corded drywall screw gun. Pros have been using these for decades. They're very fast, setting screws almost instantly, but since you have to load the screws one at a time by hand, it takes a lot of practice to get proficient. **($50 to $100)**

3 Adapter for cordless drywall screw gun. If you have only a few sheets of drywall to hang, you'll be fine using your cordless drill/driver. But do yourself a favor and buy a drywall screw adapter. It automatically sets the screw head just below the surface of the paper without breaking through, leaving a small dimple that you fill with joint compound. **($5 to $10)**

The Basics:
The key to driving drywall screws is to set the screw heads slightly below the surface of the drywall without breaking the paper facing.

FINISHING TRIM

Get a pro-quality finish with these expert tips

by **Mark Petersen,**
Senior Editor

A beautiful finish is all about proper preparation, a suitable workspace and the right products. We asked Gary Hakkinen, a painting veteran of 40-plus years, to show us his best practices for perfection. Here are a few of his favorite staining, sanding and finishing tips to help you create rich silky-smooth trim.

MEET AN EXPERT

Gary Hakkinen is the sole proprietor of Empire Painting in Lake Elmo, Minnesota. He's been painting, staining and varnishing residential homes and commercial buildings for more than 40 years.

Sand wood for even finishes

The trim you bought may look perfect, but it likely has imperfections from machining that won't show up until you stain it. Sand every contour and flat area in the direction of the grain with a combination of medium-grit sanding sponges and pads. When necessary, fold 120-grit paper to get into a tight crack.

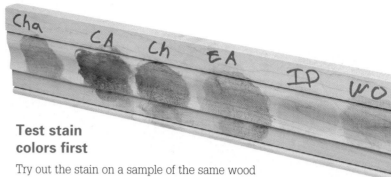

Test stain colors first

Try out the stain on a sample of the same wood you plan to finish. You can create your own custom color by mixing two or three stains (of the same type) together. If you go this route, it's important to mix up a batch big enough to finish all the wood. The odds of achieving identical results on the second batch are slim. Keep a little extra on hand for touch-ups and repairs.

Dry-brush crevices

Stain will pool in cracks. Use a dry paintbrush to remove it from each piece after it's been completely wiped. Wipe brush on a clean rag or brush it on newspaper to clean off the stain between strokes.

Stain one piece at a time

Saturate the wood with a liberal coat of stain using a natural-bristle brush. Wipe off stain with clean cotton rags in the same order you put it on. That will enable the stain to soak into all areas of the wood for about the same amount of time. Wipe with light, even pressure. Refold the wiping rags frequently so you have a dry cloth for most strokes, and grab a new rag whenever one gets soaked. Work on one piece of trim at a time to keep the stain from drying before wiping.

Apply sanding sealer first

Sanding sealer is the perfect foundation for the clear coat. It's formulated to dry quickly and has more solids than conventional clear coats, making it very easy to sand. And varnish adheres better to a well-sanded, sealed surface. Pick a sealer that's designed for the overlying finish, preferably the same brand. After the sanding sealer dries, sand it with fine-grit sandpaper and sanding sponges. Remove dust with a tack cloth.

Long strokes = a smooth finish

If you can, arrange your trim boards in such a way that after you brush on the desired amount of finish, you can make your last couple strokes in one continuous pass. That will ensure no overlap marks. If you do end up with imperfections after the finish dries, sand them out when you sand before the next coat.

Clean the room

If possible, do your sanding and finishing in different rooms. All that sanding dust will affect the clear coats. If you have to sand and finish in the same area, do whatever you can to clean the room before applying the sanding sealer and clear coat. If you're in a garage, open the overhead door and use a leaf blower to blow dust outside. Use a shop vacuum on the floor, and damp-mop it so your feet don't stir up dust.

Don't skimp on the brush

Buy a 2-in. or 2-1/2-in. brush, and don't spend less than $10. If you take care of it and clean it well, a top-quality brush will last a long time. A cheap brush is more likely to leave brush marks and shed bristles that could get stuck in the finish. China (natural) bristle brushes are the choice for oil-based products; synthetic for water-based.

Oil vs. water-based topcoats

Oil-based finishes are a little more durable than water-based, but the difference isn't nearly as great as it was 10 years ago. Oil will yellow unstained wood more than water-based products will, which can be good or bad depending on the look you're after. Yellowing isn't an issue with stained wood. Water-based products dry faster, which helps keep dust from settling into the finish, but fast drying may be a disadvantage for slower, meticulous workers. Cleanup is easier with water-based products, and the odor isn't nearly as strong.

Dispose of the rags

Rags soaked with oil-based products can spontaneously combust and burn down your house. Spread out stain-soaked rags away from other combustible items, and let them dry before disposing of them.

Polyurethane vs. varnish

What's the difference between polyurethane and varnish? The quick-and-dirty answer: Varnish contains a resin and a solvent (oil or water). Once varnish is applied to wood, the solvent evaporates and the protective resin is left behind. Varnish can contain one of a few different resins, and polyurethane is one of them. Varnish that contains polyurethane just goes by the name polyurethane. The upside to polyurethane is that it's tougher (like a plastic coating) than the other varnishes. The downside is that it can appear cloudy when it's applied too thick, and it's harder to sand between coats.

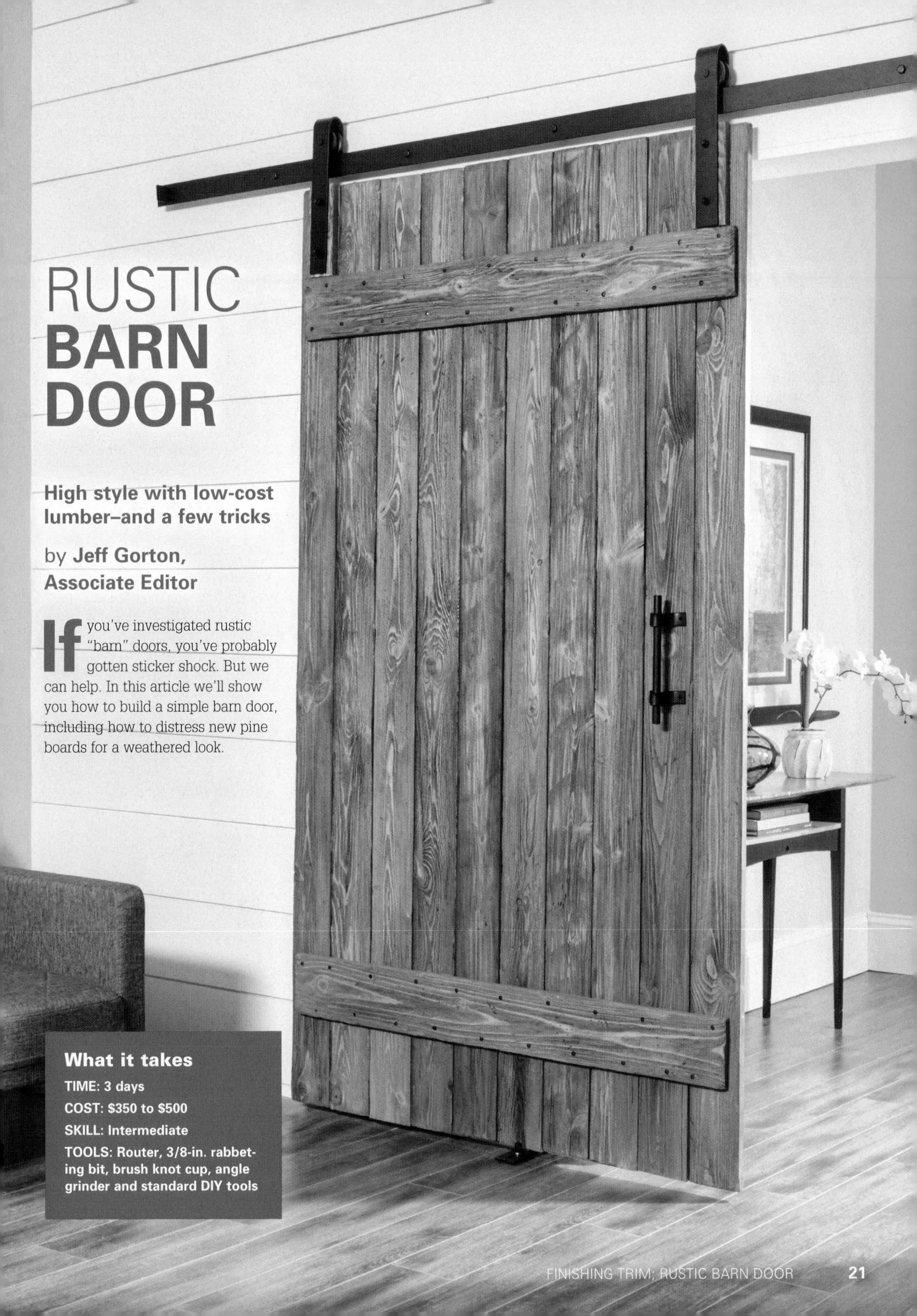

RUSTIC **BARN DOOR**

High style with low-cost lumber–and a few tricks

by **Jeff Gorton, Associate Editor**

If you've investigated rustic "barn" doors, you've probably gotten sticker shock. But we can help. In this article we'll show you how to build a simple barn door, including how to distress new pine boards for a weathered look.

What it takes

TIME: 3 days

COST: $350 to $500

SKILL: Intermediate

TOOLS: Router, 3/8-in. rabbeting bit, brush knot cup, angle grinder and standard DIY tools

BEFORE:
STANDARD
PINE BOARD

AFTER:
HOMEMADE
BARN WOOD

Fooled by a forgery

I've harvested loads of lumber from abandoned farmsteads. But Jeff's fake barn wood fooled me. I really thought it was genuine until I took a close look. Even then, I was impressed with the quality of the counterfeit. And in some ways, fake barn wood is better than the real thing: There are no rotten, splintered boards, lead paint or musty odors filling the air. In fact, Jeff's forgery made me wonder: Was collecting real barn wood—with all the sweat and splinters—a waste of my time?

To see how Jeff got a great look with standard home-center lumber, check out photos 2-6, starting on p. 23.

–Gary Wentz, Editor-in-Chief

THREE SLIDING OPTIONS

Before you start shopping for hardware, take a careful look at the area where you would like to install the door and figure out what door setup works best. If you want to cover the opening with one door, you'll need an area on one side of the opening that's wide enough for the door. Make sure there aren't any obstructions like light switches, sconce lights or heat registers that would be covered by or interfere with the door. If there's not enough wall space on one side of the opening, you can install a pair of doors that slide to opposite sides, or buy special bypass hardware that allows the doors to stack.

Single door. This is the most popular choice, but you'll need enough wall space. Order a track that's at least twice as wide as the door.

Double doors. If you don't have the wall space on one side of the opening for a single large door, you can use two doors instead. Centering the track on the opening will allow the doors to slide to the sides of the opening.

Bypass doors. If you want to install barn doors on a closet opening, or on an opening that goes wall to wall, you can order bypass hardware that allows you to stack the doors on one side of the opening.

1 Make shiplap boards. Mount a 3/8-in. rabbeting bit in your router and set the cutting depth to 3/8 in. Cut rabbets on two scraps and check the fit. Adjust the depth until the rabbeted joint is flush. Then cut rabbets on the door boards. After rabbeting one edge of a board, remember to flip it over before rabbeting the other edge.

RABBETING BIT

2 Distress the boards with a grinder. Mount a knot cup wheel in a grinder. Put on safety gear, including goggles. Nail a board to sawhorses and use the edge of the wire cup to grind out soft wood and create a weathered texture.

KNOT CUP WHEEL

3 Make wormholes. Create "wormholes" using an awl. To make an oblong hole, tip the awl after punching it in.

Time, tools and materials

The 1x6 No. 2 pine boards we used for this door are inexpensive, so be sure to buy several extras so you can experiment with the distressing and staining techniques before you start on the boards you'll use. Preparing the boards is the most time-consuming part of this project. Expect to spend several hours cutting the rabbets on the edges of the 1x6s. We used a router with a rabbeting bit to cut the rabbets; a table saw with a dado blade set would be quicker.

The grinder and knot cup brush we used make quick work of the initial distressing. It took me about 10 minutes per board. If you don't own a grinder, you can buy one for about $30 to $150. A cheap one will work fine for this project. You could also use a knot cup wire brush mounted in a corded drill, but it would take you longer to achieve the same results.

Staining goes quickly, but set aside a day or two to get the parts cut and finished. Barn door hardware ranges in price from about $250 to $500 depending on the size and style. Some companies have ready-to-ship options, but you should plan ahead if you need something else since it usually requires longer to get in the mail.

Measure the opening

Whether you're building a door or ordering one, here's what you need to know about door size. Sliding doors should extend at least an inch beyond the sides of openings that don't have trim, or an inch beyond the moldings of openings with trim. You can add more overlap for extra privacy.

Choose your hardware before determining the door height. Then check the measuring instructions or ask the manufacturer for help arriving at the door height. In most cases, measuring to the top of an opening with no trim, or to the top of the trim, and subtracting 1/2 in. from your measurement will give you the minimum door height required.

Finally, you have to make sure you allow enough clearance above the opening to lift the door onto the track. This distance varies depending on your hardware, so again, check with the manufacturer.

Three ways to support the track

To support a door, the track needs to be solidly mounted to wall framing. There are three good options. First, you could install continuous wood

BUNDLED RAG

5 Add dark stain. Dab dark stain over the board with a rag in a random pattern. Then spread out the dabs of stain to create dark areas and streaks. Finally, wipe off the excess dark stain with a different rag.

MINI ROLLER

4 Apply a base coat of stain. Roll or brush an even coat of light-colored stain over each board. Wipe off the excess stain with a rag.

6 Finish with gray stain. Wipe on the topcoat of gray stain with a rag. Apply an uneven coat of stain, letting some of the previous layers show through. Wipe off the excess gray stain with a rag. Let the boards dry overnight.

backing between the wall studs at the track height. This allows you the freedom to install track-mounting screws at any location. But this method isn't practical in a room that's finished because you would have to remove the drywall or plaster to install the blocking.

The second option is to mount a header board to the wall surface, making sure it's securely screwed to the studs, and screw the track to the header board. One manufacturer recommends a maximum door weight of 75 lbs. if you're using this method

HEADER BOARD

because the support screws will only be engaged in 3/4-in.-thick wood.

The third option is to bolt the track directly to the studs. You have to do two things if you choose this method. First, make sure to order an undrilled track. You'll need to drill holes yourself at the stud locations. And second, ask the supplier to recommend hardware to avoid crushing the drywall. Most suppliers have crush plates or something similar to solve the problem.

Get the right spacers and floor guides

Included in the track mounting hardware will be some sort of spacers or stand-offs

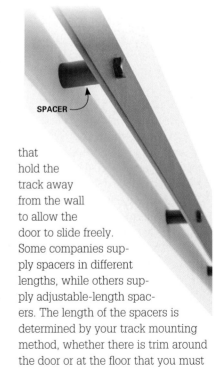

SPACER

that hold the track away from the wall to allow the door to slide freely. Some companies supply spacers in different lengths, while others supply adjustable-length spacers. The length of the spacers is determined by your track mounting method, whether there is trim around the door or at the floor that you must

PENNY SPACERS

WOOD SCRAP

7 **Square the vertical slats.** Arrange the slats on 2x4s and space them with pennies. Align the ends and screw wood scraps to the 2x4s to hold the boards in place. Then line up the ends and check the door for square by making sure the diagonal measurements are equal.

clear, and the thickness of your door. Be sure to double-check with the supplier before placing your order to make sure you're getting the correct length spacers for your situation.

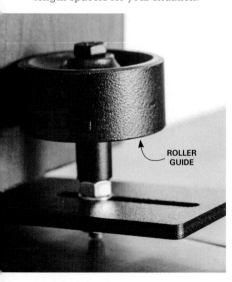

ROLLER GUIDE

You'll also need a guide at the floor to prevent the bottom of the door from swinging. The simplest guide is an L-shaped metal bracket that mounts to the floor and fits into a groove cut in the bottom of the door. If your door doesn't have a groove in it, there are roller guides and adjustable roller guides that will work. Choose the guide that works best for your door.

Make shiplap boards

We used inexpensive 1x6 No. 2 pine boards, cut rabbets on the edges to make shiplap boards, and distressed and stained them to resemble old barn wood. When you choose boards, don't worry about knots, scratches or gouges. But try to pick boards that are straight and not cupped or warped.

We divided the width of the door by the board width to see how many

boards we would need. And then we adjusted the board width until they

Check out the video!
To see how to shiplap boards on a table saw by going to **tfhmag.com/shiplap**

were all equal. When you're doing the math, remember to account for the shiplap edges.

For our 4-ft.-wide door, we cut each board 5 in. wide. Yours may be different. Cut the boards to the right width and cut rabbets on two edges of all but two boards. Cut one rabbet on two boards that will be used on the outside edges. **Photo 1** (p. 23) shows how we used a 3/8-in. rabbeting bit to cut the rabbets. A table saw with a dado blade will also work.

We also cut the boards to the right length before distressing them so we

8 **Fasten the rails.** Measure and mark for the rails. Ours are 8 in. from the top and bottom of the door. Apply construction adhesive to the back of the rails and place them on the door. Attach the rails with nails. We staggered the nails up and down on each board, but you can use any pattern you like.

WROUGHT-HEAD NAIL

9 **Mark for the hanger holes.** Follow the manufacturer's instructions for mounting the hangers. We're using a 2-1/2-in. spacer to ensure the wheel is the correct distance from the top of the door. Mark the hole locations. Then drill holes and mount the hangers on the door.

HANGER

SPACER

Add layers of stain

To achieve the look you see here, start by applying a base coat of light gold stain to the boards (**Photo 4**). We applied the stain with a mini roller to speed up the process. Wipe off excess stain with a rag. Then use a different rag to apply an uneven coat of dark stain (**Photo 5**). Wipe off excess to expose some of the base coat color. Finally, apply a thin, uneven layer of gray stain, dabbing and wiping to create an aged look (**Photo 6**). It'll look better if the stain is less consistent. Also, don't worry if the finish is different from one board to another. The variation will add an authentic look when the door is assembled. Don't forget to finish the ends and edges of the boards. Let the stain dry overnight before moving on to the door assembly.

Most stain brands have colors that will work well for aging wood. Here are the colors we used:
Base coat: Varathane Summer Oak
Second coat: Varathane Kona
Third coat: Varathane Weathered Gray

Assemble the door

Start by arranging the vertical boards on a pair of 2x4s placed flat on sawhorses or the floor. Arrange the 2x4s so they're lined up under the locations of the horizontal rails. Space the boards top and bottom with pennies. Screw scraps of wood to the 2x4s on both sides of the door to hold the boards together while you add the horizontal rail. After checking to see that the ends of the boards are still lined up, measure diagonally from opposite corners to make sure the door is square (**Photo 7**). If necessary, adjust the position of the boards until the diagonal measurements are equal.

Next mark the height of the rails on the door and attach them with construction adhesive and nails (**Photo 8**). Since the fasteners show, we decided to use 1-1/2-in. wrought-head nails that we bought at rockler. com. Since the nails protruded slightly from the opposite side, we shortened them a bit by holding them with

could make the ends look aged. At the same time, cut the two horizontal rails and the two 3-in.-wide blocks that go under the hangers. Make the horizontal rails 2 in. shorter than your door width.

Grind, scratch and beat the boards

When all the parts are cut, you're ready for the fun part—distressing the boards. **Photo 2** (p. 23) shows how to use a brush knot cup mounted in an angle grinder to abrade the soft wood and expose the grain. This gives the wood a weathered look. Pieces of wire from the cup can break off and cause serious injury if you're not protected, and there's a lot of dust. Make sure to wear safety goggles, hearing protection and a good-quality dust mask.

Start by nailing the board to the sawhorses with finish nails to hold it in place. The nail holes will add to

the rustic appearance. Tip the grinder so the wheel is on edge and parallel to the grain to wear away the soft wood. Use the wire wheel on the edges and ends of the board to create an uneven, worn look. You can also hold the wheel flat on the surface and move it in arcs across the wood to resemble saw marks. Don't worry; you can't go wrong here. Wearing away any amount of wood will look great.

If you want to take your distressing to the next level, use an awl to create "wormholes" (**Photo 3**). You don't have to put holes in every board. Some variety will add authenticity. Drag a screwdriver or other sharp object along the grain to create a fake crack. Use your hammer claw or any other tool or heavy object to create dents and gouges. When you're done distressing the boards, it's time to stain them.

10 **Mount the track.** Measure carefully to determine the track height. Hold the track level and in the correct position and mark the wall at each fastener hole. Drill pilot holes at the marks. Then attach the track to the wall with the fasteners and spacers provided in your hardware kit.

11 **Hang the door.** Set the door on the track. Carefully roll it to each end to determine where to place the stops. Install the stops, bottom guide and any other hardware to complete the project.

locking pliers and grinding off the tips on a bench grinder. You could also mount a metal grinding wheel in your angle grinder. Drill pilot holes for the nails that are near the ends of the rails to avoid splitting the wood. If you don't mind the appearance of screw heads on the opposite side of the door, you could flip the door over and drive 1-1/4-in. screws through the boards into the rails for more strength.

If you prefer, you could brush on a coat of flat polyurethane. Test the finish on a scrap to see if you like it before you apply it to your door. We didn't put a finish on our door.

Install the hangers and mount the track

Follow the instructions included with your door hardware to install the hangers. Our instructions recommended using a 2-1/2-in. spacer between the door and the wheel to hold the hanger in the correct position while marking the bolt locations (**Photo 9**). After marking the bolt locations, drill holes for the bolts and

mount the hangers on the door.

The steps you take to mount the track will depend on your track support. If you've installed continuous backing between the studs or are mounting the track on a header board, then you may be using a predrilled track and can proceed to bolt the track to the wall.

If you're mounting the track over the drywall and bolting it to studs, you'll have to locate and mark the studs, and then transfer the stud locations to the track so you can drill holes for the mounting screws in the right place. Instructions should give a formula for determining the track height. Double-check your dimensions and math before mounting the track (**Photo 10**). You don't want to have to cut down the door or reposition the track if it's in the wrong spot.

With the track mounted to the wall, finish the job by putting the door on the track (**Photo 11**) and mounting the end stops, bottom guides and any other hardware according to your instructions.

MATERIALS LIST
(FOR A 4-FT-WIDE DOOR)

ITEM	QTY.
Barn door hardware kit	1
1x6 x 8' No. 2 pine boards	12
1-1/2" wrought-head nails	40
Knot cup brush for grinder ($20)	1
Tube of construction adhesive	1
Light gold stain	2 qts.
Dark stain	1 qt.
Gray stain	1 qt.
Polyurethane (optional)	1 qt.
Mini roller and cover	1
Rags	
Brush or roller for poly	

Barn door hardware sources:

- artisanhardware.com
- realslidinghardware.com
- barndoorshardware.com
- rustichardware.com

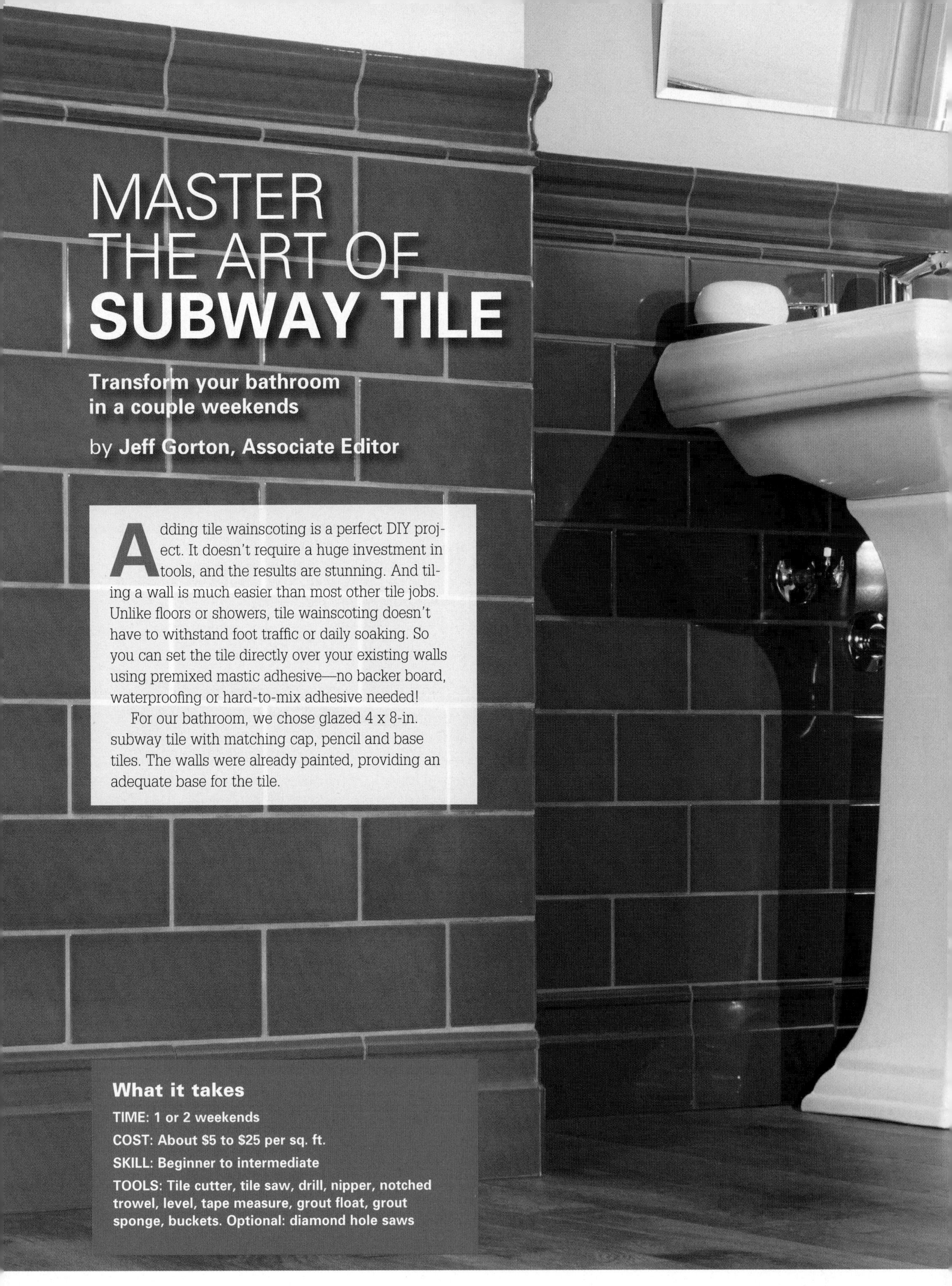

MASTER THE ART OF SUBWAY TILE

Transform your bathroom in a couple weekends

by **Jeff Gorton, Associate Editor**

Adding tile wainscoting is a perfect DIY project. It doesn't require a huge investment in tools, and the results are stunning. And tiling a wall is much easier than most other tile jobs. Unlike floors or showers, tile wainscoting doesn't have to withstand foot traffic or daily soaking. So you can set the tile directly over your existing walls using premixed mastic adhesive—no backer board, waterproofing or hard-to-mix adhesive needed!

For our bathroom, we chose glazed 4 x 8-in. subway tile with matching cap, pencil and base tiles. The walls were already painted, providing an adequate base for the tile.

What it takes

TIME: 1 or 2 weekends

COST: About $5 to $25 per sq. ft.

SKILL: Beginner to intermediate

TOOLS: Tile cutter, tile saw, drill, nipper, notched trowel, level, tape measure, grout float, grout sponge, buckets. Optional: diamond hole saws

Tile: the best bathroom wall
- Water-resistant
- Stunning appearance
- Easy to clean
- Lasts for decades

MEET AN EXPERT

"Subway tile is the same but different," says expert Dean Sorem. "In most ways, it installs just like any wall tile. But because it's set in a brick joint pattern, some steps are a little different and a little trickier." Dean has installed acres of subway tile, and in the following pages, he'll show you how to get it right.

Shop for tile

First, measure your walls and draw a sketch of the room you plan to tile. Take the sketch to a home center or tile shop where the salesperson can help you order the right amount of tile and trim pieces. We chose to add the matching base (skirt), cap (cornice) and a long, thin piece called a "pencil."

We ordered bullnose tile for the outside corner, and special outside corner pieces for the base and cap. The field tile cost us about $6 per sq. ft., and the special trim pieces cost about $10 each. As you shop, you'll discover that not all tile has matching trim pieces. If tile you select doesn't have trim pieces, you may be able to find a trim in a complementary color. Remember to choose a grout (including the color) while you're shopping. We used sanded grout to fill 1/8-in. grout spaces on this tile, but if your grout spaces are narrower, use unsanded grout. Look for polymer-fortified grout that you mix with water.

Getting started

Before doing any tile project, it's important to check that the floor is level and the walls are flat. Use a level and straightedge to see if the floor is level. If it slopes, find the lowest point and mark it. Then hold the straightedge against the walls in the areas you plan to tile. If you find low areas, fill them with setting-type compound to flatten the walls before you start tiling.

Another thing to check at this stage is how your cap tile will look when it butts into your window and door moldings. If the cap protrudes past the moldings, one fix is to add a strip of matching wood, deep enough to hide the end of the cap tile, around the moldings. You can see how we modified our trim on p. 33.

Planning the tile layout is critical to a great-looking tile job. **Photo 1** shows how to get started. Arrange rows of tile and stack all the parts on the floor to determine the exact measurements you'll need to plan the tile layout. Check the height measurement against light switches and outlets on your walls. Add or subtract from the wainscot height to make sure switches and outlets land either above or below it.

SHIFT LAYOUT
TO AVOID SKINNY
TILE HERE

BASE TILE

PENCIL TILE

CAP TILE

1 **Plan the layout.** Arrange rows of tile on the floor, including the spacers. Shift the rows left or right to determine the width of the end spaces and the locations of the plumb lines (see Photo 2). Then stack a column of tile, starting with the base and ending with the cap. Use this mock-up to determine the finished height of your wainscot.

OFFSET THE
TILE BY HALF
OF TILE WIDTH

MASTIC LINE

VERTICAL
STARTING LINE

LEVEL
LEDGER
BOARD

2 **Draw layout lines.** Install ledgers to provide a level support for the first row of tile. Then draw a "stop line" 1/2 in. below the top of the tile to show where to stop spreading mastic. Mark two plumb lines, offset by half the tile width, to create a running bond pattern.

Next, you'll need to draw vertical layout lines for starting the tile. For a running bond (brick joint) pattern like ours, you'll need two vertical lines, half a tile width apart. Start by assuming the first line will be centered on the wall. Then draw a layout for two rows of tile, offsetting the joints by the half tile width. Check to see what size the cut pieces on the ends of the two rows of tile will be. If any of the cuts are skinny, it will look better if you shift the layout a quarter tile width. For our 8-in.-wide tiles, we moved the starting line 2 in. off center, and then drew a second vertical line 4 in. from the first (**Photo 2**). Shifting the layout like this increased the width of the skinny cut by 2 in., creating a better-looking final result.

Go through this same routine on every wall, carefully planning how the end cuts will look. Plan outside corners, taking into account how trim pieces and bullnose tiles line up. If you're unsure, an easy way to do this is to draw each piece full scale on the wall to expose any potential problems.

The easiest and most accurate way to make sure your tile installation is straight and level is to screw a level ledger board to the wall and stack your tile on top. Add the height of the base tile to the width of one grout joint. Then add 1/16 in. to this measurement for a little space under the base tile. Make a mark on the wall at this height, above the lowest point on the floor, and draw a level line around the room from this mark. Align the tops of your straight ledger boards with this line and screw them to the wall. If the floor isn't level, you'll have to trim some of the base tiles to fit (Photo 12).

Install the tile

Start by spreading about 10 sq. ft. of mastic on the wall (Photo 3). We used pre-mixed water-based tile mastic and spread it with a 1/4 x 1/4-in. notched trowel. When you purchase your tile, ask the salesperson what size trowel to use. Larger tiles require larger notches. Also, if you're installing tile in a wet area, use thin-set adhesive instead.

Photo 4 shows how to get started installing the tile. Setting tile in a stair-step pattern helps keep everything lined up.

MASTIC

1/4" x 1/4" NOTCHED TROWEL

3 **Spread the mastic.** Using a 1/4 x 1/4-in. notched trowel, spread only as much mastic as you can cover with tile in about 15 minutes—usually about 10 sq. ft. If you leave the adhesive uncovered too long, it will dry on the surface and become less effective. Hold the trowel at a steep angle to make the mastic ridges as high as possible.

1/8" SPACER

4 **Set the full tiles.** Line up the end of the first tile with one of the plumb lines and embed the tile in the mastic. Set the rest of the full tiles in the row, resting them on the ledger and separating them with spacers. Start the next row by aligning the end of a full tile with the second vertical line. Build a stair step, alternating the tile joints as shown.

5 **Mark the end tiles.** Hold each end tile in place and mark it for cutting. Subtract the width of the grout joint when you make the mark. Install the tile with the cut end against the wall.

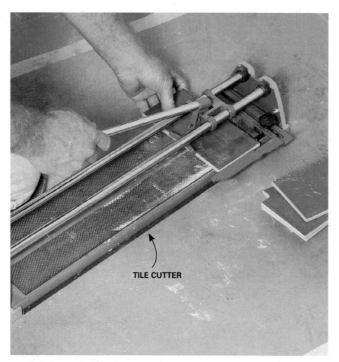

TILE CUTTER

6 Cut the end tiles. Place the tile in the cutter with the edge against the fence. Line up the mark with the cutter. Push down gently on the cutter handle and slide the handle forward to score the tile. Then pull the handle back until the breaker is over the center of the tile and push down to break the tile along the scored line.

RUBBING STONE

7 Smooth the cut end. The cutter may leave the end of the tile a little rough. Use a rubbing stone to grind off the rough edge. Several back-and-forth strokes is all it takes.

8 Miter the top cap. The inside corners of the cap pieces must be cut at a 45-degree angle where they join in the corner. Make these cuts with a wet saw tilted to cut a 45-degree bevel.

When you reach the ends, you'll have to cut tile to fit (**Photos 5 and 6**). For glazed tile like ours, with a soft bisque core, a tile cutter like the one shown in **Photo 6** is fast and convenient for making straight cuts. But if you're using porcelain, stone or glass tile, you'll have to cut it with a diamond wet saw instead. However, you'll still need a wet saw if you have trim pieces to miter (**Photo 8**) or notches to cut. You can rent a wet saw for about $50 per day, or buy one for $100 and up.

If cut ends of your tile will be visible, clean up the jagged edge with a rubbing stone (**Photo 7**). You'll find rubbing stones for about $10 where tiling tools are sold.

If the holes for plumbing pipes fall near the edge of the tile, you can simply mark the hole location and nip away the tile with a tile nipper. Or you can use a wet saw to cut a series of fingers and break them off.

Cutting a hole in the center of a tile is trickier. One method is to use a diamond hole saw. You can get a 1-in. hole saw large enough for copper water supply lines for about $20, but a larger one for the drain will run you about $40.

WOOD STRIP

BUILD OUT THE TRIM IF NECESSARY

We added a 3/4-in. x 1-1/8-in. wood strip around the perimeter of our window and door trim to cover the end of the cap tile. If your cap tile doesn't extend past the window and door moldings, you can skip this step.

9 **Install the mitered cap.** Embed the mitered inside corner in mastic. Use spacers under the cap to create a grout joint.

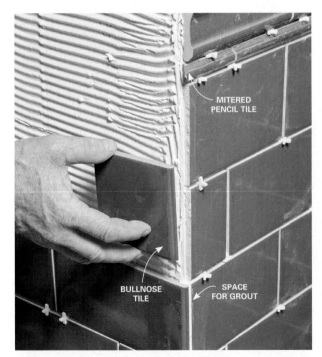

MITERED PENCIL TILE

BULLNOSE TILE

SPACE FOR GROUT

10 **Install the bullnose.** Finish the outside corner with bullnose tile. When you set the tiles on the side opposite the bullnose, make sure to cut them so they're back from the corner the width of a spacer to allow room for a grout joint.

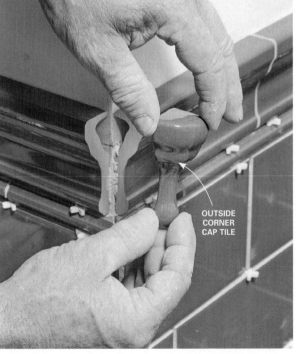

OUTSIDE CORNER CAP TILE

11 **Add the corner cap tile.** Spread a small amount of tile mastic on the back edges of the corner piece and press it into place. If the piece feels loose, use masking tape to hold it in position until the mastic sets up.

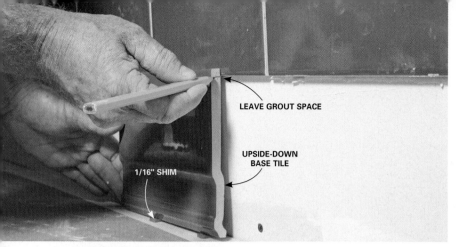

12 **Mark the base tile.** After removing the ledger boards, cut the base tile to fit. Hold the base tile upside down and rest it on 1/16-in. spacers. Then mark for the cut, making sure to subtract for the grout joint. Cut the tile at the mark and install it.

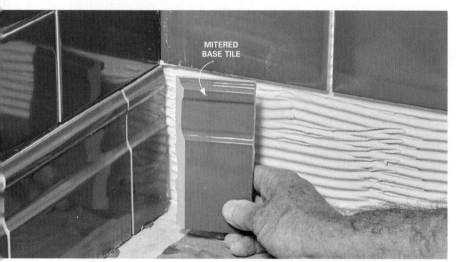

13 **Miter the base at inside corners.** Cut 45-degree bevels on the baseboard pieces that meet at inside corners. Leave a grout space between the two mitered base pieces.

14 **Grout the tile.** Mix the grout and spread it with a grout float. Remove excess grout with the edge of the float. After the grout starts to firm up, begin cleaning it with a damp grout sponge. When the grout is firm, complete the cleanup with a microfiber cloth.

The base and cap style we chose was available in outside corner pieces (**Photo 11**), so we didn't have to miter the outside corners. But we still had to miter the inside corners. We used a wet saw for this (**Photo 8**). Remember to cut your miters short by one half of the grout joint width to allow for grout.

After you've finished installing the wall tile, let the adhesive set up for a few hours before removing the ledger boards. Then install the base tile. **Photo 12** shows how to mark a tile for cutting. Remember to subtract the width of the grout joint when you make the mark. Cut the base tiles to fit, and set them in place on top of 1/16-in. shims. Miter the inside corners of the base (**Photo 13**). Finish up by gluing in the outside corner piece.

The last steps: grout and caulk

When you're done setting tile, let the mastic dry overnight. Then mix your grout according to the instructions on the package. Mix only enough grout to cover about one wall at a time. Spread the grout with a grout float (**Photo 14**), making sure to pack the joints completely. Wipe off excess grout with the edge of the float, working diagonally to the tile. Avoid getting grout into the inside corner joint or the 1/16-in gap at the floor.

Wait about 15 minutes, depending on the room temperature and humidity, for the grout to begin firming up. Pressing your fingertip into the grout should barely leave a mark. Then begin working the grout with a damp, not wet, sponge. Wring out the sponge frequently in clean water in a bucket (not a sink). When all of the grout is removed from the face of the tile, and the joints are consistent and smooth, let the grout set up for an hour before polishing the tile with a damp microfiber cloth.

Finish the project by filling the inside corners with caulk that matches the color of the grout. If you have a wood floor, don't caulk the gap at the floor.

Tons of tile tips online!
For more tips, details and projects, go to familyhandyman.com and search for "tile."

UNDER-CABINET
DRAWER

Extra storage right where you need it!

by **Travis Larson, Senior Editor**

Coffee pods, knives, utensils, spices—there are so many good uses for an extra drawer or two under your upper cabinets. You can put one under almost any upper cabinet as long as there's enough space underneath to fit your countertop appliances. So take a look at what's currently cluttering your countertop and make a nice, neat home for it above!

What it takes

TIME: 1 hour*

COST: $20*

SKILL: Beginner

TOOLS: Basic hand tools, jigsaw or circular saw, drill, 18-gauge nailer

(A miter saw and a table saw will speed things up and give you better results.)

*Per drawer

Two boards and 1/4-in. plywood

This really is a simple project. For lumber, you'll need 1/4-in. plywood for each drawer bottom (see **Figure A**), 1x3 for the drawer box and 1x4 for the drawer supports, drawer front and trim board. (You'll need two trim boards if the drawer is visible from both sides.) We used poplar for all the parts because the exposed parts will be painted to match the cabinets. But if you have natural wood cabinets, choose your wood and finish to match. Paint or finish the drawer front and trim boards before installing them.

Side-mount drawer slides made easy

Ordinarily, installing drawers with side-mount slides is very challenging. But with this technique (**Photos 4 – 6**), everything is built around the drawer, making it very easy.

Most upper cabinets are 12 in. deep. If that's the case with yours, you'll need a pair of 10-in. side-mount drawer slides ($15 per pair) for each drawer. You won't find 10-in. slides at home centers; you'll have to search for them online or shop at a woodworking store. If you have unusually deep cabinets, you can create deeper drawers and use 12-in. slides, which are readily available at home centers.

The cavity defines the drawer sizes

Peek under your cabinets and you'll see the cavities (**Photo 1**). You can put several drawers under a row of cabinets if you wish, but each cabinet needs a separate drawer. If you're putting in adjoining drawers, hold off on cutting the drawer fronts until all the drawers are installed so you can cut them to fit with even gaps between them. For single cabinet drawers, go ahead and cut the fronts the same length as the cabinet face. You won't need any drawer pulls. Because the drawer front drops about an inch below the drawer, you'll have a built-in lip on the underside for a finger pull.

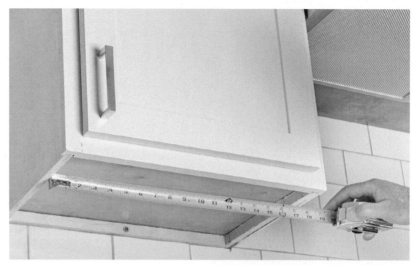

1 **Size the drawer.** Measure the cavity under the cabinet and cut a piece of 1/4-in. plywood 2-1/2 in. narrower and 1/4 in. shallower than those dimensions.

2 **Build the drawer frame.** Cut 1x3 frame parts to match the plywood dimensions, then glue and nail them together with 1-1/2-in. 18-gauge brads.

3 **Add the drawer bottom.** Glue and nail the plywood to the frame using the plywood to square up the frame as you fasten it.

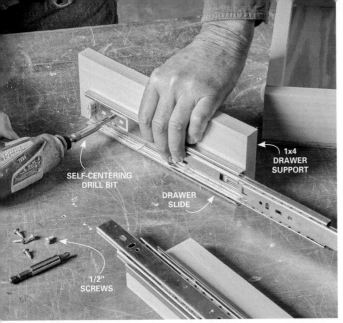

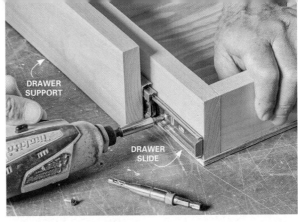

5 Join the slide to the drawer. Pull out the slide on each drawer support a few inches to expose the mounting holes, then pre-drill and screw the slides to the drawer sides flush with the front.

4 Attach the drawer slide. Cut two 1x4s to the same length as the drawer sides, then attach the slides to the drawer supports, holding them flush with the bottom and the end. Use a self-centering drill bit in the round slide mounting holes before sinking the 1/2-in. screws.

Matching your cabinets

Matching the finish on your existing cabinets can be tricky. Take a cabinet door with you to a paint store and get some help. Unscrew the hinges or, if you have European hinges, just unclip them. At the store they'll be able to match up paint colors, sheens and stain colors to get a finish that will make your new drawers look like they were built right along with the cabinets.

Figure A
Exploded View

Before you adhere and screw the assembly onto the cabinet, have someone help you hold it in place to make sure the drawer clears the cabinet face frame. If it doesn't, rip 3/4-in. strips of 1/4-in. plywood for spacers (as many as needed) and nail them to the drawer support before mounting the assembly.

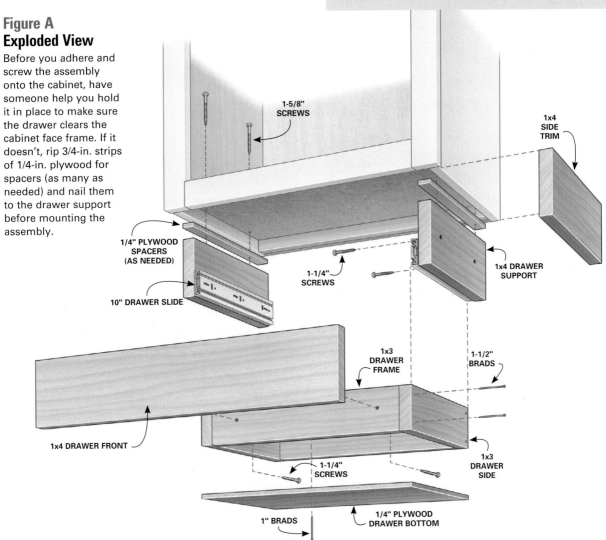

1-5/8" SCREWS

1x4 SIDE TRIM

1/4" PLYWOOD SPACERS (AS NEEDED)

1-1/4" SCREWS

1x4 DRAWER SUPPORT

10" DRAWER SLIDE

1x3 DRAWER FRAME

1-1/2" BRADS

1x4 DRAWER FRONT

1-1/4" SCREWS

1x3 DRAWER SIDE

1" BRADS

1/4" PLYWOOD DRAWER BOTTOM

6 **Finish attaching the drawer slide.** Pull the slide out the rest of the way to mount the slide to the back end of the drawer.

DOUBLE-FACE TAPE

7 **Stick the assembly to the cabinet.** Use double-face tape to temporarily stick the assembly to the underside of the cabinet. (Center it in the opening.)

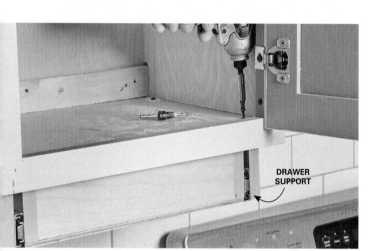

DRAWER SUPPORT

8 **Screw the drawer supports to the cabinet bottom.** Drill two 1/8-in. pilot holes through the cabinet bottom, then screw into the drawer supports.

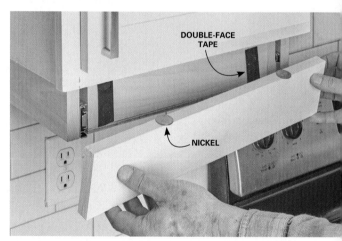

DOUBLE-FACE TAPE

NICKEL

9 **Stick on the drawer front.** Cut the 1x4 drawer front exactly the same length as the cabinet face frame. Use two nickels to space it from the cabinet frame while you attach it with double-face tape.

DRAWER FRONT

10 **Attach the drawer front.** Drill, then permanently attach the drawer front to the drawer frame from the inside with 1-1/4-in. screws.

1x4 SIDE TRIM

11 **Clamp and screw the side trim into place.** Drill pilot holes above the drawer slide and attach the 1x4 side trim with 1-1/4-in. screws.

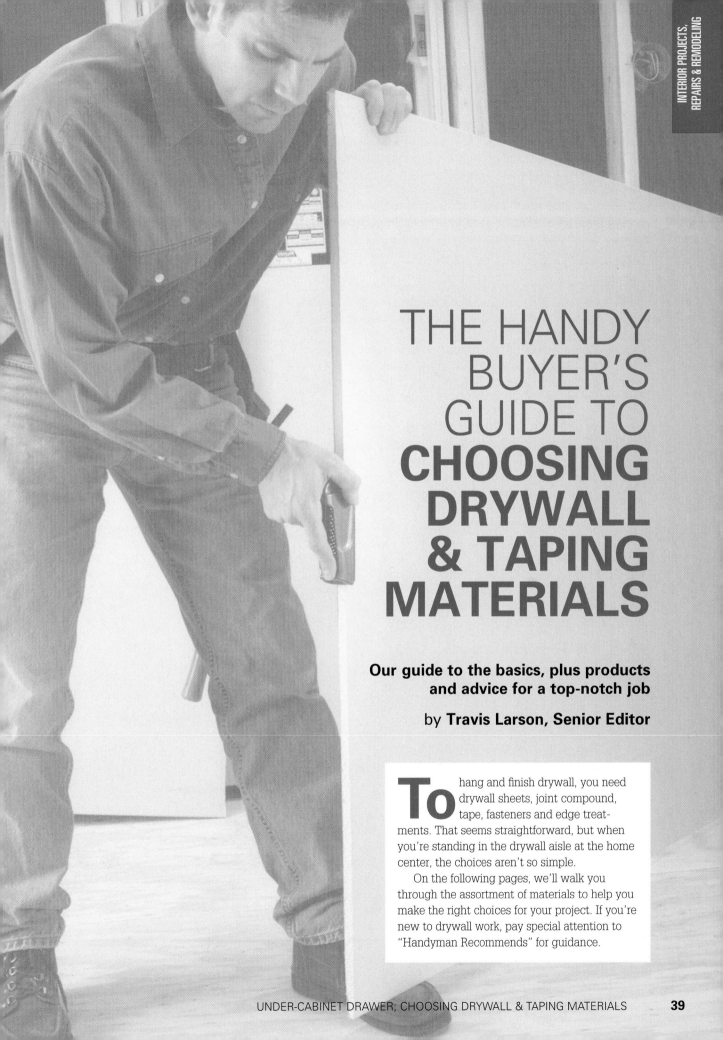

THE HANDY BUYER'S GUIDE TO CHOOSING DRYWALL & TAPING MATERIALS

Our guide to the basics, plus products and advice for a top-notch job

by **Travis Larson, Senior Editor**

To hang and finish drywall, you need drywall sheets, joint compound, tape, fasteners and edge treatments. That seems straightforward, but when you're standing in the drywall aisle at the home center, the choices aren't so simple.

On the following pages, we'll walk you through the assortment of materials to help you make the right choices for your project. If you're new to drywall work, pay special attention to "Handyman Recommends" for guidance.

A 1/2-in. drywall

This is the best choice for most walls and some ceilings. There are standard and lightweight versions. Lightweight is stronger and weighs 25 percent less.

HANDYMAN RECOMMENDS: Spend a few extra bucks and get "ultralight" or "lightweight" drywall. It's easier to handle and stiffer, so it can cover ceilings that have joists spaced at 24-in. That's why stores no longer even carry standard 1/2-in. drywall.

B Fire-resistant drywall

"Type X" drywall is 5/8 in. thick and designed to slow the spread of fire. It's often required on garage walls and ceilings that adjoin living spaces, ceilings between living spaces inside the house, and under stairs.

HANDYMAN RECOMMENDS: Talk to your local building inspector to find out where and which kind of Type X is required. There are many and each with a different fire rating. If you install the wrong type, an inspector can require you to tear it off and replace it.

C Mold- and moisture-resistant drywall

Also called "greenboard," mold- and mildew-resistant 1/2-in. drywall is a somewhat different animal. Manufacturers use various methods to eliminate or treat the paper that covers the gypsum core. Getting rid of the organic paper food source was supposed to keep mold and mildew from growing. Builders used to install it in wet and damp locations, placing it behind tile in shower and bath enclosures. Those enclosures have already been or soon will be replaced as the greenboard fails.

HANDYMAN RECOMMENDS: Although you'll still find greenboard at home centers, we advise against using it, especially for tile backing in wet areas. There are better alternatives for tile in wet locations—cement board, for one.

D 3/8-in. drywall

If you're doing repairs in a house built in the '50s or '60s, you may very well have 3/8-in. drywall. You'll want to match that thickness to patch an existing wall. Measure the existing drywall or take off a switch plate cover to find out.

HANDYMAN RECOMMENDS: Unless you're matching existing drywall, there's rarely a good reason to use 3/8-in. drywall. Remember that window and doorjambs are generally sized to be flush with 1/2-in. drywall.

E 1/4-in. drywall

This thin material is mostly used to cover bad walls: cracked plaster or unremovable wallpaper, for example. Because it's more flexible, it's also sometimes used on arches or applied in two layers on curved walls. Specialty stores carry drywall that's very bendable—enough to drywall the inside of a barrel!

HANDYMAN RECOMMENDS: Screws don't countersink well in 1/4-in. drywall, so construction adhesive would be a better choice if you're covering bad surfaces. Tack it in place with a few nails until the adhesive sets.

What length should you buy?
Longer sheets mean fewer "butt" joints to tape. So choose the longest sheets you can wrestle into the room. Home centers typically carry 8-, 10- and 12-ft. lengths. Specialty suppliers carry 14- or even 16-ft. sheets.

Tip:
Pros often layer various thicknesses of drywall to achieve the perfect thickness to match up with adjoining surfaces.

Joint compound

Drying type

Drying compound comes premixed in buckets and boxes. As the name suggests, it hardens as the water in it evaporates. There are variations, but these are the two basic types:

1 **All-purpose**

All-purpose compound contains a lot of adhesive, making it the hardest, strongest type of drying compound. That strength makes it a good choice for the first coat (when you embed paper tape). You can use it for following coats too, but sanding will give you a workout.

2 **Lightweight all-purpose**

The main advantage of lightweight joint compound is that it's easier to sand. The downside: It's not as hard or strong, so it's a bit more likely to dent when bumped or crack at joints. Look for the term "lightweight" on the label. Don't use lightweight compound to embed mesh joint tape; that combination sometimes leads to cracks.

Setting type

Setting compound is a powder that you mix with water just before use. It hardens by chemical reaction rather than by drying. The working time—the minutes before it begins to harden—is usually the number that's in the name: Quick Set 20 or Pro-Set 90, for example. Besides hardening fast and allowing you to apply the next coat, setting compound has two advantages: It's harder and stronger than drying compound, and it shrinks much less as it hardens. The disadvantages are the hassle of mixing it and the more difficult cleanup (especially after it begins to harden).

HANDYMAN RECOMMENDS: If you're after the smoothest finish and great crack resistance, here's one recipe: Embed fiberglass tape with lightweight setting compound or paper tape with all-purpose compound. Use lightweight all-purpose for the rest of the coats.

BOXED VS. BUCKET
Boxed joint compound is identical to the compound sold in premixed buckets. It's packaged in a plastic bag to keep it fresh. Pros buy the boxed type because it's more economical.

1 **Regular setting compound**

This compound is very hard, very strong—and almost impossible to sand. DIYers should avoid it.

2 **Lightweight setting compound**

Lightweight versions sacrifice a little toughness but are much easier to sand than regular setting compound, making them a good choice for DIYers.

Tape

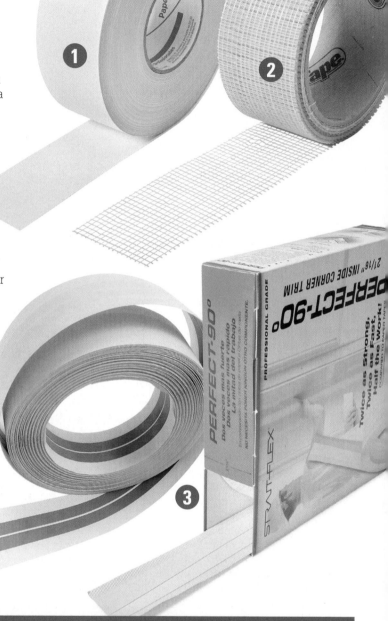

Three types of tape

1 Paper

Paper tape is cheap and, surprisingly, stronger than fiberglass tape. And unlike fiberglass tape, it's pre-creased in the middle so you can fold it to tape inside corners. However, it takes a bit more skill to embed it in drywall seams.

2 Fiberglass mesh

Mesh is far easier to use than paper. It has adhesive on one side; you just stick it to the wall and finish over it. Mesh tape is super forgiving for first-time tapers. But you'll still have to use paper tape or reinforced paper tape for corners at wall-to-wall and wall-to-ceiling joints. Since it's not as crack resistant as paper tape, setting compound (standard or lightweight) is usually recommended for embedding mesh tape.

3 Reinforced paper

Designed for inside corners and wall-to-ceiling angles, reinforced paper tape has plastic or metal strips on the back. They don't make the joint stronger, but they do provide a stiff guide for your knife, allowing amateurs to keep corners straight.

HANDYMAN RECOMMENDS: For novice tapers, the best choices are fiberglass mesh for flat joints and reinforced paper for inside corners. Stick mesh over flanges on corner beads too.

Fasteners

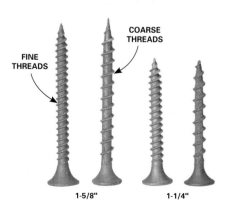

FINE THREADS

COARSE THREADS

1-5/8"   1-1/4"

Choose drywall screws rather than nails—nails are far more likely to work loose and cause ugly craters or "pops." The screw length depends on the drywall thickness: 1-5/8-in. screws are for 5/8-in. drywall; 1-1/4-in. screws are for anything thinner. Coarse threads are for wood studs; fine threads for steel studs.

HANDYMAN RECOMMENDS: You'll find drywall screws with thin (No. 6) and thick (No. 8) shanks. Choose the thin ones. Thick-shank screws are harder to drive, break out drywall near edges and leave shredded paper around the screw head.

NO. 6   NO. 8

Edge beads

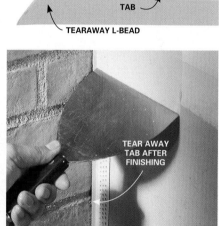

PLASTIC L-BEAD

METAL L-BEAD

FLANGE

PLASTIC J-BEAD

TAB

TEARAWAY L-BEAD

Whenever drywall meets another surface like stone, brick or paneling, you need a neat way to finish the edge. You can always use wood trim, but here are some other options:

L-bead

L-bead slips between the drywall and the adjoining wall. Then you staple plastic or nail metal L-bead to fasten it. Tape the edge and use the lip as a guide to complete filling and feathering out the edge.

J-bead

J-bead comes in metal or plastic versions. Staple it to the framing and work the edges of the drywall into it as you hang it. It doesn't require any additional work, but you'll see the exposed flange.

Tearaway bead

Tearaway bead is easier and faster to install than either J-bead or L-bead edges. Cut the drywall about 1/4 in. short of the adjoining surface, slip and staple the tearaway L-bead into place and you're ready to tape and fill the raised, beaded shoulder. Once you get a couple of coats in place, you're ready to sand and paint. Then, just tear away the scored tab and you're done.

HANDYMAN RECOMMENDS: We think tearaway bead is the way to go for finishing exposed edges. It's easy to install, and the little tearaway tab keeps compound and paint away from the adjoining surfaces. Go with J-bead if you want to skip some taping and sanding and don't mind seeing the exposed but painted plastic flange.

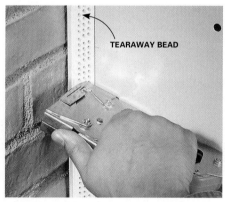

TEARAWAY BEAD

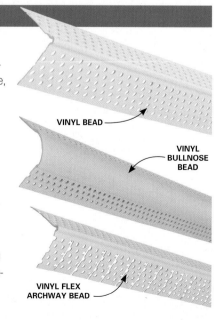

TEAR AWAY TAB AFTER FINISHING

Corner beads

PAPER-FACED COMPOSITE BEAD

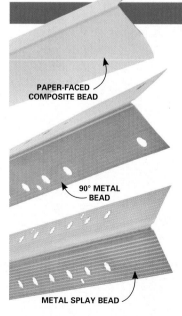

90° METAL BEAD

METAL SPLAY BEAD

You have many choices for outside corners: metal or vinyl, square or bullnose, even bead for non-90-degree corners or arches. The big difference is how they're installed. Standard metal can be nailed on and then taped; vinyl corner bead should be applied with special adhesive and staples. Paper-faced versions get "glued" into place with joint compound.

HANDYMAN RECOMMENDS: Choose metal corner bead instead of vinyl or paper-faced bead. It's easier to install and requires only ordinary tools. Exception: In damp areas like bathrooms and spas, vinyl is a good, rust-proof choice.

VINYL BEAD

VINYL BULLNOSE BEAD

VINYL FLEX ARCHWAY BEAD

CHOOSING DRYWALL & TAPING MATERIALS **43**

DIY RADON REDUCTION

You can save $1,000 in a weekend! Here's what you need to know before you begin

by **Jason White, Associate Editor**

FAN

If you've tested for radon and found you've got a problem, your next question is probably "Can I fix it myself?" This story will help you answer that question. And if you decide to go for it, we've got some great tips from professional installers to help you get it done.

In most cases, pros charge about $1,500 to install a radon mitigation system, but you can do it yourself for only about $500 in materials. So if you're fairly handy and have some carpentry, plumbing and electrical skills, you can install your own system in a weekend and save yourself a thousand bucks!

What is radon?

Radon is an invisible, odorless radioactive gas that seeps out of the soil and into the atmosphere. It's almost everywhere. In fact, you're probably breathing in tiny traces of it right now. But when it's trapped inside a home and reaches high levels, radon can cause lung cancer. Your house can have high levels of radon even if your house is new and your neighbor's house doesn't have any. The highest levels are normally found in basements, but it's possible for radon to reach other parts of your house too.

SEAL HOLES AND CRACKS FIRST

If the radon levels in your home are only slightly elevated, try sealing holes and cracks in concrete walls and floors and test again. In most cases, sealing doesn't solve the problem. But you'll have to seal before you install a mitigation system anyway, so it's worth a try. Sealing is usually simple; caulk small openings and fill larger gaps with expanding foam or hydraulic cement.

TEST FOR RADON

It's important to fix the radon problem in your house if a test shows a concentration of 4 picoCuries per liter (pCi/L) or higher, so buy a test kit. You can get one at a home center for about $10—plus a $40 lab fee—and perform the test yourself. You just let the tester sit in your house for a few days and then mail it to a lab for analysis. Electronic radon monitors that monitor continuously for radon are available online for about $130 and don't require a lab.

PVC PIPE

SHALLOW PIT

> **How a radon reduction system works**
> A fan pulls radon gas from beneath the floor and exhausts it outside. In cold climates, it's better to run the pipe inside the house rather than outside as shown here.

Planning your system: 7 questions to answer

More than most projects, a radon mitigation system requires detailed planning. The planning process will also help you decide whether you're willing and able to tackle the job yourself. Here are seven questions you must answer before you charge ahead:

1 **What does your building inspector require?**

Make a quick phone call to your town's building department to ask about local code requirements, permits and inspections. In some areas, only licensed pros are allowed to install systems.

2 **Where will the pipe begin?**

In most cases, you'll want to locate the PVC pipe that sucks radon from under your concrete floor near an exterior wall so it's out of the way and easy to route outside. This is also where sump pump basins and footing drainpipes (aka "drain tile") are located in some homes—perfect places from which to suck radon. If you don't have a sump basin, you will have digging to do (see p. 47). If you use the sump basin as your suction point, be sure to seal around any pipe and wire penetrations in the lid. Special supplies for dealing with sump basin lids are available online at indoor-air-health-advisor.com, or do an online search for "radon sump lid."

3 **Run the pipe indoors or out?**

It's much easier to route the pipe outside the house, but that can cause a problem in cold climates. Condensation can form inside, causing ice to build up and stop the fan from working.

4 **What's the pipe path?**

If you'll be routing your pipe outdoors, it's no big deal. Just run it up along an exterior wall. But running pipe indoors can be a real nightmare. Most professional installers in cold-weather areas try to avoid condensation problems by routing the pipe up through a closet or finished garage and to a fan in the attic that blows the radon out above the roof. Be ready for a big, dusty mess if you have to route your pipe indoors. Also keep in mind that the pipe has to terminate 12 in. above the roof and be at least 10 in. away (horizontally) from any dormer windows. Ask your city's building department about any additional requirements.

OUTLET

5 Where will you put the fan?

If you'll be mounting the fan outside, put it in a place where you can get electricity to it easily. If it's indoors, the fan must be located in an unfinished attic. Never install the fan in your basement or any living space because, if there's ever a leak, the fan could pump highly concentrated radon right into your home.

6 How will you get power to the fan?

The toughest part of any electrical job is getting cable from point A to point B. If there's a junction box nearby that you can extend the circuit from, you're golden. If not, you might be spending lots of time fishing cable to where you need it. Fans draw very little power—usually less than 100 watts—so you can tap any nearby circuit. You can also hardwire a fan or plug it into an outlet. In an attic, it's best to install an outlet because it makes replacing the fan easier. Outside, it's best to hardwire the fan using watertight conduit.

FAN

Tips for installing your system

Find the footing

If you'll be installing your PVC pipe close to a basement wall, drill a test hole in the floor and feel around for the foundation's footing. Concrete slabs are typically about 4 in. thick, so use a masonry bit that's a couple of inches longer than the thickness of the floor (our installers use a 12-in. one) to see if the footing under the foundation walls will be in the pipe's way. If you do hit the footing, try again a couple inches farther from the wall. You can patch the test holes later with patching cement.

Help for cutting & gluing pipe
Cutting and gluing PVC pipe for a radon system is done the same way as for any regular plumbing job. For tips, go to **tfhmag.com/joinplasticpipe**

FOOTING TEST HOLE

7 What's under the slab?

You may not know what kind of base material you have under your concrete slab until you punch a hole in the floor. (See "Make a Big Hole with Several Small Ones," below.) Soil conditions affect how readily radon flows underneath the slab, so don't buy a fan until you know what you're dealing with. You'll need to provide this information when you buy a fan. (See "Buy Your Fan from an Expert" at right.)

Buy your fan from an expert

Radon fans cost $140 to $250, depending mostly on size. Some radon mitigation systems require a big, powerful fan. Others work fine with a smaller model. Sizing a fan requires expertise, so we strongly recommend that you buy from an expert who will ask questions and supply you with the best fan for your situation, as well as exchange the fan for a bigger one if the smaller one doesn't fix your radon problem. One such expert is Val Riedman, a professional radon system installer who runs a website where you can get more DIY information and buy supplies. *The Family Handyman* editors have purchased fans from him. Visit http://www.indoor-air-health-advisor.com/radon.html for more information. Val also contributed to this article.

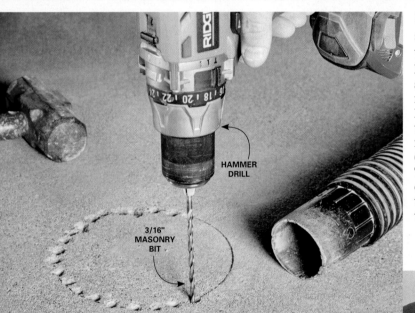

HAMMER DRILL

3/16" MASONRY BIT

Make a big hole with several small ones

You'll need a hole in the basement floor a little bigger than the PVC pipe to give you some wiggle room and make it easier to remove soil and gravel. You could rent a large rotary hammer drill and coring bit from the home center, but save yourself some money and try this trick instead: Just draw a 6-in. circle where the pipe will be installed. Then, using a 3/16-in. masonry bit, drill several holes close together. Now just whack the center of the large hole with a hammer to break through.

SHOP VACUUM HOSE

Make a suction pit

Creating a shallow pit underneath the hole gives the radon a place to collect before getting sucked up the pipe. You'll need to remove several gallons of whatever base material is under your slab. The tighter the soil, the more material you'll have to remove so the radon fan can do its job. For loose gravel, you need to remove only about 5 gallons. For tighter soils like sand, dirt or clay, plan to remove 15 gallons or more. A shop vacuum helps suck up the loose stuff. For tighter soil, you'll probably need to do a combination of hand digging and vacuuming.

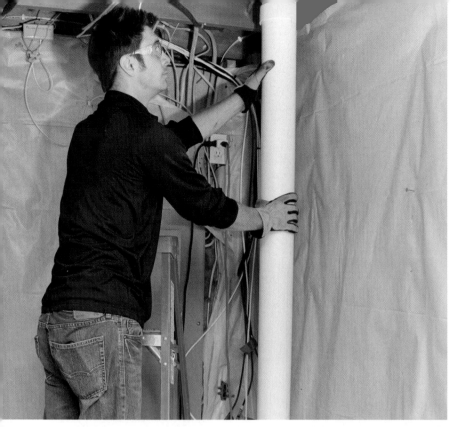

Dry-fit all the piping

Doing a "dry fit" before gluing the PVC pipe and fittings ensures that everything will fit together properly after you apply the glue. Once you commit to gluing, you only have seconds to push and twist everything together before they're permanently fused.

FIRE-STO
COLLA

Install fire-stop collars in garages

If you route part of your radon piping through a garage, then you must install fire-stop pipe collars (also called fire barriers) wherever pipe goes through a finished wall or ceiling. The collars seal around the pipe, preventing—or at least slowing down—fire from spreading to other parts of the house. You can buy fire-stop collars for $40 to $50 online.

RIM JOIST LOCATOR HOLE

CUT HOLE FROM OUTSIDE

RIM JOIST

Exit through the rim joist

If you'll be running pipe directly outside from the basement or out through an attached garage, you'll need to cut a nice, clean hole in the rim joist. A hole saw ($25 to $40 at home centers) is the perfect tool for this job. Buy the cheapest one you can find since you'll probably use it only once or twice in your lifetime. The installers we worked with use a 4-1/2-in.-diameter hole saw, which matches the outside diameter of 4-in. PVC pipe, giving it a very snug fit. Drill a locator hole from inside the basement first, then use the hole saw to cut the hole from outside.

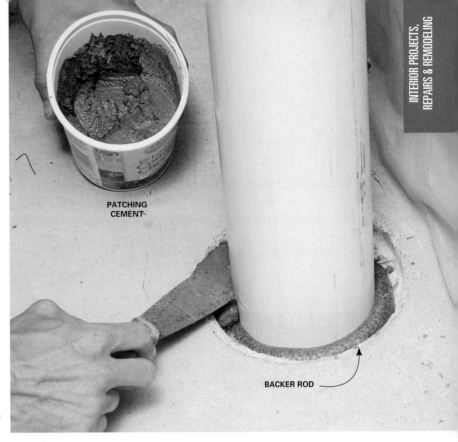

MEET THE EXPERTS

Gary and Jake Vaness are professional radon system installers. They run Radon Reduction Inc., in Minnetonka, Minnesota, and let us tag along on one of their installations for this article.

Seal around the pipe with patching cement

After you've installed all the pipe, stuff some foam backer rod into the gap between the pipe and the concrete and apply fast-setting concrete patching cement. Trowel the cement flush with the top of the concrete floor.

PATCHING CEMENT

BACKER ROD

MANOMETER

Install a manometer

Radon fans don't run forever (typically 7 to 10 years), so you need a warning device to tell you when it stops working. One option is a liquid-filled manometer ($10 to $30 online) mounted on the PVC pipe. When the liquid level drops, the system isn't working. Electronic monitors that measure radon in the air are another option. The Safety Siren Radon Detector, for example, sounds an alarm when radon levels become dangerous ($130 online).

Do another radon test

After installing your radon system, do another test. If that test shows you still have high levels of radon, contact the company you bought the fan from. Chances are, you'll need to install a more powerful fan. But in some cases, a second suction point (where pipe enters the floor) is the solution. (See "Buy Your Fan from an Expert" on p. 47.)

THE SIMPLEST CURE FOR
WET BASEMENTS

The basic solution is often the best solution.

by **Jeff Gorton, Associate Editor**

Water in your basement? Don't call the basement waterproofing company yet. According to our expert, many basement leaks can be cured with a weekend's work and a few hundred dollars' worth of dirt and plastic.

We talked to Robert Vassallo, owner of Complete Building Solutions, an engineering firm that specializes in solving water-related building problems. His firm takes on many complicated wet basement jobs, but he was quick to point out that a huge percentage of wet basements can be remedied by simply regrading the landscape, and adding or upgrading gutters and downspouts. The graphic at right shows the key elements for an effective solution.

Of course, this fix will work only if the water entering your basement is coming from rain or melting snow. But it's pretty easy to tell. If you get water in your basement shortly after a storm, or when the snow is melting, or if a wet inverted-V pattern appears on the wall, the cause is most likely improper grading or a downspout that's emptying water near your foundation. And even if there are other factors contributing to your wet basement, the solutions we show here will help keep your basement dry and should be done before you take more extreme measures.

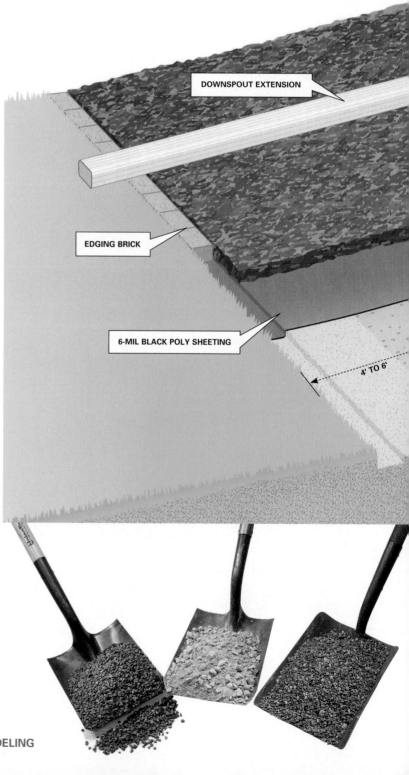

DOWNSPOUT EXTENSION

EDGING BRICK

6-MIL BLACK POLY SHEETING

4' TO 6'

WHAT YOU'LL NEED:

- Compactable fill
- 6-mil poly
- Edging
- Mulch or gravel

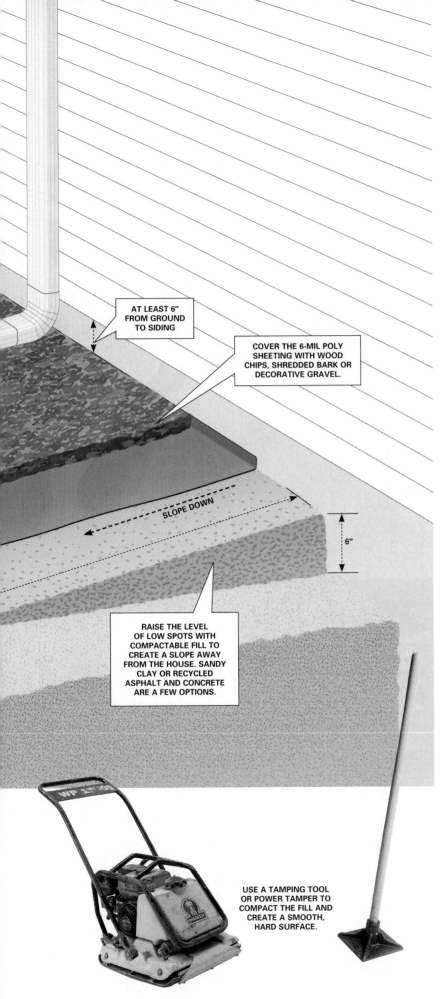

AT LEAST 6"
FROM GROUND
TO SIDING

COVER THE 6-MIL POLY
SHEETING WITH WOOD
CHIPS, SHREDDED BARK OR
DECORATIVE GRAVEL.

SLOPE DOWN

6"

RAISE THE LEVEL
OF LOW SPOTS WITH
COMPACTABLE FILL TO
CREATE A SLOPE AWAY
FROM THE HOUSE. SANDY
CLAY OR RECYCLED
ASPHALT AND CONCRETE
ARE A FEW OPTIONS.

USE A TAMPING TOOL
OR POWER TAMPER TO
COMPACT THE FILL AND
CREATE A SMOOTH,
HARD SURFACE.

4 steps to fixing a leaky basement

1. Check the landscape around your house

You'll need to do a thorough check of the ground around your foundation. For this you'll need a 4-ft. level, a tape measure and a notepad. First draw a simple sketch of your house and yard on your notepad. Then use the level to check the slope of the ground around your foundation. Look for areas of sunken soil, garden beds with edging that protrudes to form a dam, and ground that slopes toward the house. Make notes on your sketch with arrows to show which way the ground slopes. This step will help you develop a plan for redirecting the water away from the foundation.

2. Make a plan and order material

With the sketch in hand, you can figure out where the problem areas are and what you need to do to fix them. The goal is to create a 6-ft.-wide perimeter that slopes away from the house. Aim for a slope of about 1 in. per foot, but if this isn't practical, get as close to it as you can. There are two ways to change the slope of the ground near your foundation. You can add soil or some other compactable fill near the house, or you can move soil from the high area to the foundation. In either case, keep in mind that you should maintain 6 in. between the soil surface and the siding to prevent rot and discourage insects.

If you need a lot of fill, it may be cheaper to have a dump truck deliver a load. Otherwise you can buy bags of soil at most landscape supply stores or home centers. You'll also need enough 6-mil black poly sheeting to cover the area between the foundation and 6 ft. out. And if you like our idea of using bricks for the edging as shown in the illustration, you'll need to order these too. Finally, you'll need some mulch or other decorative material to cover the poly.

③ Create the slope

If you have shrubs or trees near the foundation, they may be part of the problem. In some cases, their roots form a channel for water to reach the foundation, or they penetrate cracks in the foundation and create new paths for water to enter. Remove shrubs and trees that you don't need. You'll have to work around any that are a valued part of your landscape.

Next, spread the new fill, using a level to check the slope. Or simply regrade the soil near your foundation to create the slope. Use a garden rake to smooth and level the ground. When you're happy with the slope, tamp the soil to compact it. If you're doing the entire perimeter, it may be worth renting a gas-powered tamper for this. Otherwise a hand tamper will work.

If your plan includes adding bricks along the edge, dig a trench deep enough so that the top edge of the brick is level with the ground. Then lay 6-mil poly over the ground and into the trench. Finish up by placing the bricks and covering the poly with mulch, wood chips or some type of decorative stone or gravel.

④ Check your gutters and downspouts

If you don't have gutters and downspouts, consider adding them. Otherwise most of the water from the roof ends up right near the foundation where you don't want it. If you do have gutters, or if you're adding them, make sure to attach extensions to the downspouts so that the water discharges at least 6 ft. away from the house.

MEET AN EXPERT

Robert Vassallo is the owner of Complete Building Solutions in Golden Valley, MN. The company specializes in finding solutions to tough water problems in residential and commercial buildings.

If at first you don't succeed...

These four simple steps will solve most basement leaks caused by surface water like rain and snow melt. But if your basement still leaks after you've made these corrections, consider hiring an engineering firm experienced in solving water leakage problems to propose other remedies.

Be cautious about hiring companies that offer only their own solution, because it may not be the best one for your situation. And if you're looking for more informaiton on solutions to wet basements, how to deal with wet carpet, how to fix plumbing leaks, or how to add an interior drain and sump pump, search for the key words at **familyhandyman.com**.

Tips from Robert Vassallo

■ For a premium job, substitute EPDM for the 6-mil poly. Contact local roofers to see if they're tearing off an old EDPM roof. You may be able to get the material for free.

■ Use ground-up recycled concrete and asphalt for fill. It's cheap and compacts easily to form a hard, dense surface.

■ If you can't regrade the entire perimeter, do as much of it as you can.

■ For extra insurance against any water getting in near the foundation, seal the 6-mil plastic or EPDM to the foundation wall with acoustical sealant caulk and install a flashing over the top.

■ Consider building a rain garden if you can't easily drain water from your yard.

SUCCESS WITH **MELAMINE**

These tips will help you get the most out of this common DIY material.

by **Jeff Gorton, Associate Editor**

"**M**elamine" is the common name for particleboard that's coated with a thin layer of plastic finish. The melamine finish is similar to the plastic laminate on countertops, but it's not as thick.

The advantages of building with a melamine-coated product are its durable finish and its relatively low cost. But it can be frustrating to work with. The particleboard can be hard to fasten, and the brittle finish is tricky to cut. Here are 11 tips to make your next melamine project a success.

freud®

INDUSTRIAL

MADE IN ITALY

ITEM No. LU79R007

ULTIMATE PLYWOOD & MELAMINE

60T
-5° HOOK

1 Buy a special blade. The melamine finish chips easily when cut, especially if you're using an everyday saw blade. But you can largely avoid chipping by investing in a special blade that's designed to cut plastic materials. The teeth on these blades are less angled, which helps prevent chipping. One example is the Freud LU79R007 7-1/4-in. blade ($55). If you can't justify spending this much, you can still get good results with a less expensive blade that has at least 40 carbide teeth. But be sure to use the chip-free cutting technique that we show in **Tip 4**.

2 **Order the color you want**. You'll typically find melamine products in white at home centers, but many colors are available. Depending on the brand, you'll find 10 to 20 or more colors available for special order. Check with your local lumberyard or home center for your options.

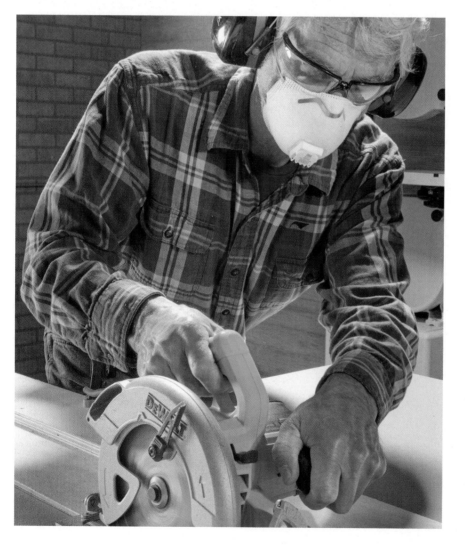

Melamine basics

Look around and you'll find melamine furniture, melamine shelves, melamine wall panels, and even melamine slatwall. It's usually labeled as melamine, but you may also see terms such as thermally fused laminate or simply prefinished panels or prefinished shelves.

You can buy 4 x 8-ft. sheets of melamine in 1/8-, 1/4-, 1/2-, 5/8- and 3/4-in. thicknesses and melamine shelves in various lengths and widths. Home centers may only stock 1/4-in. and 3/4-in. thicknesses. Melamine sheets cost about 60¢ to $1.25 per square foot. Shelving costs about $1.40 to $2 per linear foot depending on the width.

3 **Wear safety gear**. You should always wear safety gear when you're using power tools. There are particular safety concerns when you're working with melamine. For starters, the plastic finish tends to chip off as it's cut. The chips are as sharp as glass, creating a real hazard for your eyes. Safety glasses are a must.

The fine dust created by cutting the fiber core is bad for your lungs. If possible, cut outdoors. Indoors or out, wear a dust mask. Wear gloves when you're handling large sheets of melamine. The edges can be razor sharp. And don't forget hearing protection.

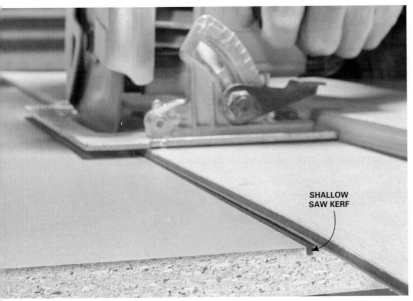

SHALLOW SAW KERF

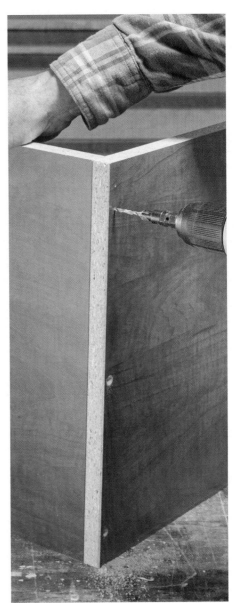

4 Cut without chipping. Making a scoring cut before the final one will result in a chip-free edge. First, use a straightedge as a saw guide. Without the straightedge, the saw might wobble slightly as you cut, and this twisting will contribute to chipping. Clamp your straightedge guide in position and set the saw to cut 1/8 in. deep. Run your saw along the straightedge and cut a groove in the melamine panel. This shallow cut shouldn't produce any chipping.

Now reset the saw so the blade extends about 1/2 in. past the bottom side of the panel and make another pass. The resulting cut will be perfectly chip-free on both sides. You can use the same technique on a table saw. Make one shallow cut. Then run the panel through the saw a second time to complete the cut. If only one side of the panel will be visible in the finished project, you don't need to use this technique because chipping occurs only on the side where the saw blade teeth exit. Just make sure to place the "show" side down if you're cutting with a circular saw and up when you're using a table saw.

6 Drill and countersink for screws. Particleboard, whether it has a melamine finish or not, doesn't hold screws as well as solid lumber or plywood. Plus, it tends to split if you drive screws without drilling first. The key to fastening it with screws is to drill pilot holes for the screws and countersinks for the screw heads. A combination bit that drills and countersinks in one operation saves time. Choose a countersink bit that's labeled for use with No. 8 screws.

COUNTERSINK BIT

5 Pin panels, then add screws. The melamine finish is slippery, making it difficult to hold the panels in alignment while you drill pilot holes for the screws. Solve this problem by first pinning the panels together using an 18-gauge brad nail gun. The small holes left by the brads are nearly invisible, and you'll save yourself a lot of time and frustration.

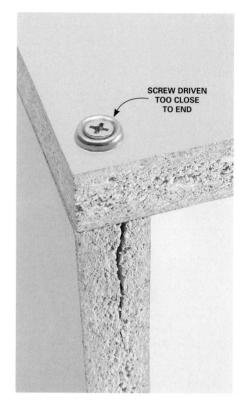

7 **Strengthen shelves with nosing.** Melamine shelves will sag over time, especially if they're more than a few feet long. Strengthen shelves by gluing a solid wood nose to one or both edges of the shelf. Here we've slotted the nosing and the melamine shelves with a biscuit joiner to allow the use of wood biscuits. The biscuits add strength and help align the edging perfectly. No nails needed; just apply wood glue, insert the biscuits and clamp the edge to the shelf until the glue sets.

WOOD BISCUIT

SOLID WOOD NOSING

SCREW DRIVEN TOO CLOSE TO END

8 **Prevent splitting.** The particleboard core is rather brittle and can split if you drive screws too close to the edge. Prevent this by positioning screws at least 2 in. from the edge of panels whenever possible. Drilling a pilot hole will also help prevent splitting (**Tip 6**).

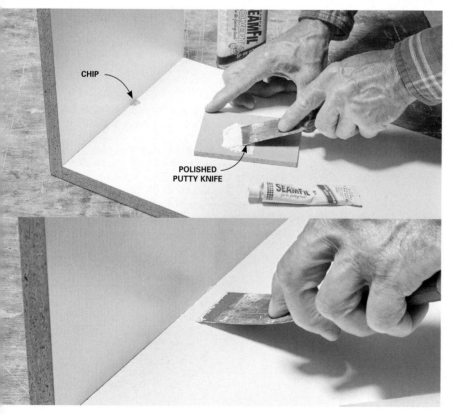

CHIP

POLISHED PUTTY KNIFE

9 **Repair chips with a special filler.** SeamFil plastic filler paste comes in a tube and is commonly used by pros who work with plastic laminate to repair chips. And since the surface of melamine panels and shelves is also a type of plastic laminate, the repairs blend in well.

SeamFil paste is available for about $5 per 1-oz. tube online or where plastic laminate (used for countertops) is sold. It's available in 20 standard colors that can be mixed to create custom colors.

To use the SeamFil paste, first clean the area with the special SeamFil solvent (available for about $9 per half pint where the paste is sold). Then spread a small amount of the paste on a scrap of wood or plastic laminate. Work the paste around with a polished putty knife until some of the solvent starts to evaporate and the paste starts to thicken. Then press the thickened paste into the area to be repaired and smooth it with the putty knife. It may take a few coats to get a flush surface. Clean off excess paste using a rag dampened with the solvent.

10 **Hide screw heads**. To conceal screw heads, you have a couple of options. You can buy plastic caps that snap onto or over your screw heads. These work fine but leave a protruding cap.

The other option is to cover the screw with FastCap self-sticking plastic screw covers ($3 to $5 for 56 1/2-in. covers). These are available at some retailers, online or directly from FastCap. Go to fastcap.com to see the huge variety of sizes and colors. If you're really picky and want to install a nearly invisible, flush screw cover, you can buy a special FlushMount drill bit system ($55 at fastcap.com) that makes a perfect-depth recess for the plastic screw covers.

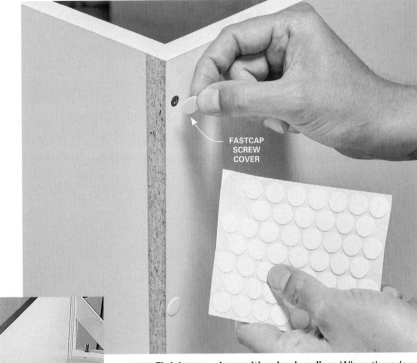

FASTCAP SCREW COVER

11 **Finish raw edges with edge banding**. When the edge of a melamine panel is visible but you don't want to add solid wood nosing, apply edge-banding tape. You can buy iron-on edge banding at most home centers. But an even easier solution is to apply self-adhesive or peel-and-stick edge banding. FastCap is one company that supplies peel-and-stick edge banding in a wide variety of colors, widths and lengths. Called Fastedge, it's available online and at woodworking stores.

1 **Cover edges with edge banding**
Move a hot iron quickly over iron-on edge-banding tape to melt the glue. If you're using self-adhesive edge banding, you can skip this step and simply peel off the paper backing and stick the edge banding to the particleboard edge.

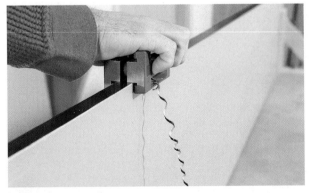

2 **Trim the tape to finish the edge**
Trim the overhanging edges of the tape flush to the melamine surface with an edge-banding trimmer. You'll find edge-banding trimmers at home centers, woodworking stores and online for about $20.

Buy shelving with edges finished
You can skip edge banding altogether if you just need shelves. Shelving with finished edges is readily available at home centers and hardware stores. The only drawback is that the color selection may be limited.

PROTECT YOUR FLOOR DURING REMODELING

Whenever you're remodeling, it's important to protect any uncarpeted floors from demolition debris and dropped tools. When canvas cloths aren't enough, I use 4x8-ft. sheets of 1/8-in. tempered hardboard, commonly called Masonite.

Start by thoroughly vacuuming the floors so grit doesn't scratch the flooring under the hardboard. Then cut and lay down the hardboard and duct-tape the pieces together at the seams.

If you'll be running the HVAC system during the remodel, be sure you don't cover grilles or registers. Finally, seal around the perimeter with masking tape so grit can't get underneath the hardboard at the edges. A sheet of 1/8-in. hardboard costs about $5 at home centers.

— Gary Wentz, TFH Editor-in-Cheif

VACUUM COMB

A paintbrush comb is perfect for removing thread that gets wrapped around a vacuum's beater bar and for cleaning stuff like lint and hair from the bristles.

— Tom Parrent

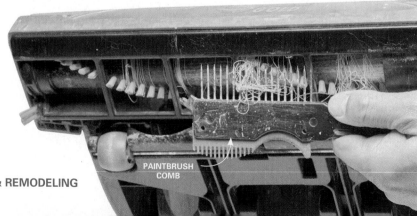

PAINTBRUSH COMB

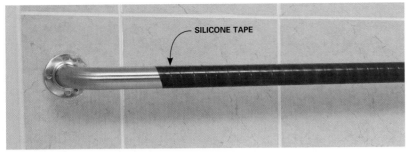

SILICONE TAPE

NONSLIP GRAB BAR

Sometimes the grab bars in my shower can get a little slippery. My quick fix was to wrap them with Stretch & Seal silicone tape. It grips well and stays where you put it. Just be sure to stretch it as you wrap it so it sticks to itself. I've also used it to get a better grip on lots of other handles.

— Bruce Knott

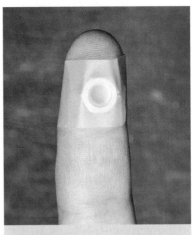

STICKY FINGER

When you need to screw on a nut in a tight space, hold it on your finger with a piece of Scotch tape. That makes it easier to get the screw started (the tape is thin enough for a machine screw to poke through).

— Gordon Watson

DON'T CARRY IT— SLIDE IT

You can buy furniture slides in many shapes and sizes at home centers and online. It's also easy to make your own sliders from plastic container covers, Frisbee discs, bedspreads, moving blankets, towels and carpet remnants. Use hard plastic sliders for carpeting and soft, padded sliders for hard flooring.

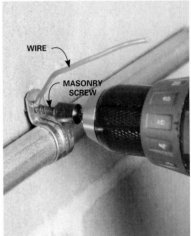

WIRE

MASONRY SCREW

WIRE IN THE HOLE!

If you've ever used masonry screws to attach something to a block wall, you know you have to predrill holes for the screws. But concrete block is hollow and crumbly, and sometimes a screw won't tighten; it just spins inside the hole. To fix the problem, I back out the screw and put a piece of insulated wire inside the hole and drive the screw alongside it. Then I snip off the excess wire. Makes a nice, tight connection!

— Josiah Grunwald

PLYWOOD SAVVY

In the United States, there are four common grades of construction plywood: A, B, C and D. Each sheet will have two grades, such as AC. The first letter is the face veneer grade, and the second is for the back veneer. Some plywoods have a third letter, X, that designates them for exterior use. From highest quality to lowest, here's what to look for:

"A" Grade. Sanded smooth, paintable. Though some neatly made manufacturer repairs are acceptable, you should have little trouble finding A-grade sheets that are free of repairs and knots.

"B" Grade. Solid surface with some repairs, usually football-shaped patches and/or wood filler. May have tight knots (no chunks of wood missing) up to 1 in. Some minor splits.

"C" Grade. Tight knots to 1-1/2 in. and knotholes to 1 in., some splits and discoloration.

"D" Grade. Knots and knotholes up to 2-1/2 in. Some splits. Generally no repairs.

Hardwood plywoods used for furniture and cabinets have a different rating system.

— Timothy Borg

D — BIG KNOT
C — OPEN KNOT HOLE
B — FOOTBALL PATCH
A — CLEAR & SMOOTH

LADDER TOPPER

I often work overhead on a ladder, and my heavy tool belt takes a toll on my back and legs. Now instead of wearing it, I cinch it around the top of my ladder, which keeps all my tools right where I need them.

— Tom Boward

PLYWOOD CUTTING GRID

I wanted an easier way to cut sheets of plywood into smaller pieces with my circular saw, so I built this cutting grid from 2x4s. I just set my grid on a couple of sawhorses and let the sawdust fly. When I'm done, I lean the grid against the wall for next time. I don't worry about cutting into a wooden grid, and the screws are located low enough that the blade won't hit them.

— Harold Niekamp

GETTING NEW CARPET? SEAL PET STAINS

If your old carpet has the lingering smell of pet urine, there's a good chance the urine also penetrated the subfloor. So it's smart to treat the subfloor after the old carpet is out and before the new carpet goes in. Wet any stained areas with a 50/50 mix of water and bleach. After a five-minute soak, wipe up the water and let the floor dry. Then paint over the spots with a stain-blocking primer such as KILZ, BIN or 1-2-3.

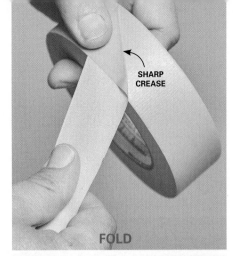

CRAYON MARK

WET-SAW MARKING TIP

Use a crayon to draw the cutting line on tile before using a wet saw.
Unlike a pen or pencil line, a crayon mark won't wash off and is easier to
see in the muddy water.

— Mike Winter

SHARP CREASE

FOLD

TEAR DOWN

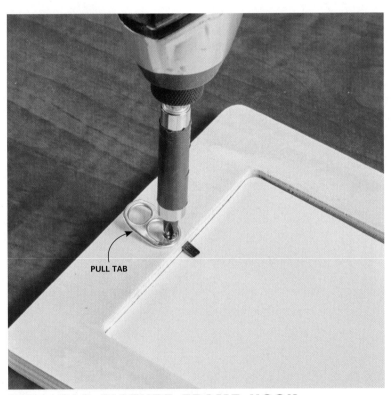

PULL TAB

PULL-TAB PICTURE FRAME HOOK

If you're hanging pictures and run out of those sawtooth hangers, just
grab the nearest soda can. Bend the pull tab back and forth until it breaks
off. Then screw it to your picture frame. Bend the free end out slightly and
hang the picture.

— Carrie Tegeler

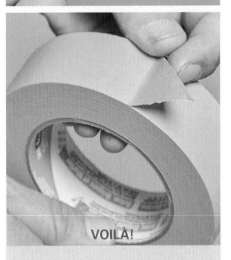

VOILÀ!

TAPE-TEARING TIP

Here's an easy way to tear tape
and get a starting edge at the same
time. Simply fold the tape under at
a 90-degree angle to the roll. Then,
with a snapping motion, pull the
tape against the edge of the roll. The
tape tears, leaving a triangular starting tab. This won't work with plastic
tapes; those must be cut.

— Chris Henrichs

MIRROR AND MESSAGE BOARD

My family is always on the go, so staying in touch with one another can be tough. We thought about putting a whiteboard near the door so we could write messages, but we wanted something better looking. So we bought a full-length mirror, turned it on its side, and mounted it on the wall. Now we can write on it with dry-erase markers and give ourselves one last look before heading out for the day.

— Matthew Kelly

DESIGN ON THE WALL

Planning to remodel? You can get a preview of the remodeled space by creating a full-scale layout on walls and floors with tape, chalk and paper. This trick is especially helpful in kitchens and bathrooms.

ALL ABOUT EURO HINGES

They make cabinet doors easy!

by **Tom Caspar, Contributing Editor**

3 reasons to love euro hinges

Euro hinges—also called "cup hinges" or "concealed hinges"—look complicated.
But they're actually much easier to install than traditional hinges.

Easy to install
Traditional hinges are fussy to install. And if you get it wrong, you're stuck. With Euro hinges, you just bore one large hole and drive some screws. Get that hole in the right spot and the rest is goof-proof.

Easy to adjust
With traditional hinges, you can spend hours getting the fit right: planing or sanding the door, shimming or moving hinges ... With Euro hinges, you can move a door in and out, up and down, or side to side just by turning screws.

Instant on and off
With traditional hinges, you have to remove screws or hinge pins to remove doors. Euro hinges like this one just snap onto mounting plates so you can instantly check the door's fit. Then pull a release lever to remove the door for finishing.

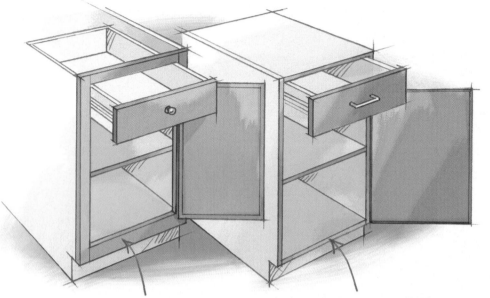

FACE FRAME

FRAMELESS

You need to answer 4 basic questions

Most Euro hinges cost about $2 each, though some specialty hinges cost $10 or more. To get hinges that suit your situation, you need to answer these questions:

1 **Face frame or not?** A frameless or "Euro-style" cabinet is basically a box. A face frame cabinet has a frame surrounding the opening of the box.

FACE-FRAME HINGE

FRAMELESS HINGE

MOUNTING PLATE

Hinges like this one mount onto the face frame, typically with a single screw.

Hinges like this one attach to a mounting plate that's screwed to the cabinet. They're made for frameless cabinets but can be used with face frame cabinets if you buy special mounting brackets.

2 **Inset or overlay doors?** Inset doors are flush with the front of the cabinet; overlay doors cover all or part of the front. Some doors, called "partial inset" (not shown) are a combination of both. We show frameless cabinets here, but the same terms apply to face frame cabinets.

3 **How much overlay?** If you choose overlay doors, you'll have to decide how much. With some frameless hinges, the amount of overlay is determined by the thickness of the mounting plate; a thicker mounting plate results in a lesser overlay.

4 **How far do you want your doors to open?** The simplest, smallest and least expensive hinges usually open to 105 or 110 degrees. If you want your doors to open farther for easier access inside the cabinet, the hinges will be bulkier and more expensive.

INSET DOOR

CABINET

OVERLAY DOOR

3/8"-OVERLAY DOOR

Installing euro hinges

No matter what type of hinge you choose, the hinges are mounted on the door first and then the cabinet.

You'll be drilling two sets of holes in the door. First, there's the "cup hole," the large hole that the hinge drops into. This hole is 35 mm (1-3/8 in.) diameter for all Euro hinges. You'll need a Forstner bit to drill it ($20 at home centers or online).

Second, you'll drill two pilot holes for the screws that fasten the hinge to the door. The instructions will tell you what bit to use.

Some Euro hinges come with a full-size template for marking both sets of holes, but many hinges don't. In that case, the instructions will include a scale drawing in millimeters (not inches) and you'll have to make a template yourself.

Make the template from an old business card. Fold the card around the edge of a scrap of wood (**Photo 1**). Measuring from the fold, draw a line indicating the mounting screw locations. Cut the card along this line.

Draw a centerline on the card, then measure the distance from the folded edge to the center of the cup hole. Poke a hole here using an awl.

Install the hinge on the door

Determine the location of the hinges on the door. The distance from the top or bottom of the door to the hinge's centerline is usually about 2 in. to 3 in. Draw centerlines for the hinges using a square or a wood scrap.

Align the template with the centerline, then trace the edge of the card (**Photo 2**). Use the awl to mark the center of the cup hole.

MEET AN EXPERT

Tom Caspar is a professional furniture maker and the former editor of *American Woodworker* **magazine.**

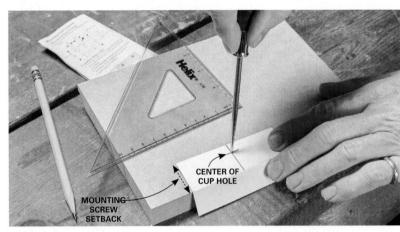

1 Make a template. Fold a business card around a scrap of wood, then cut the card to match the setback of the hinge's mounting screws. Poke a hole in the card to mark the distance to the center of the hinge's cup hole.

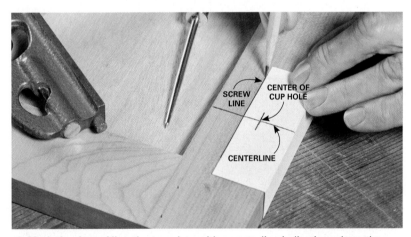

2 Mark the door. Align the template with a centerline indicating where the hinge will go. Trace the edge of the card to mark the mounting screw line, then use an awl to mark the center of the cup hole.

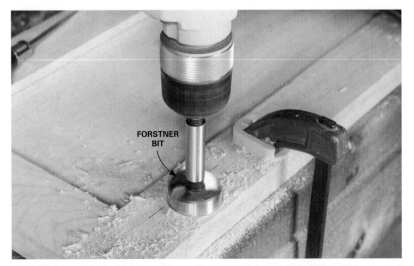

3 Drill the cup hole. Using a 35-mm (1-3/8-in.) Forstner bit, drill until the top of the bit is about level with the wood. Close is good enough.

CENTERLINE

SCREW LINE

4 **Mark screw holes.** Place the hinge in the cup hole, then mark the locations of the mounting screws. Drill pilot holes and install the hinge.

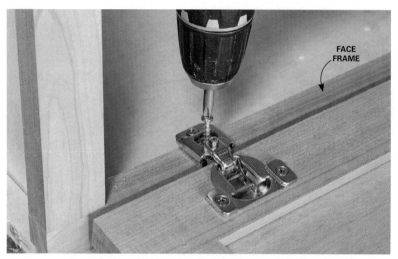

FACE FRAME

5 **Face frame: Fasten the hinge.** For a face-frame cabinet, simply position the door and screw the hinge to the face frame.

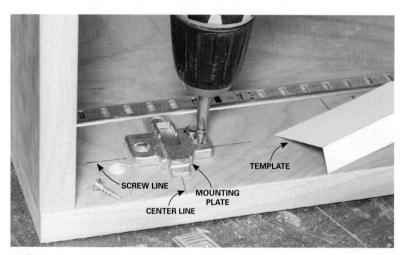

SCREW LINE

TEMPLATE

MOUNTING PLATE

CENTER LINE

6 **Frameless: Install a mounting plate.** For a cabinet without a face frame, make a second template to mark the screw line. Fasten the plate to the cabinet, then snap the door hinge onto the plate.

Shop online

Home centers carry a limited selection of Euro hinges, so it's smart to browse online as well. Sources like rockler.com and wwhardware.com carry hinges with features like soft close or cover plates to hide screws. They also have experts available to help you choose the right hinge system.

Drill the cup holes (**Photo 3**). These holes must be at least 1/2 in. deep. Most Forstner bits are about 1/2 in. thick, so it's easy to use the bit itself to judge how deep you've drilled.

Place the hinge in the cup hole, then mark the hinge's mounting screw holes (**Photo 4**). Drill pilot holes (making sure you don't drill through the door!), then fasten the hinge to the door.

Install the hinge on the cabinet

To install hinges on face-frame cabinets, turn your cabinet on its side, then place the door alongside it. Rest the protruding parts of the hinges on the face frame. Center the door.

Make sure the tabs on the hinges are butted up to the face frame, then use an awl to mark the centers of the mounting screw pilot holes. Drill the holes and install the screws (Photo 5). Stand up the cabinet and fine-tune the door's position by turning the hinge's adjusting screws.

Hinges for frameless cabinets have a separate mounting plate. The instructions will show you the correct distance from the front edge of the cabinet to the screw line. Draw screw lines inside the cabinet.

Attach the mounting plates to the hinges. Place the cabinet on its side, then butt the door to the cabinet. Center the door side-to-side. Align the mounting plate's holes with the setback lines. Mark the centers of the holes.

Pull the door away from the cabinet and remove the mounting plates. Drill pilot holes, then fasten the mounting plates to the cabinet (Photo 6). Snap the hinges onto the plates, then stand up the cabinet and adjust the hinges as needed.

Tips for euro hinges

Mark your template

Store-bought templates like this one include lots of holes to accommodate various hinges. It's all too easy to use the wrong holes. To prevent that, mark the holes you need with paint or a marker.

Go metric

In the world of Euro hinges, everything is metric. You'll need a metric ruler to make your own marking template, for example. For about a buck, you can pick up a metric ruler at any store that carries school supplies.

A corded drill is best

You can bore cup holes with a cordless drill, but that strains the drill and drains the battery fast. A corded drill does the job faster and better.

Buy before you build

Having your hinges on hand makes the planning and building details much easier and prevents major mistakes.

Drill shallow starter holes

The tiny screws that come with Euro hinges often strip out in softwoods or plywood. So instead of drilling a full-depth pilot hole for screws, just create a divot to position the screw using a drill bit, awl or even a nail.

Don't forget the bumpers

Most Euro hinges are self-closing, which means doors slam hard and loud. Pick up sheets of adhesive-backed cabinet bumpers at any home center for a couple bucks.

Fast, goof-proof centerlines

To mark perfect centerlines for the hinges, lay the cabinet box on its side and center the door against it. Then trace along a marking block (2 to 3-in. wide). Use masking tape labels to match doors to their locations.

Leave adjustments for last

Euro hinges allow for absolutely perfect alignment. But don't bother with that until cabinets are installed. Fussing with adjustments before your cabinets are squared up and level is a waste of time.

TEXTURED CEILINGS

**3 solutions for a popcorn ceiling—the best method
depends on your situation and your skills**

by **Jason White, Associate Editor**

Millions of homes have "popcorn" texture applied to ceilings. And while it does a pretty decent job of masking small imperfections in old plaster and drywall, this texture is a little out of fashion and notorious for trapping dust and cobwebs. It's also tough to make a good-looking repair with it. There's good news, however: You've got some options for dealing with an old popcorn ceiling.

1 Cover it with drywall

It's not an easy project, but there are some good reasons to consider installing drywall directly over your popcorn ceiling (and some good reasons not to).

Pros:

■ **No texture to scrape off.** Scraping, even wet-scraping, is hard, messy work. And if the popcorn texture is painted, it will be even harder to scrape off.

■ **Lower asbestos risk.** Popcorn texture applied before 1980 might contain asbestos, which poses a lung cancer danger if disturbed and inhaled. Covering the ceiling with drywall minimizes your risk because there's no scraping involved.

■ **No repairs to make.** If you have problems like flaking texture, stains, cracks or holes in your ceiling, you can skip trying to fix all those things by covering them up. Hanging new drywall over the old ceiling gives you a fresh start!

Cons:

■ **It's a big job.** Drywall is heavy, and lugging full sheets around—especially up and down stairs—is hard work. Plus, most of the work you'll be doing is overhead, so be ready for a sore neck and shoulders. Applying tape and joint compound to seams also takes skill and practice to master.

■ **It's time consuming.** There's the time needed to hang the drywall, plus the time it takes to apply the tape and joint compound. It can easily take you a week to finish one room.

■ **Finishing requires skill.** Screwing the drywall to the ceiling might seem easy enough, but making your seams look good is another story. Applying tape and joint compound is a bit of an art. Remember, this is your ceiling! And ceiling flaws are much more visible than wall flaws.

■ **It costs money.** For a 12 x 12-ft. room, your cost will be about $160 for all the materials, including drywall, joint compound, paint and the rental fee for a drywall lift.

Other key considerations:

■ **Do you have time?** You'll need a week or more to get the drywall hung, the seams taped and several coats of joint compound on and sanded. And it might take you even more time if you're a drywall newbie. Plus, don't forget you'll still have to paint the ceiling when you're done.

■ **Tight on space?** Ever try to maneuver a full sheet of drywall up a narrow staircase, around a corner and into a small room? Cutting it into smaller pieces is an option, but that means you'll have more seams to tape and finish.

■ **Existing crown molding?** If you have crown molding on the ceiling, you'll have to remove it before installing new drywall and reinstall it afterward. That's not a big deal, but it's one more thing you'll have to do. The good news about crown molding, however, is that you won't have to finish along the perimeter of the room because the crown molding will cover the seams between the ceiling and the walls.

Hire a pro?

Covering a ceiling is a big job, and taping drywall—especially on a ceiling—takes skill. So even if you think you can do it yourself, it's a good idea to get a bid from a pro to know how much money your hard work will save. Costs vary widely by region, but expect to pay $600 to $1,800 for a 12 x 12-ft. room.

2 Cover it with wood

Installing tongue-and-groove (T&G) planks on a ceiling is another good way to hide popcorn texture. Most of what you'll find in home centers and lumberyards is 1x6 or 1x8 pine or spruce, although you can special-order other kinds. And if you're working solo, it's a lot easier to handle T&G boards than 4 x 8-ft. or 4 x 12-ft. sheets of drywall. To see how to install T&G boards on a ceiling, visit familyhandyman.com and search for "tongue and groove."

Pros:

■ **It's easier to install than dry-wall.** Since T&G planks are much smaller than 8-ft. or 12-ft. sheets of drywall, you'll have an easier time installing them, especially if you're working alone. And because you'll be covering the old ceiling, you won't have to worry about asbestos or patching and painting the drywall or plaster.

Cons:

■ **Cost.** Wood isn't cheap. A single 1x8 pine T&G plank costs about $7. Covering a 12 x 12-ft. ceiling will cost at least $175.

■ **Tools.** Cutting and installing T&G boards requires several power tools (miter saw, router, pneumatic finish nailer and a compressor). Altogether, those tools will cost at least $400.

3 Scrape it off

Scraping off popcorn texture is a lot of work, but totally doable and worth the effort if your ceiling is in decent shape and you're not afraid to get dirty.

Pros:

■ **Less work than covering with wood or drywall.** However, if the ceiling has been painted, water won't penetrate easily and you might have to dry-scrape it first--a tough and dusty job.

■ **Wet popcorn often comes off easily.** Plus, if you mist the popcorn texture with water and scrape it off while it's still wet, you'll practically eliminate air-borne dust.

Cons:

■ **Risk of asbestos exposure.** Any popcorn texture applied to a ceiling before 1980 might have asbestos in it. Scraping releases asbestos fibers into the air, which can be inhaled and cause lung cancer.

■ **Repairs.** After scraping, you might be left with lots of gouges, dings, loose drywall tape and other imperfections that you'll have to repair after you remove all the texture. And as with taping and mudding drywall, it takes time and skill to fix them.

Knockdown Texture:
A slick solution for an imperfect finish

Whether you cover your ceiling with new drywall or scrape off the texture, you're going to be left with some finishing and taping to do. And unless you're really good at it, getting a smooth ceiling will be slow or difficult or both. Instead, considering applying "knockdown texture." You basically spray texture from a hopper onto the bare drywall and knock down the high spots with a big squeegee. Your ceiling won't be perfectly smooth, but the texture hides small imperfections and looks more up to date than popcorn.

For step-by-step instructions on how to install drywall over a popcorn ceiling or how to apply knockdown texture, visit familyhandyman.com and search for "popcorn" and "knockdown texture."

Another way to remove popcorn texture

We ran a story on how to remove popcorn texture from ceilings, and one of our readers, John McKinney, wrote to us with a tip of his own. "I use a Homax Popcorn Ceiling Scraper," says John. "It's a rect-angular scraper that you screw onto a painting pole or broom handle. The rect-angular part accepts a plastic grocery bag that catches most of the texture as you scrape it off. You can dump the bag when it gets too heavy or put on a new bag." The Homax popcorn scraper is available at home centers and online for about $20. Thanks for the tip, John!

POPCORN CEILING SCRAPER

PLASTIC BAG

MEET AN EXPERT

John McKinney is a retired aerospace engineer and property manager who has scraped many popcorn ceilings in his rental properties.

11 TIPS FOR SCRAPING OFF POPCORN TEXTURE FASTER & EASIER

P opcorn ceilings were all the rage back in the '60s and '70s. Applying the texture to drywall and plaster ceilings was a quick and easy way to hide imperfections and didn't require any painting afterward. But the rough texture catches lots of cobwebs and dust, and it can be a real pain to match if you have cracks or holes in need of patching.

Removing popcorn texture from a ceiling is a messy chore but worth the effort if the substrate underneath is in good shape. Here are some tips to take some of the pain out of scraping the popcorn texture off your ceiling.

TEXTURED CEILINGS **73**

1 Do a scrape test

Before you go to all the trouble of prepping the room, try scraping a small area. Try it dry first, then dampen the texture with water (see p. 75) and try again. Some texture comes off easily without water, but in most cases wetting is best. If the water doesn't soak in and soften the texture, the ceiling has probably been painted or paint was added to the texture mix. In that case, wetting the ceiling may not help, and you'll have to decide whether you want to tackle a really tough scraping job or choose another way to hide your popcorn ceiling.

2 Prep for a big mess

Cover floors and walls with plastic drop cloths. Don't use canvas drop cloths because water can soak through. Cleanup is easier with plastic too, because you can just ball it all up when you're done working and throw it in the trash. Leave the plastic in place after scraping to catch the mess you'll make repairing and sanding the ceiling later.

3 Get the furniture out

If possible, remove all furniture from the room you'll be working in. Scraping popcorn is messy work, and you won't want furniture in your way every time you move the ladder around. If moving everything out of the room isn't possible, cluster it and cover it with drop cloths.

4 Remove ceiling fixtures and fans

You might think it's easier to leave light fixtures and ceiling fans in place, but they'll just be in your way and get covered with wet popcorn. Plus, you don't want to accidentally spray water into an electrical fixture.

JUNCTION BOX

5 Cover electrical boxes

Shut off the power to any electrical junction boxes in the ceiling and cover them with painter's tape to keep the wiring dry when spraying water on the popcorn. Overlap the sides of the junction box with the tape, and then trim around the perimeter with a utility knife, being careful not to nick the wires.

6 Protect can lights from water spray

If you have recessed "can" lights, stuff newspaper or rosin paper inside them to keep them dry. Also, make sure the power to those fixtures is turned off at the circuit breaker panel or fuse box.

7 Wet it with a pump sprayer

For easier scraping and practically no dust, use a garden pump sprayer to mist the ceiling and let it soak in for about 15 minutes before scraping. Only give it a light misting—too much water could damage the drywall or loosen the joint tape. If the texture hasn't softened after 15 minutes or so, spray it again and wait another 10 to 15 minutes.

If the texture still hasn't softened, it might be painted, or paint might have been mixed into the texture before application. In either case, water won't easily penetrate. If the texture is painted, you might be able to dry-scrape it first to expose some of the unpainted texture and follow up with wet scraping. If the texture has paint mixed in, you might have to dry-scrape the whole ceiling or cover it up with drywall or T&G boards.

8 Work in small sections

Only spray and scrape a small area at a time—about 4 x 4 ft. If you work too large of an area at once, the popcorn might dry before you have time to scrape it off. If that happens, respray the area and wait another 10 to 15 minutes before scraping.

9 **Tame the mess with a mud pan**

Use a mud pan—the kind for holding joint compound—to catch the wet popcorn before it hits the floor. That way, you're not tracking it all over the place when you walk and move the ladder around. Also, use the edge of the pan to clean off your scraper when it gets loaded up with wet popcorn. A mud pan costs $6 to $20 at home centers.

10 **Get two scrapers**

A stiff 6-in. putty knife ($8) works great for smaller areas, and a 12-in. drywall taping knife ($10) helps you get a wide area done faster.

After scraping...

Scraping alone won't leave you with a paint-ready ceiling. You'll probably have small dings and gouges to fix. At a minimum, you'll have to sand the ceiling to get it perfectly smooth before painting.

For more tips on fixing drywall and getting it ready to paint, visit familyhandyman.com and search for "preparing walls for paint."

11

Prevent gouging

Round off the corners of your scraper—whether it's a wide putty knife or drywall taping knife—so it won't gouge the ceiling and leave you with dozens of ceiling wounds to repair. Use a file, a sander or an electric grinder to do this.

AVOID **FRAMING MISTAKES**

12 tips from construction pros

by **Mark Petersen, Senior Editor**

Minor framing mistakes can lead to wavy walls and squeaky floors. More serious mistakes can leave a house vulnerable to high winds, heavy snow loads and earthquakes. We wanted to know which mistakes were the most common and how to avoid them. So who better to talk to than a building inspector? He shared his experiences, his insight and a few horror stories. We walked away with some great tips on how to build a rock-solid house, build it code compliant and build it right the first time.

MEET AN EXPERT

Don Sivigny saw a few framing mistakes and code violations in the 13 years he spent as a construction manager and general contractor, and the 21 years he worked as a building inspector. Today Don is a construction code representative in the Construction Codes and Licensing Division for the State of Minnesota. He also represents the state when new building codes are being drafted.

1 Stagger the joints in the top plates

It's best to have one continuous top and tie plate, but that's not possible on longer walls. When multiple plates are necessary, keep top plate end joints a minimum of 24 in. away from tie plate end joints. And keep end joints at least 24 in. from the end of the wall as well. If the two end joints are not kept apart, they create a hinge point, which weakens the wall. But 24 in. is a bare minimum; most conscientious framers prefer at least twice that distance.

2 Nail to the framing

When you're securing the bottom plates of walls to the floor, nail into the floor joists/trusses below. Nailing through the plywood keeps the wall from moving side to side, but expansion and contraction of the roof system could cause the wall to lift if it's not also nailed to the floor joists/trusses. Plus, the nails will be out of the way when contractors need to cut holes in the plates for pipes, ducts and wires. For the same reason, nail top plates to overlying floor joists or roof trusses near studs whenever possible.

3 Don't forget the connectors

Structural connectors are designed to hold framing members to the foundation and to one another. They help a building withstand heavy loads, strong winds and earthquakes. Building codes that require structural connectors have been changing as connector technology improves, so make sure to review your local codes and contact your local building department if you still have questions. The foundation straps shown here prevent high winds from blowing these small garage walls off the foundation.

4 Include finished flooring when laying out stairs

The highest riser (step) height cannot be more than 3/8 in. higher than the shortest riser height throughout the entire flight of stairs. Those measurements include finished floor heights. So mock up and plan for the absolute finished floor heights, top and bottom, before you begin doing the math and laying out the stair stringers.

Installing 3/4-in.-thick hardwood floors on a 1/4-in. subfloor will raise a floor height 1 in. Some carpet, vinyl and laminate flooring options are less than 3/8 in. thick. If you don't account for those height differences, you could fail your inspection, and ripping out stairs is an expensive callback.

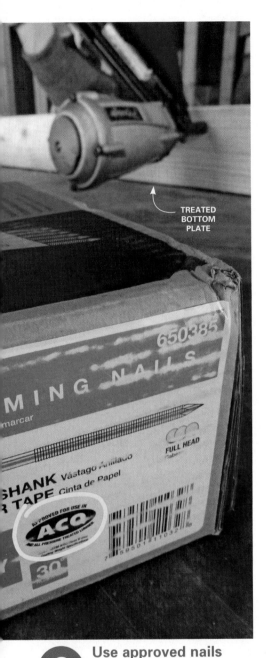

TREATED BOTTOM PLATE

TWO JACK STUDS

HEADER

5 Double up jack studs

Jack studs, or "trimmers," are the framing members that support headers. The number of jack studs needed depends on the length (and sometimes the width) of the header. If the blueprints don't specify, a good rule of thumb is to install two on each side if the opening is wider than 6 ft., the typical patio door size.

6 Use approved nails on treated lumber

Today, treated lumber intended for residential construction is protected with a copper-based preservative system called alkaline copper quaternary (ACQ). Whenever you're working with ACQ lumber, be sure to use only ACQ-approved nails. ACQ treated wood is extremely corrosive to standard framing nails; they will actually dissolve when in direct contact with ACQ lumber. And if there are no nails holding wall studs to a treated bottom plate, foundation bolts/anchors are ineffective. It's also important to use ACQ nails to secure the sheathing to a treated bottom plate.

7 Check for crowns in the studs

This may seem like a "duh!" tip, but some carpenters don't take the time to check the crown (bow) in every stud before assembling a wall. No one will notice if two studs with a 1/4-in. crown are aligned the same way. But if those same studs are installed on opposite sides of the wall, that 1/2-in. difference will be noticeable on both sides of the wall. Also, the studs may continue to warp as they dry, making the wave even more prominent. When you're assembling walls on the ground, keep the crown side up. If the crowns face down, the studs behave like a rocking chair and make it harder to assemble the wall. Some builders use engineered lumber on walls where cabinets will be located because it's super straight and stable.

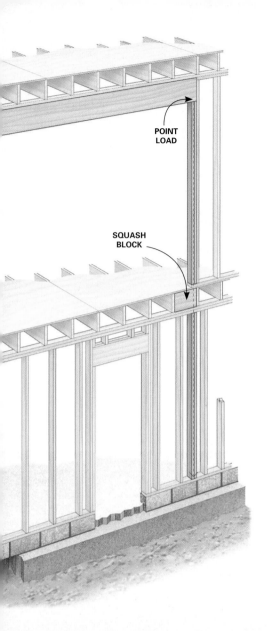

8 Add squash blocks to carry loads

When a heavy load-bearing beam sits atop a wall, extra studs are needed to help carry that "point load" down to the bottom of the wall. But the story doesn't end there; that load has to be carried all the way down to the foundation. Squash blocks are often required to bridge the gap between a beam-supporting wall and the wall beneath it. Either vertical blocks (photo above) or horizontal blocks (illustration at left) could work.

9 Don't forget drywall backing

Most framing assemblies require extra backers to secure the drywall. Even if you're conscious of installing drywall backers as you build, it's easy to forget a section now and again. Don't treat missing backers lightly; they can be a lot more difficult to install if there are wires, pipes or ducts in the way. Also, a grumpy drywall guy may have to rip off moisture barrier, pull out fiberglass insulation or chip out spray foam in order to hang the drywall. To make sure all the backing is there, one simple trick is to walk from room to room and scan every single wall and ceiling intersection with the thought of hanging drywall. And don't forget the closets.

Don't install joists under toilets

All blueprints should indicate the size and spacing of floor joists/trusses, but many don't spell out their exact locations. Avoid installing floor joists/trusses directly in the path of large drain-pipes and mechanical chases. Toilet locations usually cannot be moved, which means the plumber will have to cut into a joist/truss, which can mean hiring an engineer to design a repair, which takes time and costs money.

10 ### Reinforce doorway walls

A wall that supports a door takes a lot of abuse. Some solid-core doors weigh more than 100 lbs. Add an emotional, door-slamming teenager, and you have a door frame that needs to withstand a lot of force. It's important to add extra support to doorway walls, both on the hinge and on the latch side. Do that by applying construction adhesive under the bottom plate on each side of the opening and by adding a couple of 3-in. toe screws.

11 ### Shelter your materials

A little moisture isn't going to hurt most building materials, but if a project is delayed or you know you're in for a long run of wet weather, cover your materials with a tarp. Long exposure to wet conditions can promote mold as well as cause engineered lumber to delaminate and framing lumber to warp and twist. Plus, no one wants to work with wet lumber! Keep the tarp a little loose at the bottom for air circulation.

12 ### Talk to the masons about anchor locations

Meet with the masons before they build the foundation. They should know that anchor bolts are required to secure wall plates every 6 ft. on center and within 12 in. from the ends and each side of joints. But sometimes anchors end up where they don't belong, like in door openings or under jack studs. A short meeting to discuss locations of openings and splices could spare you from cutting out misplaced anchors and installing new ones.

WORKING WITH SELF-LEVELING UNDERLAYMENT

13 tips help you do this job right

by Mark Petersen, Senior Editor

Whether you're installing ceramic tile, laminate planks or carpet, self-leveling underlayment is a great choice for floors that are rough, uneven or out of level. And it's the absolute best choice for tile installations over an in-floor heating system.

Self-leveling underlayment is easy to work with and doesn't require a lot of fancy tools or years of training. However, there is a fair amount of prep work that needs to be done—and done right, because once the pouring starts, you'll need to work fast. We'll show you the step-by-step process to achieve a perfectly flat and level underlayment that's smooth as glass.

MEET AN EXPERT

Josh Risberg, our lead carpenter, is a certified tile installer. He also has 10 years under his tool belt as a lead carpenter for high-end remodelers and home builders.

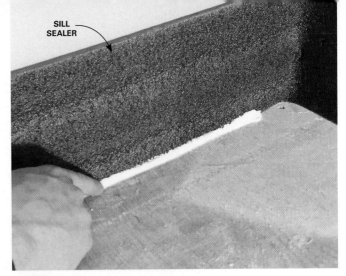

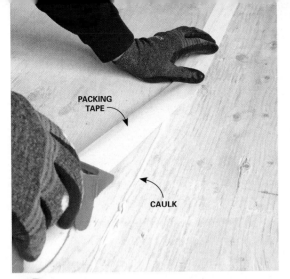

1 Seal every hole and crack

Thoroughly sweep and vacuum the entire floor, and then seal all holes and seams in the plywood with caulking. The self-leveler will drain through an opening as small as a nail hole, so be thorough. Get the type of caulk that goes on white but turns clear when it dries so you can tell when it's done setting up.

Taping over the caulk with packing tape isn't required, but it's a terrific way to avoid stepping in a glob and tracking it around the rest of the house. When working on an older house with floor planks instead of plywood, cover the whole floor with self-adhering roofing underlayment.

Cost:
One 40-lb. bag of self-leveling underlayment costs about $38 and will cover about 20 sq. ft. at 1/4-in. thick.

3 Build dams around big openings

Isolate large holes like heating vents and floor drains with cardboard. Just shape the cardboard to the hole and tape it in place. Caulk the cardboard to the floor.

2 Make the walls leakproof

Sill sealer (a foam gasket that carpenters use to seal between the foundation and the bottom wall plates) makes a great barrier to keep the self-leveler from escaping into other rooms or into the basement. Hold it in place with staples from a staple gun. Keep the staples low enough so the staple holes will be hidden by the base trim. Sill sealer that's either 3-1/2 in. or 5-1/2 in. wide will work, but the wider sealer does a better job of protecting painted walls from splashes.

Caulk the sill sealer to the floor. Smear the caulk with your finger to make sure it adheres to both surfaces. Once the pour is complete, the sill sealer can easily be cut with a razor. The small void near the wall won't affect finished floor installation.

4 Strengthen the floor with lath

Lath adds strength to the underlayment the same way rebar adds strength to concrete. Use plastic lath instead of metal when working with in-floor heating. Check with the manufacturer of the heating system as to whether the lath should be installed over or under the mat/cables.

Overlap the lath at least 3 in., and secure it with a hammer tacker stapler. Keep the lath an inch or so away from the walls so it doesn't poke through the sill sealer when you're installing it. Try to keep the lath as flat as possible; you don't want any part of it projecting through the leveler after it's placed.

Always check the continuity of the heating cables or mats before you start mixing. If you accidentally sever or nick a cable, it's easier to repair it before the underlayment is poured...that's an understatement!

WORKING WITH SELF-LEVELING UNDERLAYMENT **83**

⑤ Build dams in doorways

Dam up doorways with strips of wood. Make sure you seal the wood to the floor with caulk as well as the area where the wood strip meets the sill sealer. Think through the placement. For the best look, the joint between the newly finished floor and the adjoining floor in the next room should typically fall directly under the middle of the door.

DAM

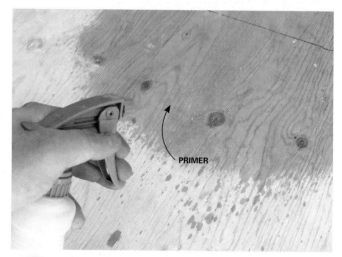

PRIMER

⑦ Prime the wood

Covering the floor with two coats of primer will prevent the plywood from absorbing water. Waterlogged wood swells. It shrinks back down when it dries, which could create cracks in the underlayment and tiles above. Floor primer can be rolled on or brushed, but our expert prefers spraying it on because it's fast and easy and there are no brushes or rollers to clean up. He uses a pump-up sprayer on larger jobs and a simple spray bottle on smaller ones. No primer is needed if you use self-adhering underlayment.

⑥ Keep bags dry

Bags of self-leveler can be ruined by wicking up moisture from concrete out in the garage or on the basement floor. Keep your bags dry by setting them on a pallet or a sheet of plywood resting on scrap 2x4s.

Order 20 percent extra

Running out of self-leveler before a pour is finished is a big hassle, so don't let that happen. Buy 20 percent more than you think you will need. A large room poured even 1/16-in. thicker than planned can gobble up several additional bags. You can return any unused bags.

8 Prep the bags

Most bags filled with dry cementitious mixes have a vent in the top. It's there so the bags don't break open when they're handled. Minimize the mess by keeping the vent side up. Line the open bags up next to the buckets. Mixing is a messy business, so do it outdoors whenever possible, or protect the floor. Extreme temperatures can affect the time it takes the leveler to set up, so store the bags at room temperature before use.

GARBAGE
CAN →

9 Fill a separate bucket for the mixer

Keep the paddle mixer in a bucket of water between pours to prevent the paddle from getting crusty. Fill the bucket at least three-quarters full so the mixer won't tip over.

10 Pull water from a garbage can

Drill holes in your fill bucket at the fill line so the bucket will drain to the proper level. For fast filling, dip a bucket into a barrel or garbage can filled with water. At this stage of the game, speed is important.

11 Mix a lot at once

Mixing self-leveler in 5-gallon buckets is a messy proposition. Get yourself 6-gallon buckets if you can. Many flooring stores carry them. Fill all your buckets with the recommended amount of water first, and then add the self-leveler. Keep the buckets close to each other to reduce the mess when moving the mixer from one bucket to another, and keep all the bucket handles facing out so they're easier to grab (every second counts).

Once you've mixed all the buckets, go back to the first, and mix it up again for a few seconds in order to stir up the sand that has settled. After dumping each bucket, fluff the sand in the next one before hauling it in. Set the mixer in the next bucket to be hauled in, and then store it in the bucket of water between batches.

12 Spread as you pour

Move the bucket along the floor as you pour. Keep the bucket low to minimize splashing. If you do splash on the wall, try to resist the temptation to wipe it off right away because small drops can quickly become large smudges. You'll have better luck letting it dry and scraping it off.

Completely cover the heating cables/mats with self-leveler to avoid damaging them with a trowel while installing the thin-set. The depth of your pour may vary depending on your project, but shoot for a thickness between 1/2 in. and 3/4 in. Anything over 3/4 in. will likely require two pours, but confirm that by reading the instructions printed on the bag of the product you're using. Check the thickness with a gauge rake, a junky tape measure or just a stick with the desired thickness marked on it.

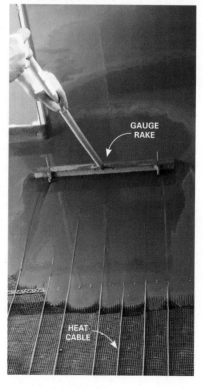

GAUGE RAKE

HEAT CABLE

13 Move self-leveler with a gauge rake

A gauge rake is a metal squeegee that rides on two adjustable depth guides. This tool isn't absolutely necessary, but it does work well at spreading the selfleveler, and it helps gauge how thick the self-leveler is. It's especially useful for large pours. Be careful to work the rake very gently near the heating cables or mat. Gauge rakes cost about $45 at flooring stores and online.

Start at the far end of the room and work your way to the door. If you pass other entry points along the way, lock the doors and hang "keep out" signs.

Wash buckets right away
Wash your buckets as soon as you're done pouring, and never dump the dirty water down a drain.

GreatGoofs®

Screwy pocket door

My daughter had recently bought a house with her fiancé, and there was a problem with the master bedroom closet. The weight of their clothes was too much for the flimsy shelving, held in place with only hollow wall anchors. No problem for "Handy Dad," though.

During their honeymoon, I went to work reattaching everything in the closet, being careful to drive screws into the studs of the closet's back wall. A few days later, my daughter called. The closet was fine, but she couldn't open a pocket door in the bedroom. Turns out the pocket door shared a wall with the back of the closet, and my screws had gone through the pocket door's frame. Some shorter screws fixed the problem, but not my red face.

— Mike Fritz

No spaghetti for you!

During a kitchen remodel, we decided to buy new pots and pans the day before our countertops arrived. We couldn't wait to put them away in our new cabinets, and since the countertops weren't on yet, we set the cookware in through the tops of the lower cabinets. A couple of days later after the countertops were installed, we went to grab the big spaghetti pot, but it wouldn't fit through the door opening. Maybe the next homeowners will be able to get it out if they remodel the kitchen.

— Sean Donley

Ask before you borrow

After a big demolition job, I needed a big shop vacuum—just like my neighbor's new one. He wasn't home, but I figured he wouldn't mind if I went into his garage and helped myself. Then I got to work. I was so focused on the cleanup that it took me a while to notice the haze in front of me. Behind me, I could see nothing but a swirling cloud. The vac had picked up piles of demo dust and blasted it into the adjoining rooms.

As I was returning the vac, the garage door opened and my neighbor pulled in. I just stood there, coated with white dust, holding the vac like a trapped thief. He got out of the car and smiled. "I could have told you there's no filter in it, Jerry," he said, trying not to laugh.

— Jerry Sommers

Paint
like a Pro

13 TIPS FOR
SPRAY-PAINTING

Every DIYer needs to know how to spray paint!

by **Travis Larson, Senior Editor**

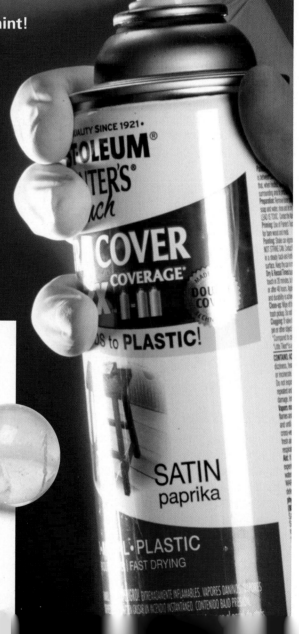

The telltale signs of a bad spray-paint job are easy to spot. Stripes of uneven coverage, paint buildup in the corners, a stray hair in the finish —the list goes on. Worst of all is the dreaded run, an obvious sign that the painter applied too heavy a coat.

Here are a dozen tips to help you get a smooth, consistent finish on your next painting project. For more on this topic, including how to build a spray-paint booth, search for "spray painting" at familyhandyman.com.

Spray-can trivia

Ever wonder what gives spray cans their rattle? It's a glass marble most likely made by Marble King, a company in West Virginia. Marble King makes spray-can marbles and most of the marbles sold in the U.S.A., 1 million a day, 365 days a year.

1 Disassemble if you can

Before you start spray-painting, examine your project. If you can take it apart without too much trouble, do it! You'll have much better luck getting even coverage, seeing what you're doing and avoiding runs. But don't just dismantle the piece willy-nilly. Mark the parts for easy reassembly.

SECOND COAT

FIRST COAT

2 Apply coats in different directions

To achieve the most even coverage, it's a good idea to put on subsequent coats in different directions. Changing directions will help you get into all those nooks and crannies and reduce the chance of zebra stripes.

3 Always clean out the nozzle

Even though nozzle-cleaning directions are on every single can of spray paint, it's an easy step to skip. After use, hold the can upside down and press the nozzle until no more pigment shows in the spray, and then wipe the tip with a rag or paper towel. If you skip this step, you could end up with a nozzle completely clogged with dried paint or a partial clog that'll affect the spray pattern next time.

4 Dust: public enemy no. 1

For a flawless finish on small parts, paint them inside a cardboard box. If you have larger projects, create a poly booth. In basements, dust will shake down from the floor joists, especially if someone is stomping around upstairs, so staple painter's plastic to the ceiling. Damp-mopping the floor will keep your feet from stirring up dust. Don't use a fan to speed up drying time. Wear clean clothes and a hat to keep hair out of the finish. An hour or so before you paint, shut off furnaces, the A/C and ceiling fans to let the dust settle.

5 Start with a tack coat

If you're spraying a vertical surface, it's always smart to apply a "tack" coat before applying the first full coat. A tack coat is a light mist that you allow to set for five minutes. The texture of the tack coat will help hold the paint in place and reduce runs.

NEW NOZZLE

PLUGGED NOZZLE

6 Swap plugged nozzles

Most nozzles have a universal fit. If you end up with a plugged nozzle and have other cans of spray paint with good nozzles, just swap the bad one for a new one. They lift right off and push on. If you don't have any good nozzles, remove the plugged one and soak it in nail polish remover, acetone or even mineral spirits.

7 Spray anything

The Spra-Tool is a simple product—a plastic jar plus an aerosol can. You just pour the liquid into the jar and pull the trigger. We had great results with thin liquids like stain, shellac and household cleaners. With thicker material—polyurethane and latex paint—we had to add thinner to achieve a smooth coat. In some cases, we added more thinner than the paint manufacturer recommended. (Using too much thinner can affect the paint's durability, but we didn't have a problem.) Still, we got smooth, perfect finishes—fast. The Spra-Tool kit (about $12) is available at some home centers and online.

8 Need a custom-color spray paint?

If you want to paint radiators, electrical cover plates, a shelf or anything else to match your wall or trim color, go online and search for "custom spray paint." You'll find many companies (one is myperfectcolor.com) that can custom-mix just about any color, provided you know the paint manufacturer and color name. If you want a different shade of an existing color, choose one of the other shades from the paint swatch you got at the home center or paint store and have that color custom-mixed.

ACTIVATED
CARBON
RESPIRATOR

9 Authentic-look hardware...for less!

When I bought my 1923-vintage house, the two exterior doors were original, as were the doorknobs. Unfortunately, the previous owners had installed shiny new brass dead bolts and escutcheon plate—a bad mismatch. Instead of scouring local antiques stores to find replacements, I decided to try painting the brass.

After removing the hardware, I scuffed the brass finish with fine sandpaper. Then I sprayed on a coat of primer and a few coats of Rust-Oleum's hammered-finish spray paint. The hammered finish provided the aged bronze look I was after. I was amazed at how well the repainted hardware matched the old doorknobs, and the paint job has held up, inside and out, for more than 10 years. So here's my advice: Don't replace ugly metal hardware. Save money by refinishing it with a metallic spray paint.

— Vern Johnson, Art Director

10 Hang 'em high

If the project parts are small enough, you can suspend them for painting. You'll be able to paint all sides at the same time and have everything at eye level. Use coat hangers, wires, thumbtacks, screws—whatever you have on hand. Wear an activated carbon respirator when you spray-paint, especially if you're painting indoors.

11 Read the directions!

This sounds obvious, but few people bother to read the directions on the can. If the manufacturer says to apply a tack coat or start with a primer, there's probably a good reason for it. One of the most important pieces of information is the drying time between coats. Often, you can apply a second coat soon afterward. But if you miss that window, you may have to wait a long time to apply the next coat.

Directions: Use outdoors, or in well-ventilated area, when temperature is above 50°F (10°C) and humidity is below 85% to ensure proper drying. Do not apply to surfaces that exceed 200°F. Avoid spraying in very windy, dusty conditions. Cover nearby objects to protect from spray mist. Remove loose paint and rust with a wire brush or sandpaper. Lightly sand glossy surfaces. Clean with soap and water, rinse and let dry. Shake can vigorously for one minute after mixing balls begin to rattle. Shake often during use. Hold can upright 12-16" from surface and spray in a steady back-and-forth motion, slightly overlapping each stroke. Keep the can the same distance from the surface and in motion while spraying. Apply 2 or more light coats a few minutes apart. May recoat within 1 hour or after 48 hours. Dries to the touch in 2-4 hours, to handle in 5-9 hours, and is fully dry in 24 hours, at 70°F (21°C) ~50% relative humidity. Allow more time at cooler temperatures. When finished spraying, clear spray valve by turning can upside down and pushing spray button for 5 seconds. If valve clogs, twist and pull off spray tip and rinse it in a solvent such as mineral spirits. Do not stick a pin or other object into the stem. Throw away empty can in trash pickup. Do not burn or place in home trash compactor.

12 Many light coats

It is common knowledge that you should apply several light coats rather than one or two heavy ones. But few have the discipline to follow this simple advice. When you're spraying, resist the temptation to fill in thinner areas on one pass to completely cover the surface. Or welcome to dealing with runs—yet again.

Paint like a Pro

13 All-in-one paint and primer

Ever wonder if it's OK to skip the primer and use a "paint and primer in one"? The answer is yes for about 90 percent of DIY painting projects, according to John Gilbert at Behr. All-in-one products are not simply primer and paint mixed in a can. Special polymers were developed to make them sticky enough to use without a separate primer.

Traditional primer is still best for metal, plastics and substrates like drywall and plaster with water stains or smoke damage. It's also recommended for woods like redwood or oak that contain tannins that might bleed through, says Gilbert.

MEET AN EXPERT

John Gilbert is the chief research and design officer at Behr Process Corp.

HandyHints®

FROM OUR READERS

Paint mix-up

I had part of my living room ceiling patched and retextured, and took on the job of repainting the entire ceiling myself. The popcorn ceiling was soaking up more paint than I expected, so I bought a second can of ceiling white (or so I thought). When I finished painting, I pulled off all the masking tape and painter's plastic, folded up the drop cloths and poured myself a cold one.

However, a few hours into a "Godfather" binge-watching session, I glanced up and half the ceiling still looked wet. In a cold sweat, I checked the label on the second can and discovered that instead of flat ceiling paint, I had bought glossy enamel. And because of its shiny appearance, it always looks wet. So I was forced to repaint the entire ceiling. Next time, I'll double-check the paint can label before I leave the store.

— Rick Muscoplat, Associate Editor

12 GREAT PAINTING TIPS

Interior painting must be the No. 1 home improvement activity—everyone has to paint a room sometime! To help you master the process, check out these terrific tips from pros and DIYers alike.

SPRING CLAMP

FERRULE

FINISH SETTLES IN THE BOTTOM OF THE JAR

1 Self-cleaning paintbrushes

Just hang your brush in a jar of solvent: water for latex paint, and mineral spirits or paint thinner for oil-based. Using a clamp, suspend the brush in the jar with the bristles fully submerged almost to the ferrule, but not touching the bottom of the jar. Finish will slide off the bristles and settle on the bottom of the jar.

If you're using paint thinner or mineral spirits, set the jar outside to keep fumes out of your house. Be sure it's away from children and pets. After a day or two, remove the brush and give it a thorough rinse in clean solvent.

— Pat Gustafson, reader

Paint like a Pro

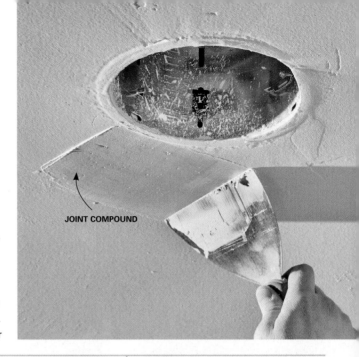

JOINT COMPOUND

2 **Patch, prime, patch, prime...**
You've done a great job of patching and smoothing over all those pesky cracks, holes and dimples in your walls and ceiling, and you've rolled on the primer. So does that mean you're ready for the top-coat? Not so fast. Take a closer look at the surfaces with a portable work light. Chances are, you still have small imperfections you'll want to touch up with spackling or joint compound. Better to take care of these now because they'll really stand out after the final coat of paint goes on.
— Matt Karl, Field Editor

STIR STICKS

3 **Baby wipes for small messes**
I always have a package of baby wipes handy whenever I paint a room. They're great for wiping up small drips before I accidentally walk through them and track paint all over the house. It beats keeping a bucket of water and rags around any day!
— Carl Edouard Denis, Field Editor

4 **Make your own stir sticks**
Forgot to grab stir sticks at the store when you picked up the paint? If you have a band saw and a hunk of 2x4, you can make your own! Take a 2-ft.-long 2x4 and draw a perpendicular line in the middle. Next, "rip" several 3/16-in.-thick strips on the band saw up to the pencil line. Then, to release the stir sticks, chop the 2x4 at the pencil line. This method keeps your fingers a safe distance from the saw blade.
— Les Eastep, Field Editor

DIY debate

Paint walls or trim first?

We asked our Facebook followers whether they preferred to paint trim or walls and ceilings first, and boy, are people divided on this! We got more than 300 comments from DIYers and pros, but no clear consensus. However, we did learn some new tricks:

Paul G. paints in this order: "Hands, jeans, cat, kid, then finally the walls and trim."

And our keep-it-simple award goes to Brian G.: "I paint everything the same color, so it doesn't much matter."

MARBLES

5 Touch-up paint bottle

When there's only a little bit of latex paint left in the can and I want to save it for touch-ups, I put a half-dozen marbles in an empty water bottle and pour in the leftover paint. When I'm ready to do a touch-up, I shake the bottle and the marbles mix the paint. A roll of tape with a rag draped over it helps hold the bottle steady while I pour the paint into it. Just be sure to use a funnel or you'll have a mess on your hands.

— Ron Hazelton,
TV Home Improvement Expert,
Ronhazelton.com

6 Shelter baseboards from splatter

When you're rolling paint onto walls or ceilings, a fine mist of paint settles on unprotected trim. For baseboards, forget about covering them completely. Just cover the top of each one with a "shelter" made from painter's tape. A single overhanging strip of 1-1/2-in. or 2-in. tape catches roller splatters just like the roof overhang on a house keeps rain off the siding. Tape doesn't stick to dusty surfaces very well, so be sure to vacuum or wipe down your baseboards before masking. Also press the tape down hard with a putty knife to prevent paint from bleeding underneath. For the best results, use "self-sealing" tape (see p. 97).

— Michael Whiting, Pro Painter

7 Take photos of paint can lids

Have you ever thrown away a paint can and later wished you hadn't because you couldn't remember the name of the color you painted the bedroom? Paint can lids usually have labels with color information printed on them. Take photos of your paint can lids, print them and tuck them away for future reference.

— Gary Wentz, Editor-in-Chief

DIY debate

Angled or straight bristles?

We asked our Facebook followers whether they preferred paintbrushes with straight or angled bristles for tasks like cutting in around windows or painting trim. Most said they preferred angled, but we did hear from a handful of straight-bristle brush fans. And lots of people use both. As Lea D. told us, "Angled for corners and cutting in, and flat for all-over coverage."

9   Kitchen-whisk paint stirrer

Paint mixers that you can chuck in a drill are nothing new, but I didn't have one on hand for a recent touchup and needed to improvise. So I found a whisk in one of my kitchen drawers, cut off the loop on the end of the handle, and put it in my cordless drill. It happened to be the right size for a 1-gallon paint can and did a great job of mixing the old paint.

— Rosie Wallent

SELF-SEALING TAPE

8   Splurge on self-sealing tape

With regular painter's tape, you run the risk of "paint bleed"— paint creeps underneath the tape, leaving a ragged line where a wall meets trim or another wall or ceiling. We like self-sealing tapes like FrogTape and ScotchBlue Edge-Lock tape because they're specially designed to prevent paint bleed, giving you crisp, straight lines. They cost a lot more than regular masking or painter's tape, but they're worth it.

— Tom Dvorak, Field Editor

Paint like a Pro

10 Foil-tape paint saver

After paint cans have been opened and closed over a couple of years, the lids and rims get all bent and gooped up, making it hard to get an airtight seal. I now wrap foil duct tape around the upper part of the can. Works great!

— John Van Der Linden

FOIL DUCT TAPE

11 Never clean a roller tray

Instead of buying liners for my plastic paint roller tray, I just let the paint dry and pour new paint right over it for the next job. When the paint starts getting thick, I peel it out and throw it in the trash. I've had this tray forever and probably won't ever need to buy another one.

— Travis Larson, Senior Editor

12 Golf tee paint helpers

When you're painting or varnishing small projects, it's best to elevate them for good coverage and to keep your project from sticking to the worktable. I use an old piece of pegboard and some golf tees. The pegboard keeps the tees in place, and I can arrange them as necessary for different size projects.

— Terry Meincke

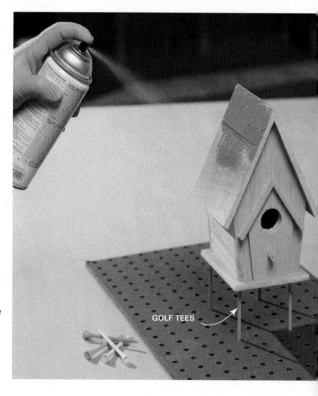

GOLF TEES

2 Electrical & High-Tech

IN THIS CHAPTER

Home Care & Repair 100
How to reset a circuit breaker, time to upgrade your electrical service?, fix a broken phone charger, easier twisting for wire connectors and more

Protect Against Electrical Surges 107

Bluetooth Wireless Speakers 110

Avoid Freeze-Up Disaster 112

Super-Easy USB Outlet 114

Great Goofs 117
Drilling debacle & hots pants!

HOW TO **RESET** A CIRCUIT BREAKER

You probably know how to reset your circuit breaker, but what about your kids or their baby-sitter? Use this tutorial to show them how.

by **Jason White, Associate Editor**

The electrical panel

You'll usually find the main circuit breaker panel—a gray, metal box—in a utility room, garage or basement. Don't worry about opening the panel's door. All the dangerous stuff is behind another steel cover. Behind the door is the main breaker for the entire house (usually at the top of the panel) and two rows of other breakers is below, each controlling individual circuits.

If the breaker trips for no apparent reason, there may be a short circuit—a much bigger problem, usually best left to an electrician to figure out. A tripped breaker isn't always easy to spot. If you're lucky, there will be a list of circuits on the back of the panel's door and you'll be able to find the tripped one quickly (sometimes those lists are labeled wrong, however). If not, you'll have to find it by eye. Look for a partially tripped breaker that's about halfway between the "off" and "on" positions (see photo above). Avoid the temptation to switch all the breakers, or you'll find yourself resetting electronic devices like clocks around the house or losing work underway on computers. You could even damage delicate electronics.

DOUBLE- POLE BREAKER

SINGLE- POLE BREAKER

TANDEM BREAKER

Three types of breakers:

You're likely to see switches for three different types of circuit breakers in a panel—single pole, double pole and "tandem." Single-pole breakers feed 120-volt circuits for ceiling lights and most wall outlets, while double-pole breakers feed 240-volt circuits for appliances like electric ranges and central air conditioning systems. "Tandem" breakers also have two switches. They take a single slot inside the circuit breaker panel and turn it into two 120-volt circuits to save space.

FIND THE SWITCH THAT'S OUT OF LINE

1 **Find the tripped breaker.** When a breaker trips (shuts off), it's usually because too many things were running on one circuit at the same time and it got overloaded. If you are running multiple high-amperage appliances like hair dryers, toasters or space heaters, and the breaker trips, shut off the devices and reset the breaker.

SWITCH OFF, THEN ON

2 **Reset the breaker.** To reset a breaker, move the switch all the way to its "off" position, then back to "on" (see photos). You might hear a few beeps from smoke detectors and appliances when you turn the power back on, but that's normal. You're good to go!

LIGHTNING: DON'T GET HIT INDOORS

Your home is probably the safest place to be in an electrical storm. But lightning can still get to you through the conductive paths in your house: your wiring, your plumbing and water. Talking on a corded phone, taking a shower or bath, working on your desktop computer and handling power tools during an electrical storm aren't much safer than standing outside. Stay away from all water and appliances until the storm passes.

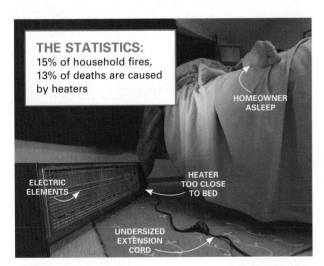

THE STATISTICS:
15% of household fires, 13% of deaths are caused by heaters

HOMEOWNER ASLEEP

ELECTRIC ELEMENTS

HEATER TOO CLOSE TO BED

UNDERSIZED EXTENSION CORD

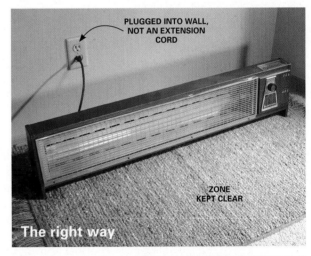

PLUGGED INTO WALL, NOT AN EXTENSION CORD

ZONE KEPT CLEAR

The right way

STAY WARM, DON'T BURN

Most deaths from household fires occur when wood stoves or space heaters are in use and ignite nearby combustibles while everyone's asleep. Wood stoves also cause fires when embers in discarded ashes smolder and ignite other trash. Creosote build-up and sparks can cause a chimney fire that ignites combustibles located too close to a wood stove.

Prevention:
- Keep space heaters at least 5 ft. away from drapes, bedding and other flammables.
- Plug space heaters directly into outlets, not into extension cords.
- If your space heater has electric elements, don't use it while sleeping.
- Empty wood-stove ashes in a metal container and store them outside away from combustibles for at least a week before dumping them into the trash.
- Have chimneys inspected and cleaned every year.
- Keep combustible objects at least 5 ft. away from the stove or fireplace.

HomeCare&Repair

DON'T FORGET SURGE PROTECTION

More and more appliances now contain sensitive electronics that can be destroyed by a power surge. And the repair bill can total hundreds of dollars. So if you buy a new washer, for example, consider spending an extra $50 or so on a surge suppressor. For more info, go to familyhandyman.com and search for "surge protection."

WHICH WIRE NUTS?

Ever wonder which color wire connector you should use to join wires in a junction box? Master electrician Rex Cauldwell has this to say:

"If the wire nut is too small to fasten properly, jump to the next size. As a general rule, use orange connectors for tiny wires; yellow connectors for 14-gauge; red connectors for 12-gauge; and big blue connectors for 10-gauge. When in doubt, read the packaging. It should list the exact number of wires that can go inside a wire connector."

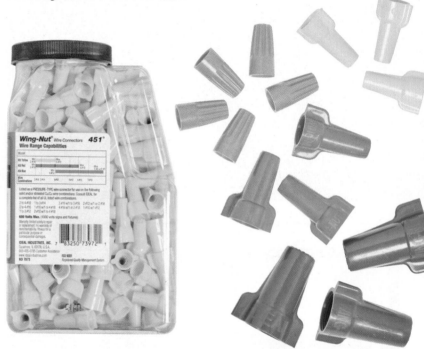

BUYING LIGHT FIXTURES? BEWARE!

Every once in a while, I show up at a home to install a new fixture that the homeowner provided and run into an obstacle. It might be a hanging fixture that won't allow a door or cabinet to open or a sconce that blocks the medicine cabinet. The worst part is that I sometimes don't recognize the problem until I've installed the fixture. Ouch. So before you shop, measure first.

— Al Hildenbrand, Electrical Contractor and *TFH* wiring whiz

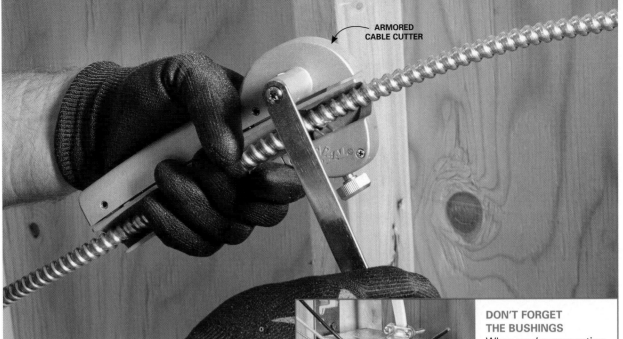

ARMORED CABLE CUTTER

CUTTING METAL-CLAD CABLE

I once lived in an old house with miles of metal-clad (MC) cable—sometimes called "BX" or "armored" cable—which is a bundle of insulated wires sheathed in a flexible metal spiral. The cladding protects the wires from damage in exposed areas like basements and garages. I had to reroute some of this cable in my basement, which meant removing metal cladding in some spots so I could join the cable to some new junction boxes.

You can remove the metal cladding by bending the cable and cutting through the armor with diagonal cutters, but that's time consuming and you can accidentally nick the wires. So I bought an armored cable cutter (shown) made for the job, and boy, is it a time-saver! It uses a hand-cranked cutting wheel that cuts through the armor only, leaving the wires undamaged. You just squeeze the tool, turn the crank a few times and slide off the metal cladding. The cable cutters cost $30 and up at home centers and online.

— Jason White, Associate Editor

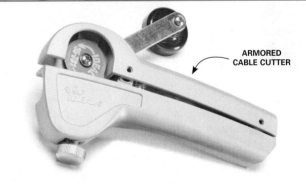

ARMORED CABLE CUTTER

DON'T FORGET THE BUSHINGS

When you're connecting MC cable to a junction box, be sure to install anti-short bushings to protect the wires inside from the metal cladding's sharp edge. Only connect MC cable to metal junction boxes using approved connectors. Also be sure to ask your local electrical inspector whether MC cable is allowed for your particular situation.

ANTI-SHORT BUSHING

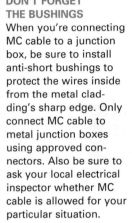

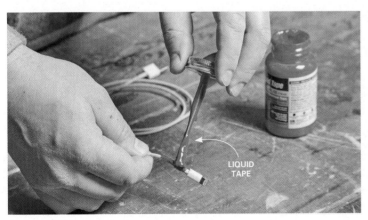

LIQUID TAPE

FIX A BROKEN PHONE CHARGER

Charger cables for cell phones usually last only a few years before the insulation starts fraying on the ends. Replacement cables cost $8 to $30, but there's a cheaper solution. If the insulation is cracked but the copper wire inside is still intact, try covering the crack with a couple of layers of liquid electrical tape ($5 to $10 per bottle). Performix and Gardner Bender are two brands that get lots of positive reviews online. Just be sure not to let the cable touch anything until the liquid tape dries completely.

HomeCare&Repair

EASIER TWISTING FOR WIRE CONNECTORS

When you have multiple or heavy-gauge wires to join, twisting on wire connectors by hand can be a real bear, even when they have wings on them. Several manufacturers have tools that make the job easier, but we especially like this one from Ideal Industries.

Ideal creates a recess in the handle of several of its screwdrivers, conduit reamers and other tools. You just insert the wire connector into the star-shaped recess as shown; the recess and the tool's large rubber grip make twisting wires much easier. You can find these tools for about $6 and up in home centers and online.

WIRE CONNECTOR GOES HERE

FASTER HOME CENTER CHECKOUT

Ever get to the cash register at the home center with a cart full of lumber, only to find the bar code stickers missing? When this happens, the cashier has to spend several minutes either looking up the item or waiting for somebody to run back to the aisle to get the item number.

I avoid this annoyance by making sure there's a bar code sticker on the product before I take it to the register. If it's missing, I grab my cell phone and snap a photo of the shelf label, which usually has the item number and bar code or price information on it. I just hand my phone to the cashier, who can then scan the bar code or punch in the item number manually. This is also helpful when something's on sale but doesn't ring up at the lower price at the register.

MEET AN EXPERT

Jason White is an associate editor at *The Family Handyman* and has spent what feels like half his life buying stuff in home stores.

TIME TO UPGRADE YOUR ELECTRICAL SERVICE?

An electrical panel upgrade can cost anywhere from $1,200 to $3,000. So why do it? Master electrician and electrical inspector John Williamson offers the following reasons:

■ If you have an old 60-amp breaker panel (or fuse box), a mortgage lender or insurance company might force you to replace it with a new 100-amp panel to prevent an electrical fire, thereby minimizing its risk.

■ An upgraded panel might help you sell your home faster because it gives a prospective buyer one less thing to worry about.

■ Some old panels won't accept modern GFCI- and AFCI-protected circuit breakers, but a newer panel will.

■ A new panel, along with a new meter socket and service entrance wires, is an opportunity to increase the capacity of the electrical system. Old 60-amp and 100-amp panels are often replaced with 200-amp and even 400-amp panels these days because of the increased number of electrical appliances people use in their homes.

■ It's an opportunity to bring your service up to code.

■ You can't beat the convenience and safety of modern circuit breakers in new panels.

MEET AN EXPERT

John Williamson is a master electrician and electrical inspector in Minnesota.

HomeCare & Repair

REPLACE YOUR THERMOSTAT BATTERIES, OR ELSE...

Some thermostats run only on batteries, and this note from one of our readers is a great reminder to replace them before they die (you'll usually see a warning on the thermostat's screen letting you know when it's time).

"Not realizing my programmable thermostat required batteries, I left on a five-month trip to Florida. A few days after I left, my neighbor went to check on the house and found that it was more than 120 degrees inside. The furnace repairman said if the furnace is running when the batteries go dead, it won't shut off. He changed the batteries in the thermostat and all was well... or so I thought. Once home, I found that the toilet was leaking. The wax ring had melted and didn't reseal under the toilet after cooling down. The bathroom sink also got clogged because a candle sitting on the counter melted and the wax flowed down the drain. The price of two batteries would have saved me two service calls. Lessons learned!"

— Irene Badini

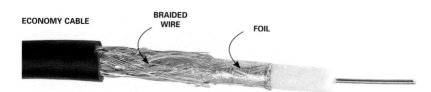

DON'T CHOOSE CHEAP COAXIAL CABLE

Shielding is what counts when it comes to cable quality. It blocks interference and keeps the signal clean. So skip the "dual-shield" or "double-shield" cable and go for a "quad-shield" product; it has twice as much braided wire and foil shielding. After spending big bucks on a TV or computer, it doesn't make sense to skimp on cable.

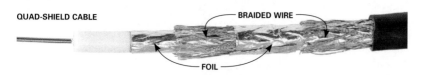

CHECK THE OUTLET

If any electronic item suddenly won't turn on, don't immediately assume it's broken. Plug in a radio or a lamp to make sure the outlet is working.

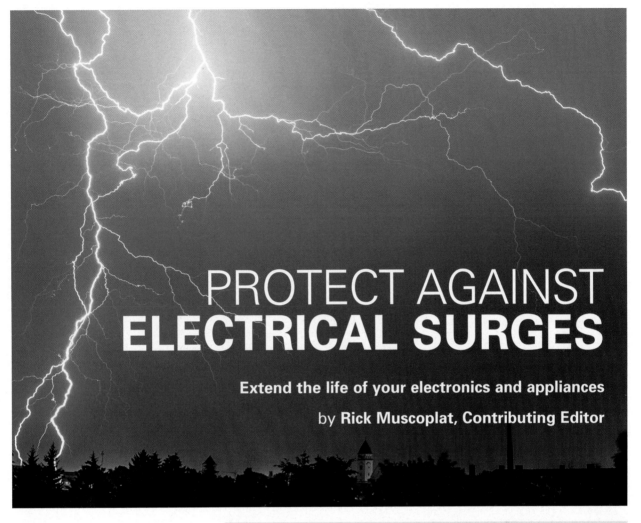

PROTECT AGAINST ELECTRICAL SURGES

Extend the life of your electronics and appliances

by Rick Muscoplat, Contributing Editor

Your home's electronic devices experience electrical surges all the time, both from outside and within the home. And every time there's a surge, it causes incremental damage to surge protection components built into your TVs, appliances, computers and every other device plugged into an outlet.

We contacted surge protection expert Karenann Brow, director of product marketing for Tripp Lite, a large manufacturer of surge protection equipment. She gave us some great tips on how to buy and implement whole-house and "point-of-use" surge protection.

No single surge protection device (SPD) can protect everything in your home. That's why Karenann recommends a two-layered approach that knocks down big surges from outside your home and absorbs surges generated inside your home.

WHERE DO SURGES COME FROM?

External surges

Lightning strikes create huge surges on nearby power lines, and those surges travel into all homes connected to those wires. External surges are also generated as power demands fluctuate and your electric utility operates switching gear to meet those demands.

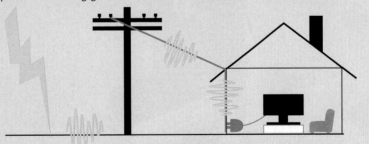

Internal surges

All motor-driven appliances—air conditioners and refrigerators, even vacuum cleaners—generate surges and electrical interference when the motor shuts down.

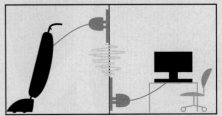

Two ways to stop external power surges

Surge protectors that mount on your electrical panel are referred to as whole-house or Type 2 SPDs. They knock down the biggest surges before they can spread through your home's wiring and wipe out your electronics. Type 2 units cost about $150 and are available at home centers and electrical supply houses.

If you're comfortable working inside the electrical panel and have a vacant spot for another 20-amp 240-volt breaker, you can install a Type 2 SPD yourself. Otherwise hire an electrician. Most Type 2 SPDs can be professionally installed in less than an hour, costing about $400 for parts and labor. If you don't have enough room for an additional breaker in your panel, the electrician can move a few existing breakers to a subpanel to make room or install a Type 1 SPD (where allowed by the utility) that fits between the meter and the meter box. The cost to install the subpanel and a Type 2 SPD or Type 1 SPD is about $1,000 for parts and labor.

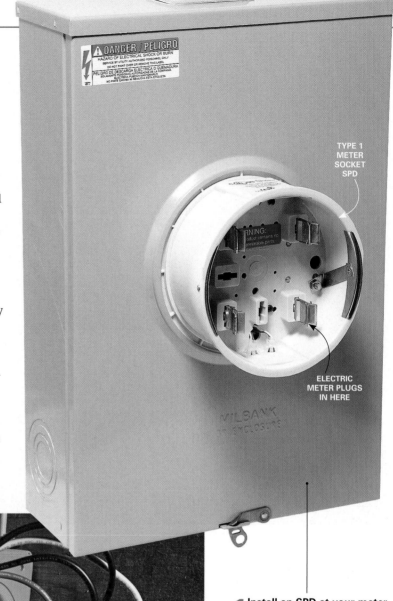

TYPE 1 METER SOCKET SPD

ELECTRIC METER PLUGS IN HERE

1 Install an SPD at your meter box. Hire an electrician to install a Type 1 meter socket SPD instead of a Type 2 SPD if you don't have enough room in your electrical panel for another 240-volt breaker. Some utilities won't allow meter socket SPDs, so check with your utility before hiring an electrician.

2 Stop surges at the panel. Install a Type 2 SPD at your main electrical panel to stop externally generated surges before they spread to the individual circuits in your house. Adding a Type 2 SPD requires the installation of a 20-amp 240-volt circuit breaker. Professional installation costs about $400.

Two ways to stop internal power surges

Power strips and surge protection strips look alike but they're completely different animals. Power strips cost less than $10 and just allow you to plug in more devices—they don't provide any protection. Surge protection power strips and receptacles are available in many configurations and surge protection ratings, so it's important to buy based on specs, not price.

Install SPD receptacles behind your refrigerator, washer and dryer, wall-mounted TVs, built-in microwave and gas range—wherever you don't have enough room to accommodate a strip. Buy an SPD receptacle with an audible alarm for applications where you can't visually inspect the outlet's status.

Cheap SPD strips ($15 or less) have short (3-ft.) cords, low surge ratings and weak warranties. A 3-ft. cord is rarely long enough, and daisy-chaining several surge protection strips or adding an extension cord are violations of the electrical code and reduce the effectiveness of the SPD. That's why Karenann recommends spending more to get an SPD strip with a cord that's long enough to reach between the outlet and your gear. If you have a newer home, chances are you'll need only a 6-ft. or 8-ft. cord. However, if you're buying an SPD for an older home or a dorm room, you'll most likely need a 12-ft. or 25-ft. cord.

Next, consider what you're protecting. For an entertainment center or office, you'll want a strip with eight or ten outlets, noise filtering to remove electromagnetic and radio interference (listed as EMI/RFI in the description) and surge protection for coaxial cable, Ethernet and telephone lines. Then choose a strip with the highest joule rating (the amount of energy the device can absorb before it fails). Karenann recommends at

1 Stop surges with an SPD strip. Connect your entertainment and office gear to an SPD strip with a surge protection rating of at least 1,000 joules. Buy an SPD strip with a long enough cord to reach between the outlet and your gear and with enough outlets to handle all your devices.

2 Install an SPD receptacle in tight space. Replace unprotected receptacles behind your refrigerator, microwave, wall-mounted TV, range, etc. with SPD receptacles equipped with an audible alarm. The alarm alerts you when the surge protection is worn out and requires replacement.

least 1,000 joules. Plan to spend at least $25 to get all those features.

However, spending more than $25 gets you more protection and better interior circuit design. Generally speaking, the higher the joule rating, the better the surge protection, and three-mode protection (listed as L-N, L-G and N-G in the specs) is better than two-mode. Higher-priced units also include more convenience features like rotatable outlets and outlets spaced for plugging in multiple AC adapters. Some higher-priced units even include internal USB charging ports to free up outlet space. Next, shop for an SPD that shuts down when it wears out instead of just turning on a red light. It's easy to

miss the light and think you're protected when you're not.

Finally, examine the company's warranty terms. The best ones offer lifetime protection against failure, while the weak ones expire in about a year.

MEET AN EXPERT

Karenann Brow is the director of product marketing at Tripp Lite, responsible for surge protection, power strips and additional product categories. She brings over 20 years of surge protection experience to the table.

BLUETOOTH
WIRELESS SPEAKERS

Everything you need to know about these high-tech speakers

by **Rick Muscoplat, Contributing Editor**

Smartphone and tablet speakers are just too small and tinny-sounding to produce good output. But crummy sound isn't limited to your smart devices; the cheap speakers in your flat panel TV aren't that good either. However, you can get great sound for your smart devices and TV, simply and inexpensively, with Bluetooth speakers.

Battery-powered Bluetooth speakers are fine if you need portability. But if you largely enjoy your smart device entertainment in one area, or plan to upgrade your TV audio, choose AC-powered units. You'll eliminate battery-charging hassles and get much better sound. Prices start at about $100 for bookshelf-size speakers and go up in price based on size, power rating and transmission technology. We'll give you some buying advice and show you

how to make Bluetooth wireless speakers work with other devices, such as your TV and old stereo equipment.

Quick primer on AC-powered wireless speakers

Wireless speakers receive sound wirelessly through Bluetooth, but they do have wires. Every pair has an "active" unit that plugs into an AC receptacle and a cable that connects the active to the passive speaker. The active unit houses the wireless receiver, amplifier, volume and tone knobs. Many active speakers also have a stereo jack and speaker terminals that allow you to connect directly to your smart device or TV using a cable.

Bluetooth technology is supposed to work up to 33 ft., but don't count on that—it's really more like 10 to

15 ft. In fact, plan on being within line-of-sight with your Bluetooth speakers because the signal doesn't travel well through walls. There are significant sound-quality differences among brands, so it's best to shop for wireless speakers at a retail store where you can compare sound quality rather than blindly ordering online. stereo equipment.

Teach old dogs new tricks with Bluetooth add-ons

You can easily retrofit your TV, computer or old stereo to work with Bluetooth. Just plug a Bluetooth transmitter (one example is the TaoTronics No. TT-BA07; $30 at taotronics.com) into the external speaker or headphone jack on your TV or computer and pair it to your speakers. To retrofit your old receiver, just add a Bluetooth receiver (such as the BrightPlay Home HD; $30 at brightechshop.com).

Broadcast sound from your smartphone or tablet

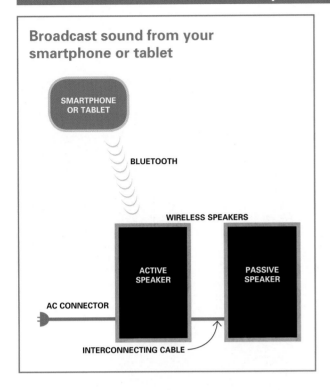

Broadcast sound from your desktop, laptop or TV

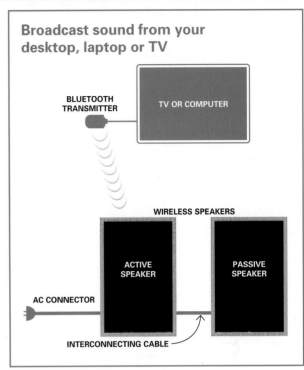

Broadcast sound from your smartphone, tablet or computer to your stereo system

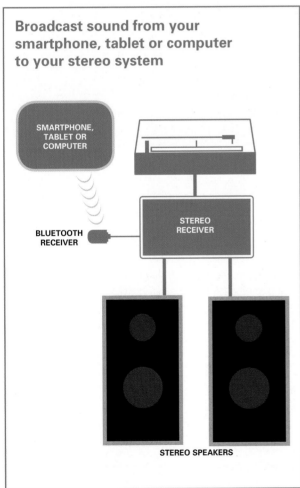

WHAT YOU'LL NEED:

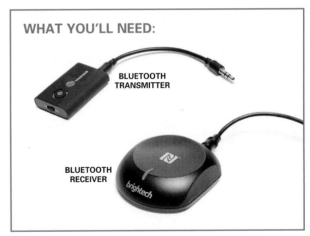

What is bluetooth?

Bluetooth is a wireless transmission technology that's used for device-to-device connections, for example, between your phone, tablet or laptop and Bluetooth-equipped speakers or headphones. Bluetooth can also be used to transmit data between two devices.

In perfect conditions, Bluetooth can transmit up to about 100 ft. But in your home, you'll find it's closer to 10 to 15 ft. Bluetooth doesn't transmit well through walls or around corners. Setting up a Bluetooth connection between two devices requires a special "pairing" procedure. Pairing has to be done only once—the devices remember each other after they're paired.

ELECTRICAL & HIGH-TECH

AVOID FREEZE-UP DISASTER

4 ways to get a wake-up call before your pipes burst

by **Rick Muscoplat, Contributing Editor**

Your tropical vacation memories can turn into a nightmare if you return home to find frozen pipes and water damage caused by a dead furnace. Asking family members or neighbors to check your home daily can't prevent serious damage if your furnace fails between visits. In the dead of winter, pipes can freeze in a matter of hours.

A freeze alert device will most likely prevent the disaster. You can install one yourself in less than an hour without any special tools. The units range from less than $100 to almost $600, depending on how you want to be notified—phone call, text message or email. There are four basic systems you can choose from.

Freeze alert systems

Deciding on the best system for your home depends first on how you, your family and your neighbors prefer to receive the low-temperature warning—verbally by phone, or text or email. Then you can choose a unit based on the communications technologies available in your home or vacation place—phone line, Wi-Fi or cell phone.

A disaster for one of our own:

When one of our editors returned home from vacation, he discovered that the furnace had died and his water lines had frozen and burst, causing all kinds of expensive damage. His son had checked the house just the day before and everything was fine. The repairs came to about $60,000. His family had to live in temporary housing for six weeks while repair crews put the house back together. If he had installed a heat loss monitor/freeze alarm, he could have avoided all that.

Wi-Fi–based ($150 to $550)

Many companies make Wi-Fi temperature monitoring systems that send email and text alerts or activate the notification feature on a smartphone or tablet app. A Wi-Fi thermostat is the least expensive way to go for Internet-based alerts and easy to install and configure.

The Sensi Wi-Fi thermostat (less than $140 at home centers and online) is one popular brand, but other Wi-Fi thermostat brands offer the same features. The Sensi thermostat is factory programmed to send an Internet alert to a smartphone or tablet app when the room temperature drops to 45 degrees F or rises above 99 degrees (an important feature if you have pets and your A/C fails).

In addition to the high/low alerts, the thermostat also alerts you if the room temperature rises or falls by 5 degrees when the thermostat is calling for either heat or cooling. That kind of temp change means your HVAC system can't keep up with the demand and can mean you've got a power outage or an equipment failure.

By notifying you way before temperatures dip dangerously low or get too high, you'll have enough time to summon a family member or neighbor to check on your home. This particular thermostat also alerts you to a high-humidity condition (greater than 78 percent) that could indicate a water leak.

If you choose a Wi-Fi unit, make sure you have a good signal in the room where it's installed and provide backup power to your Wi-Fi router. Then program the temperature set points (if equipped) and the text phone numbers and email addresses for everyone you want notified of a temperature alert.

KEEP THINGS RUNNING WHEN POWER IS OUT

Most Wi-Fi thermostats and freeze sensors require backup batteries to provide power during an outage. But if you don't provide backup power for your Wi-Fi router, the alerts won't go through. Many cable and phone company Wi-Fi routers have a backup battery compartment, but they don't supply the battery. You have to buy and install one yourself. Router backup batteries run the unit on standby for about eight hours and cost about $35. Replace the battery every few years. Or, buy an uninterruptible power system (UPS) and plug in the router and temp alert device.

Cell phone–based alert ($100)

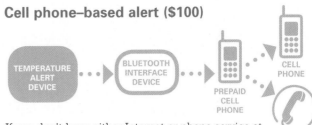

If you don't have either Internet or phone service at your home or vacation place, but do have a strong cell phone signal, purchase a phone alert unit and a prepaid cell phone that works with that carrier's signal and has the Bluetooth feature. Then buy a Bluetooth interface device (one choice is the Sensaphone FGD-0230; $110 at DIYcontrols.com).

The interface provides dial tone to the temperature alert device and completes the call through the prepaid cell phone using Bluetooth. Program the alert unit, pair the phone and Bluetooth interface and connect the components. Don't forget to make a test call.

Telephone-based alert ($80)

If your home has a landline or a voice over Internet protocol (VoIP) phone line, choose from the many freeze and high-temperature alert devices on the market. The Home Sitter unit from Control Products (HS-700; $80) has factory preset high (85 degrees F) and low temperature (45 degrees) set points and a water sensor. It calls three phone numbers.

Just add batteries, plug the unit into an outlet, program the phone numbers to call and plug the phone cable into the nearest phone jack. When the unit detects water or an out-of-range temperature, it calls all the programmed phone numbers and plays a recorded voice alert.

Add a freeze sensor to your security system ($50)

If you already have a home security system and it alerts you by email, text or central station, add a wired or wireless freeze sensor for about $50 (homesecuritystore.com is one online source).

SUPER-EASY
USB OUTLET

Adding a USB outlet is easy enough for a first-time electrician.

by **Brad Holden, Associate Editor**

Besides the tangled mess they create, bulky chargers devour outlet space. For a clean solution, add a USB wall outlet at a more convenient height than a typical wall outlet. Doing this is fast and easy if you place the new USB outlet in the same cavity as an existing outlet. Then you won't have to cut into walls to run cable through studs.

What it takes

TIME: 1 hour

COST: $40

SKILL: Beginner

TOOLS: Stud finder, drywall saw, wire stripper, noncontact voltage tester, basic hand tools

What you'll need

This a great project for electrical beginners, and everything you need is available at a home center. If you don't own any electrical tools, expect to spend about $15 on the basics.

Before you shop, determine whether your cable is 12- or 14-gauge; you'll need the same size cable for your new outlet. For reference, 12-gauge wire is about the thickness of a nickel, and 14-gauge is about the thickness of a dime.

The new junction box you'll use is called an "old work" box. It mounts on drywall and doesn't need to be fastened to a stud. We chose a "two-gang" box that allows for a second outlet. It also requires a larger hole in the wall, which makes feeding cable into the existing box much easier.

Outlets with USB ports come in various configurations and cost $15 to $30 at home centers. For a wider selection, shop online.

To comply with electrical code changes, you may have to buy an AFCI outlet ($30) to replace the existing outlet. Ours is protected by an AFCI circuit breaker.

Getting started

USB ports don't draw much power, so you can add a USB outlet to any existing outlet except a switched outlet or a dedicated outlet for an appliance, such as a stove or refrigerator.

Once you've chosen your power source outlet, switch off the breaker for that circuit. Then use a noncontact voltage tester to verify that the power is off.

You may need a larger junction box

Electrical codes contain strict rules about how many wires, connectors, switches and outlets can go in a junction box. Since you're adding wires, your existing box may not be large enough according to code. To see the formula, go to familyhandyman.com and search for "adding a receptacle." For help installing a larger box, search for "crowded electrical box."

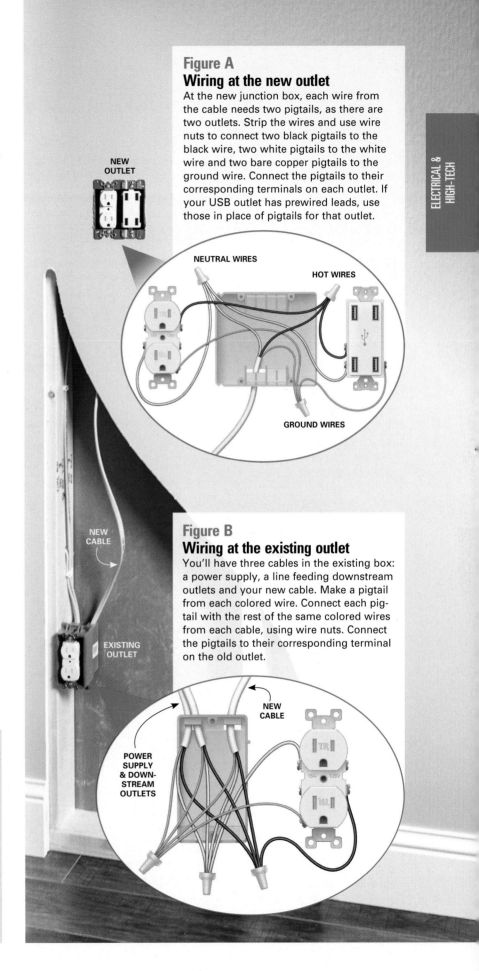

NEW OUTLET

Figure A
Wiring at the new outlet

At the new junction box, each wire from the cable needs two pigtails, as there are two outlets. Strip the wires and use wire nuts to connect two black pigtails to the black wire, two white pigtails to the white wire and two bare copper pigtails to the ground wire. Connect the pigtails to their corresponding terminals on each outlet. If your USB outlet has prewired leads, use those in place of pigtails for that outlet.

NEUTRAL WIRES

HOT WIRES

GROUND WIRES

NEW CABLE

EXISTING OUTLET

Figure B
Wiring at the existing outlet

You'll have three cables in the existing box: a power supply, a line feeding downstream outlets and your new cable. Make a pigtail from each colored wire. Connect each pigtail with the rest of the same colored wires from each cable, using wire nuts. Connect the pigtails to their corresponding terminal on the old outlet.

NEW CABLE

POWER SUPPLY & DOWN-STREAM OUTLETS

STUD
LOCATION

1 **Find the studs.** Locate the studs with a stud finder and mark them with tape. You can place the new outlet anywhere between the studs.

NEW "OLD WORK" BOX

2 **Trace the box.** Mark the cutout while holding the open end of the new box against the wall. Be sure to hold the box level.

Install the box & cable

Locate the two studs that flank the existing outlet (**Photo 1**) and find a good position in the wall cavity for the new outlet. Hold the new "old work" box in place against the wall, making sure it's plumb and level, and then trace around it (**Photo 2**).

Cut the hole as accurately as possible (**Photo 3**). An "old work" box relies on a snug fit in the cutout for stability, as it's not attached to a stud. If your new outlet is on an exterior wall, use a box that maintains the vapor seal to keep out drafts.

Disconnect the old outlet and then feed the new cable to the existing box. Don't skimp on cable; a little extra inside the wall is good, and you'll trim the ends when you're ready to make the connections. Run cable into the new box, and then mount the box to the wall (**Photo 4**).

Connect the wires and receptacles in both boxes (**Photo 5** and **Figures A and B**). Mount the outlets, reinstall the faceplates, turn the power back on and test the outlets.

3 **Cut the hole.** Stab a drywall saw into the wall and cut along your marks. Test-fit the box and enlarge the hole slightly if needed.

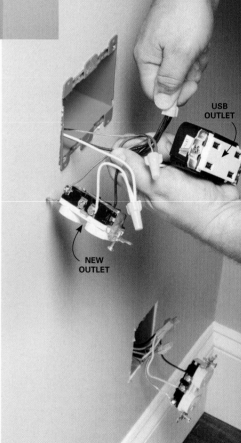

USB OUTLET

NEW OUTLET

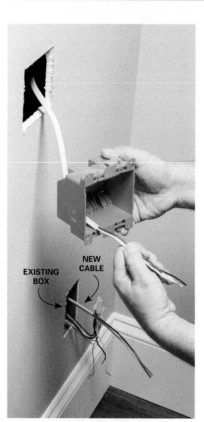

EXISTING BOX

NEW CABLE

ELECTRICAL ADVICE GALORE!
For tons of tips, techniques and expert knowledge, go to familyhandyman.com and search for "electrical wiring."

4 **Run the cable.** Reach inside the wall and feed the cable into the existing box. Then feed the cable into the new box and install it.

5 **Make the connections.** Reconnect the outlet at the power source and connect the new outlets. Our USB outlet came with lead wires. Yours may have terminal screws like those on standard outlets.

GreatGoofs®

DRILLING DEBACLE

My dad was doing some electrical work at home and had drilled a hole in a wall so he could run some new wiring. Unbeknownst to him, directly behind that wall on a shelf was a very full bottle of liquid laundry detergent. By the time we found out what had happened, most of an entire gallon of goopy, gloppy detergent was all over the floor. It took an entire roll of paper towels to clean up that mess.

— Kevin Barnes

HOT PANTS!

Working down a list of weekend chores, I found myself on a stepladder changing the 9-volt battery in a smoke detector. After I stuck the new battery into the unit, I slipped the old one into my pants pocket and headed off to the hardware store for my next task.

On the drive there, I felt a strange warmth on my thigh. It quickly escalated to dang hot followed by a worrisome burning smell. I screeched to a stop at the side of the road and hopped out of my truck—and my pants.

My pocket change had shorted out the not-so-dead battery terminals, making the coins hot enough to char clear through the lining of my pants and singe a few leg hairs.

Now I know where the Energizer Bunny gets the spring in its step.

— Walt Parker

Secret Hiding Places

15 clever ways to keep your stuff out of sight

by **Mark Petersen, Senior Editor**

Maybe it's jewelry, maybe it's cash, maybe it's just a bag of M&Ms you want to eat all by yourself. But we all have something we want to tuck safely out of sight. We asked our readers to share their best hiding places, and share them they did! Of course, we omitted their names to protect their secrets. So read on, pick your favorites, invent your own— and keep those crooks guessing!

GUN LOCK

1 **A shelf with a secret**

Floating shelves are beautiful and easy to build. With a little extra effort and a few bucks more, you could build yours with a hidden compartment.

Build a floating shelf! To find out how, go to tfhmag.com/ floatingshelves

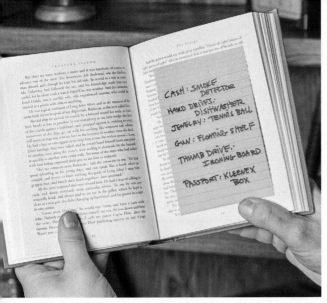

Make a treasure map

2 Having several hiding places makes sense…unless you forget where they are! Avoid this misfortune by making yourself a map of your various treasure sites. That way you only need to remember one location—the place where you hid the map.

Slit open a tennis ball

3 Slice open a tennis ball and you've got yourself a little vault just like those rubber squeeze coin purses from the '70s. Don't store the ball in the garage with the other balls or it could get tossed across the yard for your dog.

Stow a key in your yard

4 If you have an irrigation system, install a phony pop-up sprinkler head near the front door and hide a key in it. You could dismantle an extra sprinkler head or buy a fake one designed to hold a key. They cost less than $5 at home centers and discount stores.

SPRINKLER HEAD KEY HIDER

You can't take it with you

5 Prepare for the worst, and make sure your goodies are not lost forever by including all your hidey-hole locations in your will.

Sneaker subterfuge

6 Some shoes have a removable sock liner (the foam pad your foot rests on). Pull out the sock liner and slide in some cash. What thief is going to want to dismantle your stinky shoes? This is also a good place to hide emergency cash on your person while you're on vacation. Unless your sneakers are nice enough that someone would want to steal them too.

SOCK LINER

Key magnet

7 Keep a spare key hidden somewhere on your vehicle. Don't use a magnetic key box because it can fall off, and it's not easy to find a place big enough to stick them to mostly plastic modern cars. Instead, bolt your spare key to a magnet, the kind with metal on one side and a hole in the middle. Find a little nook with enough metal for the magnet to grab onto.

Secret Hiding Places

8 Who'd suspect an ironing board?

Many ironing boards have tubular legs with plastic caps on them. Pull the cap and you've got yourself a perfect little hidey-hole. Slide in a wad of paper towels first so the secret stays near the opening and doesn't rattle around.

9 Secret in the ceiling

You can stash your treasures above the suspended ceiling tiles in your basement. At that height, would-be thieves can't get at them without a ladder. Keep your goodies in a plastic container to protect them from bandits of the rodent variety. And don't stash anything heavy that could cause a ceiling tile to sag.

11 Hide a key in the keypad

It takes hours, not days, for some younger kids to lose their house keys. Here's a solution: install a remote keypad for the garage door opener. That works great until you lose power and your 12-year-old is left out in the cold … literally. If you're lucky, your key will fit right behind the nine-volt battery inside the keypad. A key in a keypad—now that's ironic.

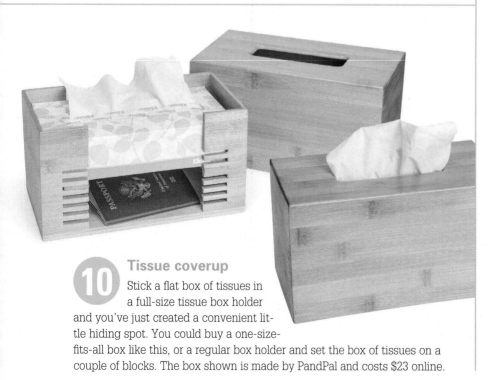

10 Tissue coverup

Stick a flat box of tissues in a full-size tissue box holder and you've just created a convenient little hiding spot. You could buy a one-size-fits-all box like this, or a regular box holder and set the box of tissues on a couple of blocks. The box shown is made by PandPal and costs $23 online.

12 Family album

Nobody ever looks at those old photo albums, but they never get thrown away either. That's why they're the ideal place to store a little emergency cash.

13 Kitchen cabinet cache

There are tons of ways to hide stuff in a kitchen cabinet. Bury a zipper-top bag full of jewelry at the bottom of a half-full oatmeal box. Open a cereal box at the bottom and shove in some cash. (Pick a healthy cereal that no one will touch.) A "smooth-edge" can opener cuts through the top in such a way that the top often fits snugly back in place.

SMOOTH-EDGE
CAN OPENER

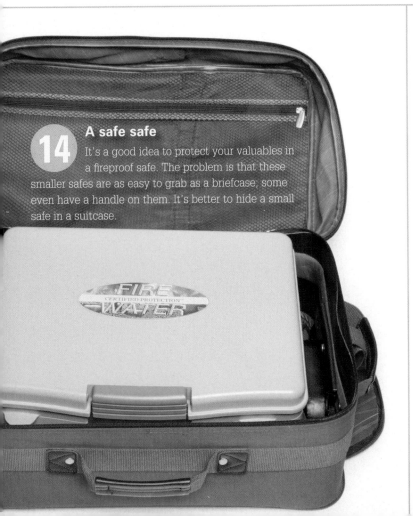

14 A safe safe

It's a good idea to protect your valuables in a fireproof safe. The problem is that these smaller safes are as easy to grab as a briefcase; some even have a handle on them. It's better to hide a small safe in a suitcase.

15 Password protection

Keep a list of your passwords on a sheet of paper near your computer. Protect the list from bad guys and nosy coworkers by putting it in a file folder. Lay the folder flat on the bottom of a file cabinet drawer under the other hanging folders.

SECRET HIDING PLACES　　**121**

Secret Hiding Places

HIDDEN COMPARTMENT
MEDICINE CABINET

Style and quality at a bargain price

by **Jeff Gorton, Associate Editor**

With medicine cabinets, your choices are mostly high cost or low quality. And sometimes both! The medicine cabinet we designed is built from solid wood and good-quality hardware, so it will hold up to the rigors of everyday use. The materials aren't expensive. And it's relatively easy to build, making it a good project for an intermediate woodworker or an experienced DIYer.

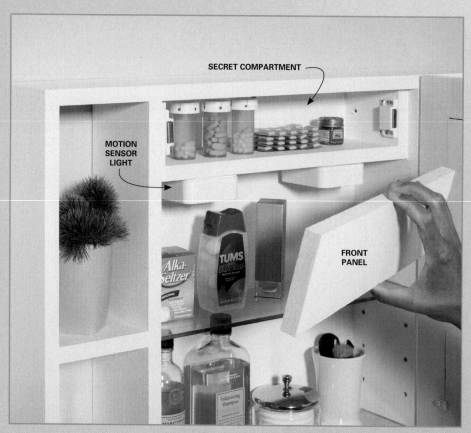

SECRET COMPARTMENT

MOTION SENSOR LIGHT

FRONT PANEL

Secret Hiding Place

The small compartment is a handy place to hide prescription medicine or jewelry. The front panel is held on with magnets. The battery-powered, motion-sensor lights make the compartment look like a lighting valance.

What it takes

TIME: 2 days

COST: $180

SKILL: Intermediate to advanced

TOOLS: Standard woodwork-ing tools, miter or table saw, router and 3/8-in. rabbet bit, biscuit joiner, 35-mm and 3/8-in. Forstner bits

This medicine cabinet has open shelves on the sides that can be used for display or storage. The mirrored door is mounted on self-closing cup hinges for maximum adjustability. There are adjustable shelves inside, and even a hidden compartment disguised as a light valance. You can paint the cabinet, apply a clear finish to let the grain show through, or stain and varnish it.

We've kept the construction simple to allow even intermediate woodworkers to build this medicine cabinet. The carcass is assembled with butt joints that are screwed together. We covered the screw heads with wood plugs, but you could substitute trim-head screws and just fill the screw holes with wood filler.

Skills, tools and materials

Even though the joinery is simple, assembling the door and cabinet requires careful measuring, accurate cutting and attention to detail. We used a table saw fitted with a table saw sled to cut the parts, but a miter saw would also work for making the end cuts. The door is held together with wood biscuits, but you could use dowels or pocket screws instead. You'll need a router and a 3/8-in. rabbeting bit to make the recesses for the cabinet back and door mirror.

It's critical that you choose boards that are flat and straight, especially for the door. Sight down the boards and reject any that are twisted or crooked. The boards should lie flat when you stack them. We built this cabinet from inexpensive aspen, which looks great when painted. Pine or poplar would also be good choices for a painted finish.

You'll find full-overlay cup hinges at home centers or woodworking stores, or you can order them online. We purchased the mirror and glass shelves from a glass shop, but some full-service hardware stores also supply them. To save money, you could substitute wood shelves.

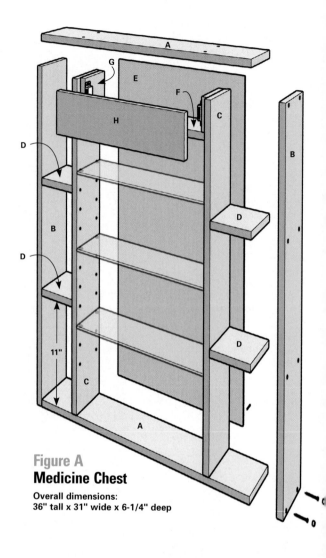

Figure A
Medicine Chest
Overall dimensions:
36" tall x 31" wide x 6-1/4" deep

MATERIALS LIST

ITEM	QTY.
1x6 x 6' boards	4
1x3 x 8' board	1
1/4" x 4' x 4' plywood	1
3/8" flat top wood plugs	32
1-1/2" multipurpose screws, 1-lb. box	1
1" nails, small box	1
Magnets	2
1/4" shelf pins	12
Screen fasteners, package	1
Full-overlay cup hinges	2
Mirror—cut to fit	1
Glass shelves—cut to fit	1
Mr Beams Night Lights (MB723)	1

CUTTING LIST

KEY	QTY.	MATERIAL	DIMENSIONS	PART
A	2	1x6 board	3/4" x 5-1/2" x 29-1/2"	Top and bottom
B	2	1x6 board	3/4" x 5-1/2" x 36"	Sides
C	2	1x6 board	3/4" x 5-1/2" x 34-1/2"	Dividers
D	4	1x6 board	3/4" x 5-1/2" x 5"	Shelves
E	1	1x4" plywood	Cut to fit	Back
F	1	1x6 board	3/4" x 4-1/2" x 18"	Compartment bottom
G	2	1x6 board	3/4" x 4-1/2" x 3-1/4"	Compartment sides
H	1	1x6 board	3/4" x 4-1/2" x 17-7/8"	Compartment panel
J	2	1x3 board	3/4" x 2-1/2" x 36"	Door stiles
K	2	1x3 board	3/4" x 2-1/2" x 14-1/2"	Door rails
L	1	Mirror	Cut to fit (subtract 1/8")	Mirror
M	1	1x4" plywood	Cut to fit	Mirror back

1 Mark the boards for shelves and screws. Cut the cabinet box parts and arrange them as shown. Square the assembled boards by placing a framing square against the ends. Then use a scrap of the same wood to check the length of the dividers (**C**). If the dividers are the right length, the scrap will line up with the ends of the sides. Next, mark for the shelves using **Figure A** as a guide. Then flip the boards over and draw a single line to indicate the middle of the shelves. This is where you'll place the screws. Also mark screw locations for the dividers on the top and bottom boards.

WOOD SCRAP

SIDE

DIVIDER

DIVIDER

SIDE

SHELF MARKS

FRAMING SQUARE

2 Prepare the boards for wood plugs. Mark screw locations 1 in. from each edge of the boards along the center lines you drew in the previous step. Then drill 3/8-in. holes about 3/8 in. deep at each mark. You'll glue wood plugs into these plug holes to cover the screws. For clean-edged plug holes, use a Forstner or brad point bit.

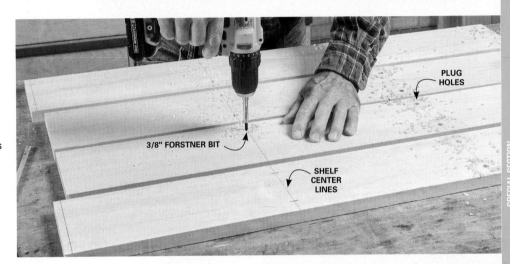

PLUG HOLES

3/8" FORSTNER BIT

SHELF CENTER LINES

Figure B
Door

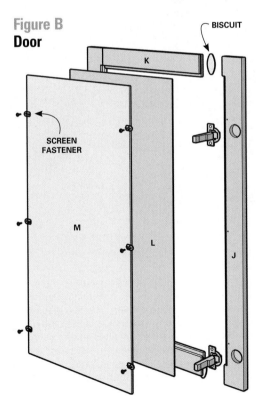

BISCUIT

K

SCREEN FASTENER

M

L

J

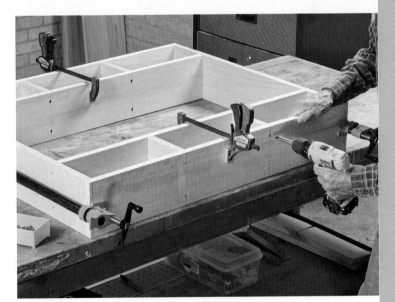

3 Assemble and clamp the parts. Arrange the parts with the shelf marks facing the inside. Line up the shelves with the marks and lightly clamp everything together. Tap the parts with a hammer to align the edges perfectly before tightening the clamps. Drill 3/32-in. pilot holes for each screw, using the divot left by the tip of the Forstner bit as a centering guide. Then drive 1-1/2-in. screws to hold the cabinet parts together.

Secret Hiding Places

Cut your own wood plugs! Watch a video on how to cut your own wood plugs. Search for "wood plugs" at familyhandyman.com

3/8" x 1/4" RABBET

4 Cover the screws with plugs. Apply a little glue to the edges of the plugs and tap them into the holes. Leave the plugs slightly proud of the surface so you can sand them flush later.

For our painted medicine cabinet, we purchased flat-top wood plugs at a home center. If you plan to apply a clear finish, or a stain and clear finish, and want the plugs to be less conspicuous, shop for face grain plugs or cut your own plugs from the same wood you use to build the cabinet.

5 Cut a recess for the cabinet back. Mount a 3/8-in. rabbeting bit in your router and set the depth to 1/4 in. If you don't already own one, consider purchasing a rabbeting bit with a set of interchangeable bearings ($25 to $40) that allow the bit to be used to cut several rabbet sizes. Place scraps of 2x6 alongside the cabinet to create a more stable base for the router. Cut slowly in a clockwise direction.

SHARP CHISEL

BACK

1" NAIL

6 Square the corners. The rounded corners left by the rabbeting bit need to be squared off so the plywood back will fit. You'll need a sharp chisel for this task. Start by marking the corner. Align a short straightedge with the edge of the rabbets and make pencil marks for the corner. Then carefully chisel out the wood to create the square corner.

7 Nail on the back. Measure the height and width of the rabbet and cut a piece of 1/4-in.-thick plywood to fit. Make sure the plywood is perfectly square by measuring diagonally from opposite corners. The two diagonal measurements should be equal. Run a bead of wood glue in the rabbet and insert the plywood back. Check to make sure the cabinet is square using the same diagonal measuring technique. If opposite diagonal measurements aren't equal, nudge the cabinet until they are. When you're sure the cabinet is square, attach the back with 1-in. nails placed about 6 in. apart.

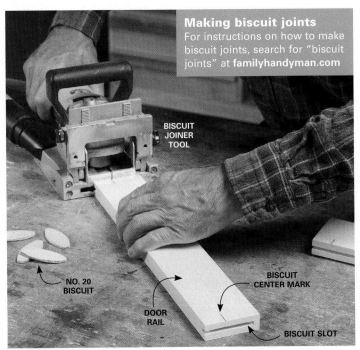

Making biscuit joints
For instructions on how to make biscuit joints, search for "biscuit joints" at familyhandyman.com

BISCUIT JOINER TOOL

NO. 20 BISCUIT

DOOR RAIL

BISCUIT CENTER MARK

BISCUIT SLOT

8 **Slot the door parts for biscuits.** Cut slots to connect the door rails (top and bottom) to the stiles (sides). The No. 20 biscuits are a little too long, so rather than center the slots, offset them so the biscuits will protrude from the top and bottom of the door where they won't be noticeable after you cut them flush to the door edge. Make marks 1 in. from the top and bottom of the stiles and rails and center the biscuit slots on the marks. Glue biscuits into the slots and clamp the door, making sure it's square.

RABBET

DOOR

9 **Cut a rabbet for the mirror and mirror back.** Cut a 3/8-in.-deep rabbet to accommodate the 1/4-in. back and 1/8-in.-thick mirror. Cut the rabbet using the same 3/8-in. rabbeting bit you used for the cabinet back. Make a first pass with the router set to about 3/16 in. deep. Then set the router to cut 3/8 in. deep and make the final pass. Square off the corners like you did for the cabinet back. Next, measure for the mirror. Subtract 1/8 in. from the width and height and take these measurements to your local hardware store or glass shop.

35-MM FORSTNER BIT

10 **Drill for the cup hinges.** Mark the hinge side and the top of the door to keep the orientation straight. Center the top hinge 8 in. from the top of the door, and the bottom hinge 3-1/2 in. from the bottom of the door. Check your hinge specifications to see how far from the edge of the door to center the 35-mm hole. Drill a 1/2-in.-deep hole with a 35-mm Forstner bit for the hinge cup.

CUP HINGE

11 **Mount the cup hinges.** Press the cup hinges into the hinge holes. Measure to make sure the center of the hinge mounting holes are equal distance from the edge of the door. This will ensure the hinge is properly aligned. Drive the included screws into the mounting holes.

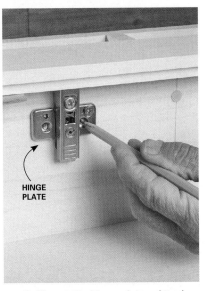

HINGE PLATE

12 **Mount the hinge plates.** Attach the plates to the hinges. Then set the door into place on the cabinet and align the top and bottom edges. Shim up the door with two thicknesses of thin cardboard and mark the screw locations for the hinge plates. Remove the door and unclip the plates. Drill pilot holes at the marked screw locations. Then mount the plates to the cabinet with the included screws.

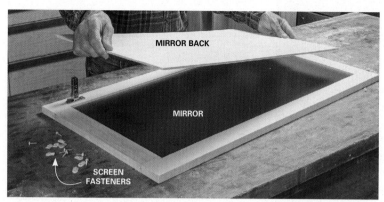

13 **Install the mirror.** Cut a piece of 1/4-in. plywood to fit the rabbeted opening. Set the mirror into the frame and place the plywood on top. Secure the back with plastic screen fastener clips, available at home centers and hardware stores. For an easier and neater paint job, remove the mirror and all other hardware before painting the cabinet. Then reinstall it after the paint is dry.

14 **Build the hidden compartment.** Build the compartment using **Figure A** as a guide. Attach magnets to the cabinet and metal plates to the removable cover to hold the cover in place. We mounted Mr Beams MB723 ($30 for three) motion sensor lights to the bottom of the compartment.

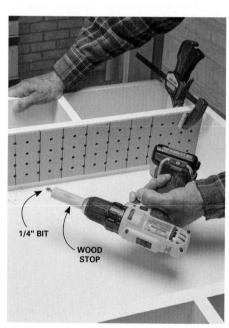

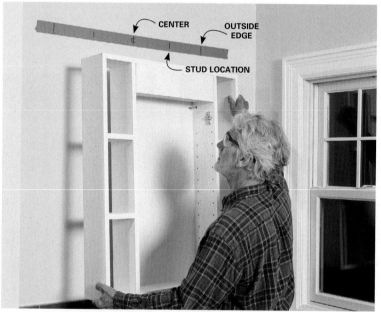

15 **Drill shelf-pin holes.** Cut a scrap of 1/4-in. pegboard to 4-5/8 in. x 29-3/4 in., making sure the distance from the holes to the edges of the template is the same on the sides and the top and bottom. This will avoid confusion by allowing you to position the template without regard to its orientation. For 2-in. hole spacing, draw lines across alternate sets of holes. Use a 1/4-in. brad point bit with a wood stop to limit the depth of the holes to 3/8 in. Press the pegboard against the back of the cabinet to drill the back holes. Clamp it flush to the front for the front holes.

16 **Install the cabinet.** Hang the cabinet by screwing through the back into one or two studs. Start making two marks, level with each other and about 30 in. apart, to indicate the top of the cabinet. Apply a strip of masking tape to the wall so its bottom-edge marks align with these marks. Mark the cabinet center on the tape. Then measure out 15-1/2 in. in both directions and make marks to indicate the sides. Finally, use a stud finder or other means to locate any studs in the area where the cabinet will be mounted and mark them on the tape.

Transfer the stud locations to the cabinet back to mark the mounting screw positions. If you hit only one stud, use toggle bolts or snap-toggle bolts to provide an additional hanging point. Prop or hold the cabinet in position and drive one screw at the top. Then use a level to plumb the cabinet sides before driving another screw at the bottom. Add the second set of screws or toggle bolts to complete the job.

3 Plumbing, HVAC & Appliances

IN THIS CHAPTER

Home Care & Repair 130
   *Water softener maintenance, clean the
   refrigerator coils, toilet shopping tips,
   springtime safety warning and more*

Finishing Up a Plumbing Job.................135

Handy Hints 138
   Recycle water, draft dodger and more

Great Goofs..112
   Toilet blues, hold on! and more

WATER SHUTOFF VALVE

TOILET

QUIET A NOISY TOILET

Whenever you flush a toilet, the "fill valve" inside the tank opens, letting fresh water back into the tank. The sound of the water rushing into the tank can be quite noisy, which is really only a problem if it's the middle of the night and people are trying to sleep.

Gary Wentz, our editor-in-chief, says to try this trick: Find the water shutoff for the toilet underneath the tank and close it a little bit. That will reduce the amount of water flowing into the tank and help quiet things down a bit. Of course, the toilet will take longer to fill.

DO YOU NEED A WATER SOFTENER?

If soap and detergent aren't doing a good job of getting you or your clothes clean, you might have hard water. This problem is easily solved with a water softener. Water softeners rid your water of "hardness"— naturally occurring calcium and magnesium ions that are in your water and leave spots on dishes, cause scale buildup on shower walls and damage water-using appliances.

But before you go spending thousands, or even hundreds of dollars, installing a water softener, go to your local home center and buy a water quality test kit ($10). These kits measure total hardness and other contaminants like iron, copper and nitrates. The results are instant—you don't have to send the samples to a lab for analysis.

WATER SOFTENER
MAINTENANCE

Three ways to get the iron out

Well water and city water with high iron content can coat the resin beads in your water softener and reduce their efficiency. There are three ways to clean the beads to keep your water softener's resin bed in tip-top shape:

1 Buy water softener salt that includes a rust removal agent (Diamond Crystal Iron Fighter and Morton Rust Remover are two examples). It costs a bit more than ordinary salt, but it's the easiest way to keep iron at bay.

2 Pour an antirust liquid or powder directly into the brine tank at the first sign of rust building on your plumbing fixtures. Track how long it takes to recur, then establish a regular treatment schedule to stay ahead of the game. (Summit Brands' Iron Out, $6, is one example.) Then send the softener through the recharge cycle.

3 Add a drip dispenser to your brine tank. Fill it with an antirust product (one choice is Pro Products' ResCare RK11K Easy Feeder Starter Kit for $20).

DISPENSING TUBE

BOTTLE BRACKET

Salt crystals or pellet salt for your water softener?

Readers often ask which form of water softener salt they should buy—rock salt, solar salt crystals or pellets. Rock salt contains the highest percentage of insoluble particles (dirt), which can muddy up the brine tank, coating the tank walls with scum. Solar salt crystals are cleaner but can still cause brine tank dirt buildup.

Salt pellets and cubes are the cleanest of the three types. However, some water experts don't recommend them because they can get mushy or form salt bridges. Yet other water experts discourage the use of solar salt crystals because of the dirt problem.

To get the scoop, we contacted Emily Arthurs, senior brand manager at Morton Salt. Emily said

that the way pellets and cubes are manufactured determines whether they'll mush and form salt bridges. Some economy-brand pellets and cubes are shaped first and then sprayed with a binding agent to hold them together. The binding agent washes off as soon as the pellets or cubes reach the brine and that's when they fall apart, turn to mush and bridge.

Emily said Morton uses a manufacturing process in which the binding agent and other key ingredients are blended throughout the batch before it's formed into pellets. Instead of washing off, the binding agent "time releases," holding the pellet together to prevent mushing and bridging.

If you've used pellets or cubes and had mushing or bridging problems, don't just give up and switch back to solar salt crystals. Try a few premium brands of pellets until you find one that stays together without mushing or bridging.

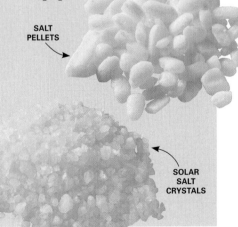

SALT PELLETS

SOLAR SALT CRYSTALS

TOILET SHOPPING
TIPS

Sick of your old, leaky, water hog of a toilet and want to buy a new one? You'll find water-efficient toilets with an array of options. Our friends at Maximum Performance (MaP) Testing make a living putting toilets through their paces and offered these tips for your next time toilet shopping.

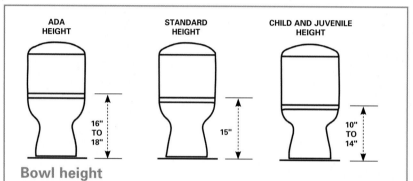

ADA HEIGHT	STANDARD HEIGHT	CHILD AND JUVENILE HEIGHT
16" TO 18"	15"	10" TO 14"

Bowl height

This is the distance from the floor to the top of the toilet bowl's rim. The standard height for toilets used to be 14 to 15 in. But today, you'll find toilets that are 16 to 18 in. high. These are often called "comfort height" or "ADA height" or something similar. The additional height makes getting on and off the toilet easier and is more comfortable for lots of people, especially the elderly. Child heights of 10 to 14 in. are also available.

Insulated tank

If summers are humid where you live and you don't have air conditioning, you've probably noticed your toilet "sweating" quite a bit. Condensation forms on the outside of the toilet, which can drip down and make a mess or even rot out your floor. Some toilets are available with insulated tanks to prevent condensation problems.

One-piece vs. two-piece

A two-piece toilet—a separate tank and bowl—is the most common design found in homes. But one-piece models are available. While two-piece toilets are less expensive, one-piece toilets often have shorter tanks and are easier to clean. Some people also like one-piece toilets for their smooth, sleek appearance.

ONE-PIECE TOILET

Cost

When it comes to toilets, expensive doesn't automatically mean better performance. In fact, some of the best models tested by MaP are relatively inexpensive, while costlier ones offer only marginal performance.

Color

Fashion is fickle. Stick with a white or an off-white toilet so you're not stuck with a color you'll hate a few years down the road. (Don't miss the blue one on the next page!)

WALL ON RIGHT →

HANDLE ON LEFT

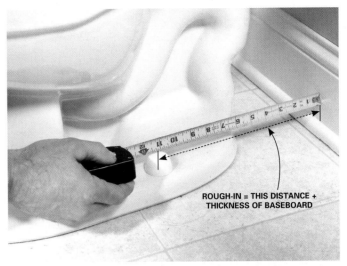

ROUGH-IN = THIS DISTANCE + THICKNESS OF BASEBOARD

Flush-handle location

If you have lots of room above or beside your toilet, this probably isn't all that important. But if your toilet will be right up against a wall or cabinet, choose one with the handle on the opposite side or on top of the tank.

Rough-in

The distance of the flange bolts—the two bolts that anchor your toilet bowl to the floor—to the wall behind the toilet is known as the "rough-in" dimension (make sure to account for the thickness of your baseboard, paneling or tile). Twelve-inch rough-ins are the most common, but in some older houses you may find 10-in. or 14-in. rough-ins. Be sure to measure your rough-in before you go toilet shopping so you'll know what to ask for.

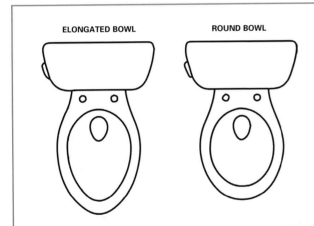

ELONGATED BOWL ROUND BOWL

Bowl shape

Most toilets sold today have either round-front bowls or elongated-front bowls. Round-front bowls are great if space is tight. Elongated bowls have a longer rim—as much as 2 in. longer—and require more space (there have been cases where doors and drawers couldn't be opened after installation). On the plus side, elongated bowls are generally more comfortable for adult use and help improve hygiene. Check manufacturer websites for dimensions of bowls and measure your space before deciding on the bowl shape.

"Wall print"

If you install a new toilet with a smaller tank, you might have to paint the part of the wall that was covered by the old toilet tank.

Footprint

If you're replacing an old toilet that has a large footprint (the base covers a large floor area), you might have to patch and repair the part of the floor that was covered by the old toilet. You may even have to replace the entire floor before installing a new toilet with a smaller footprint.

"WALL PRINT"

FOOTPRINT

MEET AN EXPERT

John Koeller is a principal at Maximum Performance (MaP) Testing and contributed his toilet expertise to this article. Visit map-testing.com for more toilet tips, product reviews and flush ratings.

TEMPERATURE DIAL

A SLIGHT TURN OF THE DIAL MAKES WATER HEATERS SAFER

Water heaters set too high send thousands (mostly children) to hospitals each year with burns from water from a faucet. Most safety experts recommend a setting of 120 degrees F. But finding that setting on the dial isn't easy—most dials aren't labeled with numbers. If the stickers on the water heater don't tell you how to set the temperature and you can't find the owner's manual, use this method:

Run hot water at the tap closest to the water heater for at least three minutes. Then fill a container and check the temperature. If the water is above 120 degrees, adjust the dial, wait about three hours and check again. Repeat until you get 120-degree water. For a final test, check the temperature the following morning, before anyone uses hot water.

COOKING THERMOMETER

SPRINGTIME SAFETY WARNING

Every spring and summer, readers tell us about their window air conditioner accidents: A/C units dropped on toes, tumbling down stairways or falling out of windows. We haven't heard about any serious injuries or deaths, but lots of close calls. In almost every case, the trouble began when someone decided to install an A/C unit solo. The lesson is this: Those things are heavy and clumsy to handle. Get help!

CLEAN THE REFRIGERATOR COILS

Dust buildup on the coils underneath or on the back of your fridge reduces airflow and wastes energy. Worse, it may lead to repairs that can cost almost as much as a new fridge. That's quite an incentive to vacuum the coils every six months.

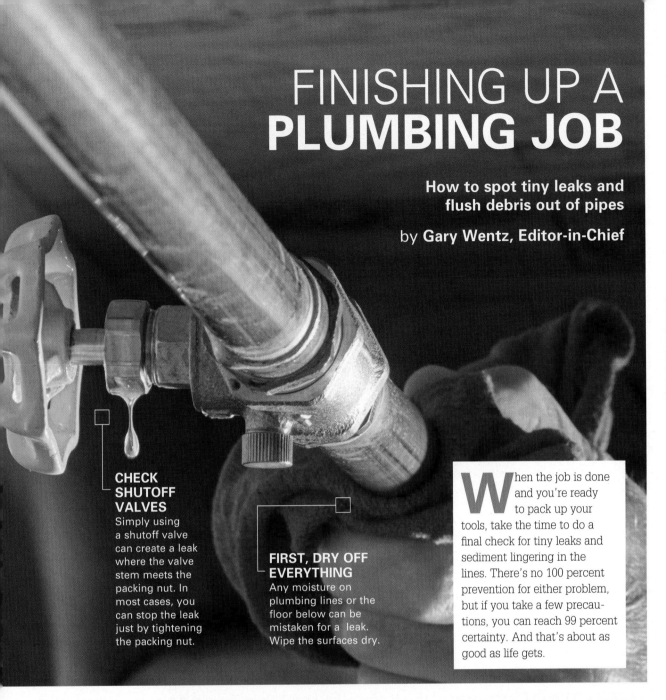

FINISHING UP A PLUMBING JOB

How to spot tiny leaks and flush debris out of pipes

by Gary Wentz, Editor-in-Chief

CHECK SHUTOFF VALVES
Simply using a shutoff valve can create a leak where the valve stem meets the packing nut. In most cases, you can stop the leak just by tightening the packing nut.

FIRST, DRY OFF EVERYTHING
Any moisture on plumbing lines or the floor below can be mistaken for a leak. Wipe the surfaces dry.

When the job is done and you're ready to pack up your tools, take the time to do a final check for tiny leaks and sediment lingering in the lines. There's no 100 percent prevention for either problem, but if you take a few precautions, you can reach 99 percent certainty. And that's about as good as life gets.

Stress-Test Drain Lines

To test drain lines under a sink, don't just turn on the faucet. Instead, completely fill the sink. (Fill both bowls on a double sink.) Then open the drain to release a gush of water. In humid conditions, fill the sink with lukewarm water. Cold water will cause condensation on the lines and prevent you from finding leaks.

MEET AN EXPERT

When Gary Wentz, editor-in-chief, did a stint as a journeyman plumber, he picked up tricks from some of the sharpest plumbers on earth.

Don't get fooled by condensation

SPOT TINY LEAKS

In high humidity, a cold water line will sweat, making it almost impossible to detect tiny leaks. Here's how to work around that: Run the water just enough to fill the line. Then take a coffee break while the water in the pipe warms to room temperature. When it's warm enough, wipe the pipe dry and look for leaks. Condensation may also be caused by cold water in drain lines.

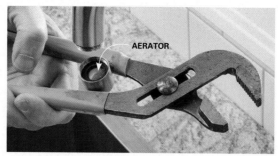

AERATOR

Remove aerators

Small particles that flow through a faucet often get caught in the aerator. So always unscrew the aerator and run the water after a plumbing job.

LET IT RUN

When flushing lines, you'll be tempted to shut off the water after 10 seconds. That's not long enough. One minute is the minimum. In a large house with long runs of supply pipe, let it flow for several minutes. Better to waste some water than to repair plugged faucets.

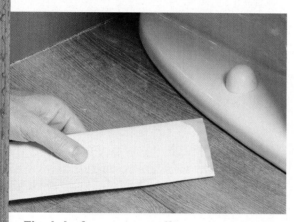

Flush before you caulk

A small leak at the toilet flange leads to a puddle. But if that puddle is dammed up by caulk around the toilet base, it may not show up for months. So before you caulk, flush a couple times and probe for leaks with a strip of paper.

Detect drips with paper

Paper towels or newspaper are great leak locators. You'll immediately see—or even hear—leaks as soon as a drip hits the paper.

TROUBLE!

Locate leaks with tissue

A wet spot on a tissue is a lot easier to see than a small droplet on a pipe. So wipe with a tissue and look at it after each swipe.

Check sink rims

Dribble water around a sink rim to check the seal. Rim leaks rarely show up right away, so wait a few minutes before inspecting from below.

Flush out the sediment

Water supply pipes contain sediment: corrosion, mineral deposits, pipe dope or solder. Plumbing work shakes that stuff loose. Water flow will carry that loose grit to fixtures—and possibly plug them. To prevent that, run water through the lines to flush out the sediment.

WHAT YOU DO DEPENDS ON THE PIPES

There's no need to take every flushing step on every job. It depends on the age and type of plumbing. In a newer home with PEX plumbing, for example, you might only have to remove the aerators before flushing.

Flush before you connect

Sediment trapped in a fill valve can make a toilet fill slowly or run constantly. To flush out this sediment, run water into a bucket before you connect the supply line.

Protect the showerhead

Low-flow showerheads have tiny openings that can be plugged by a single particle. So run the tub faucet before the shower. In a dedicated shower (no tub spout), remove the showerhead and flush the line.

Start at a high-volume, low-risk valve

To flush out debris, you need a high-volume flow of water. That makes outdoor hose bibs and washing machine supply lines great for this purpose. These faucets have another advantage too: Unlike kitchen or bath fixtures, they have big, simple ports that are less likely to get plugged or damaged by sediment. Just keep in mind that any faucet you choose for flushing should be downstream from the work area.

Watch out! Some washing machine hoses often have screens that can become plugged. Luckily, they're easy to remove and clean.

SCREEN

FLUSH HOT AND COLD SEPERATELY

To get maximum flow through a single-handle kitchen or bath faucet, swing the handle to one side and run the water full blast. Then switch to the other side and do the same.

HandyHints®

PLASTIC TUBE GOES IN PIPE

RECYCLE WATER

If you have a dehumidifier, you have a free supply of water that's perfect for houseplants. Dehumidifiers remove moisture from the air and create "condensate" that's free from chemicals and minerals found in tap water. Just don't drink it—it could contain microbes and trace amounts of metals that are harmful to humans.

— J.A. Kemble

SPRAY-BOTTLE PIPE PUMP

When soldering a fitting onto a copper pipe, you have to get the water out of the pipe or the solder won't melt. But removing the water from vertical pipes is tricky. That's when I grab the spray nozzle from a plastic bottle. I just stick the plastic tube down into the pipe and pull the trigger a few times. It helps to have a small cup to shoot the water into.

— Dean DeBeltz

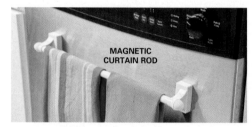

MAGNETIC CURTAIN ROD

TOWEL BAR FOR APPLIANCES

Some dishwashers don't have a handle that you can use as a towel bar, so I used a magnetic curtain rod designed for steel entry doors. Many stainless steel appliances won't hold magnets, but some newer ones will.

— Lucie Maggio

DRAFT DODGER

My house has round ceiling registers for the air-conditioning system. In the winter, we'd get cold air falling from the registers. Rather than put up with the drafts, I sealed the registers with those clear plastic saucers that you put under flowerpots. I temporarily glued them in place with White Lightning SEASONSeal Clear Removable Weather Stripping ($5). It's a rubbery sealant that you apply with a caulk gun and peel off in the spring.

— James Herrenknecht

FLOWERPOT SAUCER

GreatGoofs®

A FLUSH TO REMEMBER

After removing an old toilet, I did the classic handyman trick of stuffing a bunch of plastic bags into the sewer opening. This kept the stench from seeping into the bathroom while I installed the new toilet over the weekend.

After setting and hooking up the new commode, I did a test flush. It was very satisfying to watch the water swirl down and the bowl fill up—and up and up! The toilet gushed water all over the floor.

Turns out the other half of that trick is removing the bags from the sewer opening.

— Rob Kiesling

THE COST OF NOT KNOWING

A few weeks after I moved into my first home, a washing machine hose burst, releasing a geyser in my laundry room. I knew enough to try the valve behind the washer, but it was ancient. And stuck. What I didn't know about was the main valve, which could have shut off the water to the whole house. So I just stood there like a dummy, waiting for a plumber to show up while water flowed from the laundry room into adjoining rooms. Insurance covered most of the damage, but I paid the deductible, plus higher insurance premiums for years afterward. Make sure everyone in your home knows where the main water valve is.

— Andy Carson, *The Family Handyman* Field Editor

HOLD ON!

We wanted to move our washer and dryer down to the basement. Although my wife was due home shortly to help, I decided to get a start on it. I loaded the dryer onto a dolly and rolled it toward the steep, narrow staircase.

I was in trouble immediately. The dryer began to pull me forward, so I dropped to the floor and lodged my feet against both sides of the doorjamb. Ten minutes later my wife arrived home to find me sprawled at the head of the stairs, sweating and holding on with all I had. She began giggling uncontrollably.

One of us had to get below the dryer quickly before I dropped it down the stairs, but the staircase was too narrow for my wife to squeeze past. The basement has an exterior door, so my wife held the dolly while I ran outside and entered the basement. Next time, I'll be more patient and wait until my wife gets home.

— John McAllister

TOILET BLUES

My wife came home with a $10 chlorination gadget that "self-cleans" the toilet bowl after flushing. The installation seemed simple enough, but within minutes I had broken the fill valve assembly at the base.

I turned off the water supply and tried to loosen the nut that secures the valve so I could replace the part. It was corroded and wouldn't budge. I decided to pull the toilet for better access to the stuck nut. I removed the flange nuts and lifted the toilet with all my might. The bowl base broke into three pieces and water spilled everywhere.

My wife and I decided I should quit while I was behind and call a plumber. The $350 bill was painful, but there's no cleaner toilet than a brand new one.

— Marcus Cherlin

SPECIAL SECTION

10 Clever Tool Hacks

Save your back, time and money with these ingenious tool tips

by **Mark Petersen, Senior Editor**

Here's a great collection of tool hacks for every level of DIYer, from beginner to advanced. These simple tips and techniques will help you get the most out of your tools. You'll learn creative ways to use everyday tools and even how to modify them to do jobs "outside the box." Got a tip of your own to share? Send it to submissions@familyhandyman.com.

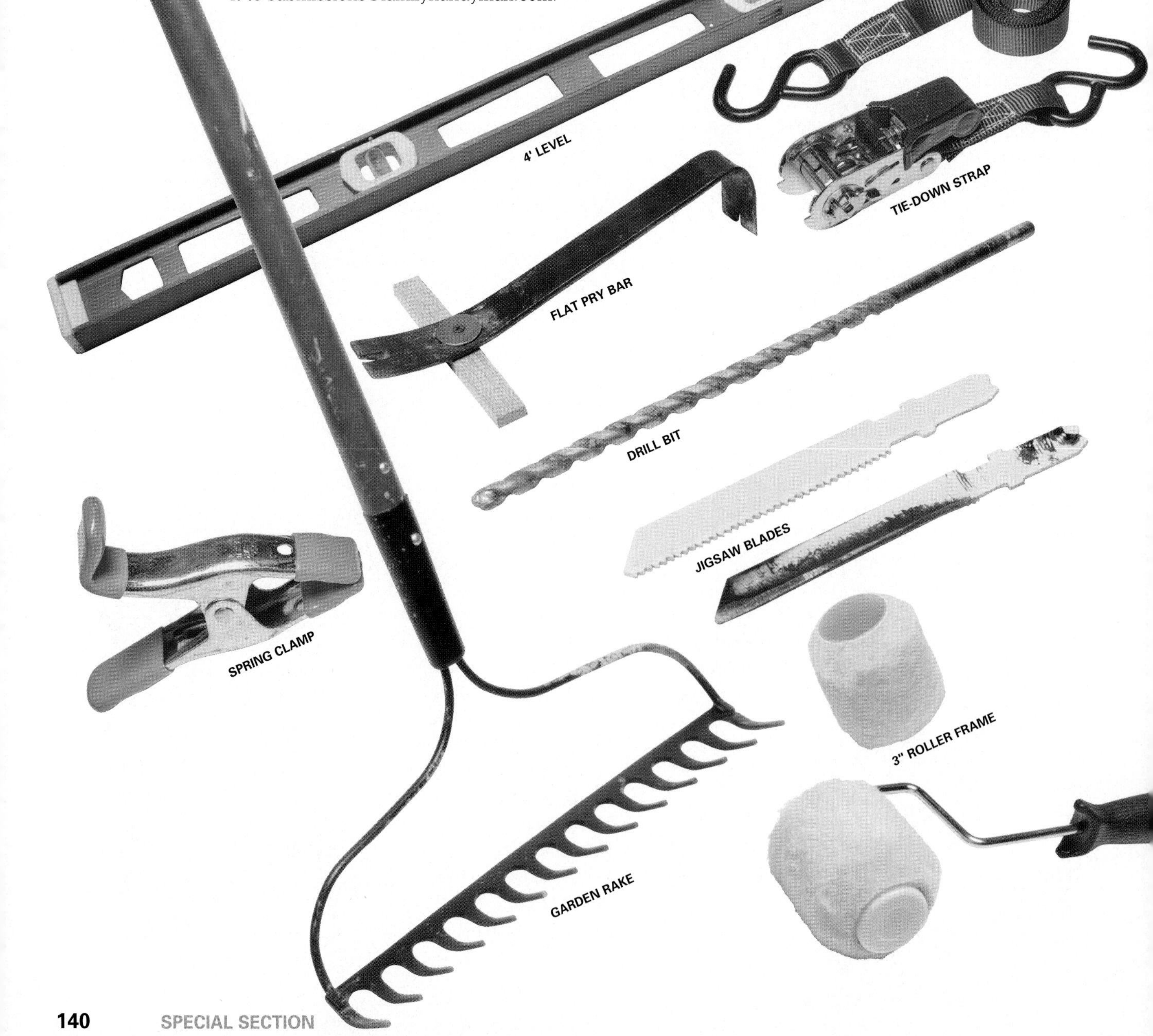
4' LEVEL
TIE-DOWN STRAP
FLAT PRY BAR
DRILL BIT
JIGSAW BLADES
SPRING CLAMP
3" ROLLER FRAME
GARDEN RAKE

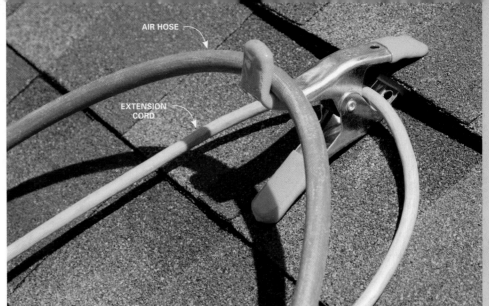

1. Hang your roofing tools

Use spring clamps to keep your hoses, extension cords, and other tools and materials from sliding off the roof. Don't try this on brittle or scorching hot shingles or you may damage them. You can create a handier hook by sticking the clamp in a vise and bending up one of the handles.

AIR HOSE

EXTENSION CORD

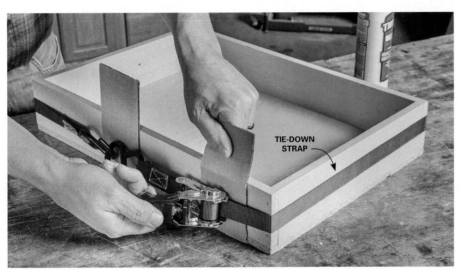

2. Clamp with a tie-down strap

If you need to clamp boxes together, a ratchet tie-down strap can often do the job just as well as band clamps. Just make sure to protect the wood under the ratchet and hooks with cardboard.

TIE-DOWN STRAP

3. Mix concrete with a rake

Try a garden rake instead of a hoe the next time you have to mix concrete. The rake won't splash as much water over the edge, and the tines do a good job of combining the water with the powder. With a hoe, you waste a lot of time just pushing powder around the tub. A medium mixing tub like the one shown costs $7 at home centers.

10 Clever Tool Hacks

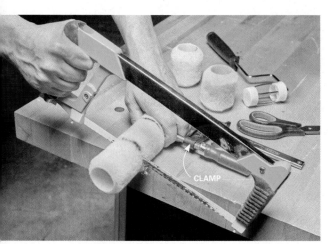

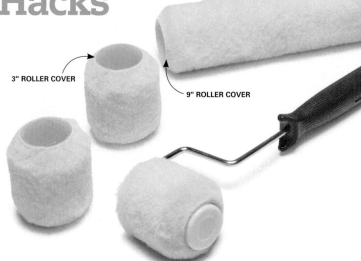

3" ROLLER COVER

9" ROLLER COVER

CLAMP

4 **Make mini roller covers**

Next time you're in the paint department, pick up a 3-in. roller frame, the type that takes the same diameter cover as a standard 9-in. roller. You can then cut any 9-in. roller cover into three 3-in. covers to fit it. A 3-in. roller is perfect for painting trim or small stuff like a mailbox, but not every store carries 3-in. covers.

This little trick will also cut the cost of the 3-in. roller covers in half.

Mark the 9-in. roller covers 3 in. in from each end. Cut into equal pieces with a hacksaw, holding the cover steady with a bar clamp. Trim the rough edges of the nap with scissors.

5 **Use a level to extend your table saw fence**

The only way to achieve a perfectly straight cut is to keep your material tight up against the table saw fence. But that's hard to do when you're cutting a large sheet of plywood on your own. Extending the fence with a 4-ft. level will make it easier to keep the plywood on a straight and narrow path as it approaches and passes through the blade. Hold the level in place with a couple clamps.

CLAMP

4' LEVEL

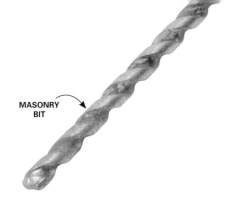

MASONRY BIT

6 Need a hole in hard soil? Use a Drill!

Have you ever waited too long to install your reflective driveway markers and discovered the ground was frozen? Or tried to install a yard sale sign in dry soil that's as hard as concrete? Well, why not treat it as if it really were concrete and drill holes into it with a masonry bit? This 3/8-in. x 12-in. bit costs less than $15 at home centers.

JIGSAW BLADE

7 Make a blade for cutting foam

A jigsaw will cut through rigid foam like butter—except butter doesn't crumble into thousands of bits that mess up your shop, basement or garage. If you remove the teeth from a jigsaw blade, it will cut the foam just as well but without the mess. Remove the teeth with a grinder, and be sure to wear eye protection. Hold on to the blade with locking pliers, not your fingers!

Clever Tool Hacks

8 Lift heavy stuff with a flat pry bar

If you've ever had to remove a solid-core door, you know how heavy they can be. Lifting them up to reinstall hinge pins can be a challenge if you're working alone, but a flat pry bar (aka "flat bar") can give you just the leverage you need.

If your flat bar won't raise the door high enough, install a small block of wood at the fulcrum point of the pry bar to increase the lifting distance. Hold the block in place with a small screw and washer. Make sure the screw doesn't poke through. If it does, grind off the end so it won't damage the floor. This same setup can be used to raise bottom drywall sheets off the floor for fastening.

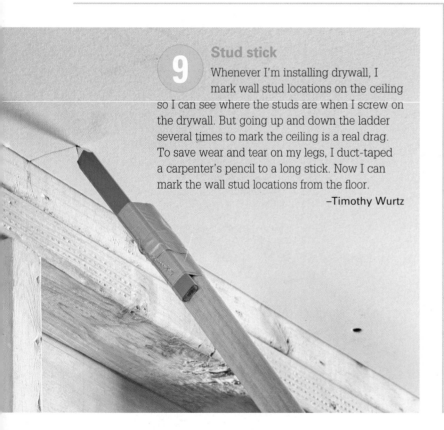

9 Stud stick

Whenever I'm installing drywall, I mark wall stud locations on the ceiling so I can see where the studs are when I screw on the drywall. But going up and down the ladder several times to mark the ceiling is a real drag. To save wear and tear on my legs, I duct-taped a carpenter's pencil to a long stick. Now I can mark the wall stud locations from the floor.

–Timothy Wurtz

10 Long-reach shears

Slip PVC pipes over the handles of your lopping shears and tape them in place to extend your reach so you can clip high branches without a ladder.

4 Woodworking & Workshop Projects & Tips

IN THIS CHAPTER

Wood 101 146

Simple Timber Bench 152

Perfect Patio Charis 158

Foolproof Dadoes & Rabbets 164

Custom Picture Ledges 168

Super-Capacity Tool Cart 173

How to Buy Rough-Sawn Lumber 180

Hot Glue—A Wood Shop Staple! 185

Ultimate Workshop Storage 189
  Benchtop organizer, drill dock, circular saw luggage, eyeglass-case hardware storage, drill bit savers and more

Handy Hints 196
  Dustless drilling & drum sanding, cardboard sawhorses and more

WOOD 101

Wood movement causes heartbreak when projects crack and warp. Learn how to master these simple techniques and save yourself some nightmares.

by **Jeff Gorton, Associate Editor**

LET IT MOVE!
If your plans don't accommodate wood movement, you'll end up with trouble, like this cracked tabletop.

When humidity is high, wood absorbs moisture and swells. When humidity drops, wood shrinks. This "movement" is gradual, so you probably won't notice weekly changes. But seasonal changes cause problems you can't miss, like sticking doors, ugly gaps in woodwork or a crack in a tabletop.

This movement occurs whether wood is fresh from the mill or centuries old, whether it was kiln dried or air dried. And it exerts tremendous force that's almost unstoppable. But with a little knowledge, you can minimize the consequences. This article will explain the basics of wood movement and show you real-world solutions.

THE ABCs (AND D!)

A Width movement is the main issue

Wood moves as its moisture content changes. Wood doesn't move much lengthwise, so you don't have to worry a lot about boards getting shorter. But a board can move quite a bit across its width. A board that's 6 in. wide during a humid summer might shrink by 1/32 in. in winter. That's not much, but it's enough to cause a crack in a tabletop or gaps between floorboards.

NOT MUCH MOVEMENT LENGTHWISE

MOST MOVEMENT ACROSS WIDTH

B Movement is caused by moisture content

When wet wood dries, it shrinks. The amount of movement is determined by the type of wood and the degree of change in its moisture content. Applying a sealer or paint can moderate wood movement. But it's nearly impossible to seal wood so completely that its moisture content stays constant.

DRY WOOD SHRINKS

WET WOOD SWELLS

C Wood can also change shape

Movement within a board isn't uniform; one section might move more than another. That leads to warping, twisting and cupping. Most of these changes happen in the initial drying phase, but wood can change shape later, too.

MOVEMENT ISN'T UNIFORM

D Vertical grain is more stable

How a board is cut from the log also affects how much it moves. Quarter-sawing yields "vertical-grain" boards, while plain-sawn boards have "flat grain." Inspecting the grain pattern on the end of a board will reveal whether the board has vertical grain or flat grain. A flat-grain board will move about twice as much as a vertical-grain board with the same change in moisture content. But because cutting quarter-sawn lumber is much less efficient, vertical-grain boards are expensive and can be hard to find.

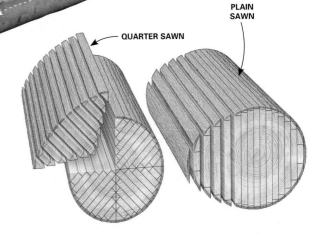

PLAIN SAWN

QUARTER SAWN

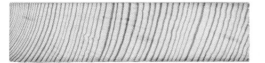

VERTICAL GRAIN

FLAT GRAIN

WOODWORKING & WORKSHOP PROJECTS & TIPS

10 TECHNIQUES: HOW TO TAME WOOD MOVEMENT

You can't keep wood from moving, but these tips and strategies can help you avoid problems

BUTT JOINT

BUTT JOINT

EXPANSION SPACE

1 Avoid miters outdoors

Miter joints hide end grain and look more refined. But the effect is ruined when the miters don't meet tightly. Huge changes in humidity, and wetting and drying from rain and sun, cause wood to move more outdoors than it would indoors. So whereas a miter joint will look good for decades indoors, it may start to look really bad after only one season outdoors. That's why it's usually better to avoid miters outdoors whenever possible. Use a butt joint instead.

2 Allow expansion space for wood floors

If you're installing an engineered wood floor, follow the instructions carefully—they include all the information you need about spacing. In general, floating wood floors that aren't nailed or glued down require about a 1/2-in. space around the perimeter and enough clearance at thresholds, doorjambs and other obstructions to allow movement. Solid wood floors also require at least a 1/2-in.-wide expansion space around the perimeter.

3 Plan for deck board movement

Deck boards can shrink or expand after they're installed, depending on how much moisture they contained when you fastened them down. To allow for this, space wet treated boards with a 16d nail (1/8 in.) and dry boards, such as cedar decking, with a carpenter's pencil (5/16 in.).

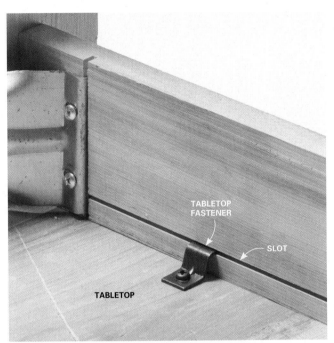

4 Let tabletops float

One of the most common errors that beginning woodworkers make is to securely fasten wood tabletops to the underlying frame. Tabletops tend to be wide, and wood moves a lot across its width. Restricting the movement with screws or nails can cause the top to crack as it shrinks. To avoid this, use special tabletop fasteners or some other method that holds the top down but still allows the top to expand and contract.

5 Avoid wide boards

Of course there are times when you have to use a wide board or you want to use one because it looks better. But always be aware that movement in wide boards, whether it's cupping, twisting or something else, will be more pronounced than in two or more narrower boards. Gluing several narrow boards together will result in a more stable tabletop than gluing two wide boards together.

6 Let wood acclimate

Since the relative humidity of your indoor space may be quite different from the humidity where your trim or flooring was stored, you should always allow time for the material to acclimate. The wider and thicker the trim or flooring boards are, the longer you should leave them in the space before installation. Thin, narrow trim may only take a day or two to reach equilibrium with the room's relative humidity. Wide or thick boards should be left in the room for at least four days before you install them. Of course the trim or flooring will still move a little after it's installed, but at least most of the change will have occurred beforehand.

Peeling paint
Outdoors, moisture in wood leads to paint problems. Search for "fix peeling paint" at **familyhandyman.com**.

WOODWORKING & WORKSHOP PROJECTS & TIPS

7 **Manufactured wood holds paint better**

If you're planning to paint an exterior project, consider building it from a manufactured product rather than solid wood. Wood movement requires the paint to flex constantly, and eventually the paint cracks and peels. Manufactured wood substitutes from companies like Louisiana-Pacific, AZEK or James Hardie are more stable than solid wood. And because these products move less, they provide a better surface for paint.

Better decking
Search for "composite decking" at **familyhandyman.com**

8 **Prefinish tongue-and-groove**

As tongue-and-groove boards expand and contract, the spaces between them change a little. If you don't prefinish the boards, you'll see exposed raw wood on the tongue when the boards shrink. But finishing the boards before you install them will solve this problem. Just be careful to avoid a buildup of finish in the groove; it could make the boards hard to fit together.

CABINET DOOR PARTS

9 Don't fill cracks on wood floors

If you have wood floors, especially old ones, you probably have some cracks between the boards. It's tempting to try to hide the cracks with wood filler, but it's not a good idea. As the floorboards expand and contract, the filler will crack and fall out, leaving you with an unsightly mess that's hard to fix.

10 Let parts warp before assembly

When you go to all the trouble to build cabinet doors, you want to make sure they aren't going to warp or twist after assembly. One way to prevent this is to cut your parts then stack them with spacer boards (stickers), and let them acclimate for about 24 hours before building the doors. Be sure to cut extra parts so you can replace any boards that warp.

Extra credit

STICKING DOORS

Sticking and rubbing doors are a common problem caused by wood movement. High humidity is usually the culprit, so some problems can be avoided or solved by keeping the humidity levels in your house low. But when this isn't practical, you'll have to resort to solutions like tightening door hinge screws or planing or sanding the door edge.

Substitute sheets for boards

As you're planning your next woodworking project, don't assume it has to be built entirely from boards. Veneered sheets of plywood and MDF are more stable and are a good alternative to solid lumber. These veneered sheets are less likely to bow or cup, and won't crack like lumber. Choices at home centers are usually limited to oak, birch or maple veneers. If you're looking for something else, such as cherry or walnut, check with a local hardwood lumber supplier or a full-service lumberyard.

Fix sticking doors

For more solutions, search for "sticking doors" at **familyhandyman.com**

MEET AN EXPERT

Jeff Gorton is an associate editor at *The Family Handyman.*

SIMPLE TIMBER BENCH

We knew what we wanted in a bench, and this one has it all!

- Low cost
- Stylish design
- Rock-solid
- Low maintenance
- SUPER EASY TO BUILD!

by **Jason White, Associate Editor**

What it takes

TIME: 1/2 day

COST: $145

SKILL LEVEL: Beginner

TOOLS: Circular saw, drill/driver, standard hand tools

aybe I'm biased, but I love this simple outdoor bench. It's massive without being clunky, rustic yet modern, well designed (if I do say so myself) and super easy to build. In fact, if you can lift the heavy landscape timbers needed for this project—about 60 lbs. each—you can build this bench! And since the bench is made from treated lumber, it's practically rot-proof, so you'll enjoy it for decades.

Time, tools and materials

Building this bench is surprisingly fast. If you have some experience with power tools, you'll have it built in just a few hours, though staining it may add a couple hours more. You can build it with just a drill/driver, circular saw and basic hand tools, but you'll get faster, better results if you also have a router and a random orbit sander.

All the materials are available at home centers. When you're choosing timbers, take the time to pick through the pile for the straightest ones. They'll twist a little after you build the bench (see "One Year Later" on p. 157), but they need to be nice and straight when you're cutting the joints and assembling the bench.

Cut the parts to size

Three of the landscape timbers will become the "beams" for the bench's seat. The timbers are slightly longer than 8 ft. when you buy them, so you'll need to cut a little off each end to make them exactly 96 in. long.

3 BASIC PARTS

This bench is made entirely from pressure-treated landscape timbers and a few galvanized lag screws and washers. Add black spray paint and exterior stain and you'll have a beautiful, low-maintenance bench. The hardest part of the project is picking through the pile of heavy landscape timbers at the home center to find the best ones.

4x6 TIMBERS

WASHERS

LAG SCREWS

Set each timber on a pair of saw-horses and use a Speed Square to draw a pencil line on all four sides (Photo 1). Set your circular saw blade for a full-depth cut. Then, using your square as a guide, make the first cut on one of the wide "faces" of the timber. You won't be able to cut all the way through in one pass; doing three passes works well (Photo 2).

When you finish the first cut, flip the timber on edge, start the saw and slip your saw's blade partway into the "kerf" (slit) you just made to align the blade for your second cut. Guide the saw with your square again, finish the second cut, then flip the timber one more time and do the same thing to make the third and final cut. Now cut the rest of the parts to length the same way and use a random orbit sander to remove any saw marks left behind (Photo 3).

Cut the notches

The joinery that connects the legs to the seat beams looks complicated, but it's really simple. The outside beams of the bench's seat are supported by L-shape notches in the legs. U-shape notches are also cut into the seat beams so the leg's faces can sit about 1/4 in. proud of the beams. The notches are all formed the same way using a circular saw, a square and a sharp wood chisel.

Tip each of the outside beams on end and, using a pencil and your square, mark layout lines for the sides and bottoms of the notches (Photo 4). Set your circular saw blade to the proper depth and then, using the square as a guide (clamp it down if needed), make a perfectly straight cut on each side of the notch (Photo 5).

continued on p. 156

MEET AN EXPERT

Jason White has 17 years of carpentry and woodworking experience and was an associate editor at *The Family Handyman.*

Figure A
Exploded view

Overall dimensions:
96" long x 19" tall x 18-1/2" deep

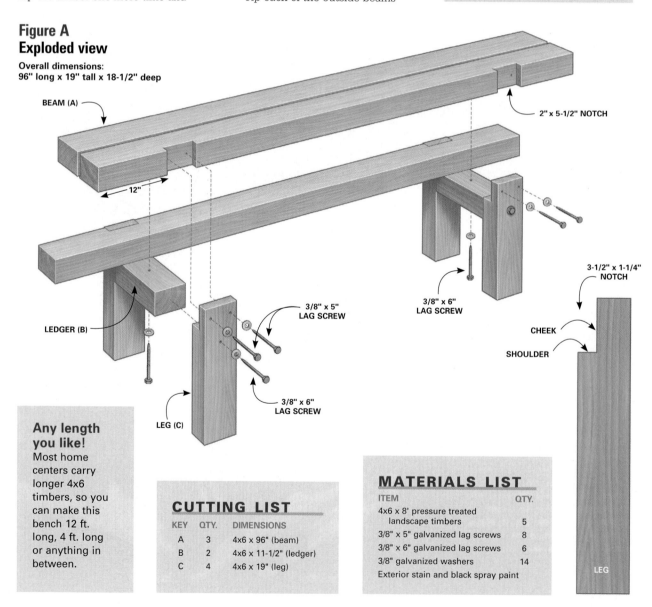

BEAM (A)

2" x 5-1/2" NOTCH

12"

3-1/2" x 1-1/4" NOTCH

CHEEK

SHOULDER

LEDGER (B)

3/8" x 5" LAG SCREW

3/8" x 6" LAG SCREW

LEG (C)

3/8" x 6" LAG SCREW

LEG

Any length you like!
Most home centers carry longer 4x6 timbers, so you can make this bench 12 ft. long, 4 ft. long or anything in between.

CUTTING LIST

KEY	QTY.	DIMENSIONS
A	3	4x6 x 96" (beam)
B	2	4x6 x 11-1/2" (ledger)
C	4	4x6 x 19" (leg)

MATERIALS LIST

ITEM	QTY.
4x6 x 8' pressure treated landscape timbers	5
3/8" x 5" galvanized lag screws	8
3/8" x 6" galvanized lag screws	6
3/8" galvanized washers	14
Exterior stain and black spray paint	

1 **Mark the lengths of the parts.** For each part, mark where you'll be cutting with a square and pencil. Draw lines on all four sides of the timbers to help align your cuts.

SPEED SQUARE

2 **Cut three times.** A 4x6 timber is too thick to cut in one pass; it's easy to do in three. Guide your circular saw with a square and rotate the timber 90 degrees in between cuts. To align the second cut, slip the saw blade partway into the kerf you made on the first cut. Repeat this for the third and final cut.

3 **Sand off saw marks.** Remove any saw marks left behind with a random orbit sander and 60-grit sandpaper.

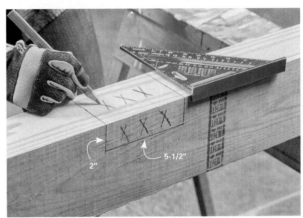

2"   *5-1/2"*

4 **Mark the notches.** Draw layout lines for the notches in the legs and beams (Figure A). Make X's to remind yourself where to cut.

SHOULDER CUT

5 **Make the shoulder cuts.** Guide your saw with the square to make dead-straight "shoulder" cuts that will define the outsides of the notches in the legs and beams (Figure A). The beams get two shoulder cuts per notch. The legs get one shoulder cut per notch.

KERF CUTS

6 **Make the kerf cuts.** Cut a series of freehand kerfs between the shoulder cuts you made for the notches in the beams. The legs have only one shoulder cut per notch, so start your kerf cuts at the ends and work toward the shoulder cut.

7 **Knock away the slivers.** Remove the thin slivers of wood left behind with the claw of a hammer.

8 **Chisel the notches smooth.** Smooth the "cheek" of each notch (Figure A) with a sharp wood chisel.

ROUND-OVER BIT

9 **Round over the edges.** Remove the sharp edges from the beams and legs with a router and 1/4-in. round-over bit.

continued from p. 154

Then make a series of freehand kerf cuts between the two outside cuts you made (**Photo 6**). The notches for the legs are made nearly the same way.

When you're done cutting, knock out the thin slivers of wood with the claw of your hammer (**Photo 7**) and use a sharp wood chisel to smooth and flatten the bottoms of all the notches (**Photo 8**).

Round over the sharp edges

The edges of the seat beams and legs are sharp and can give you splinters, so deal with them now before you assemble the bench. Lay the beams and legs on sawhorses and knock off all the sharp edges with a router and 1/4-in. round-over bit (**Photo 9**). Be sure to go counterclockwise with the router. If you don't have a router, you can do the job with a block plane, a sanding block or a random orbit sander. Don't round over the edges of the notches.

Assemble the bench

If you're planning to stain your bench, do it now before you assemble all the parts. You might need to let the wood dry out a bit before staining because pressure-treated lumber is very wet when you buy it. Be sure to read the directions on the can.

Set the outside beams for the seat upside down across your sawhorses with the U-shape notches facing out and fit the L-shape notches of the legs into each of the U-shape notches. The L-shape notches should fit snugly into the U-shape notches and the tops of the legs should be flush with the tops of the seat beams. The faces of the legs will sit a little proud of the seat beams—about 1/4 in. If the joints won't go together by hand, knock them together with a rubber mallet or dead blow hammer. If they still won't go together, you might have to fine-tune the fit of each joint with your chisel.

Set the third beam (the one without notches) between the other two beams, making sure the spaces are even—about 1/2 in. Now set the ledgers between the legs, pull everything together tightly and use long clamps to hold it temporarily. Drill pilot holes through the tops of the legs for lag screws (**Photo 10**)—two through each L-shape notch and one below each notch's shoulder (**Figure A**) and drill one hole in the center of each ledger.

Next, spray-paint the heads of the lag screws and washers and let them dry before driving (**Photo 11**). Once they're dry, drive the lag screws with washers through all the pilot holes you drilled (**Photo 12**). Touch up the tops of the lag screws with more paint if they get scuffed up (spray a little on a disposable brush).

One year later...

My bench sat outside, completely unsheltered, through a hot summer and a hard Minnesota winter and it still looks great! The timbers twisted a little, but that just added to the rustic look. The joints loosened up a bit from wood shrinkage, but that was easily fixed by tightening the lag screws.

10 **Drill pilot holes for lag screws.** Temporarily clamp together all the bench parts and drill 5/16-in. pilot holes for lag screws.

11 **Paint the lag screws and washers.** Coat the heads of the lag screws and washers with black spray paint. Save the can for future touch-ups.

12 **Drive the lag screws.** Drive lag screws with washers through the pilot holes you drilled earlier. An impact driver with a socket works great for this, but you can also use a wrench or ratchet. Touch up any scuffs on the lag screws with black paint.

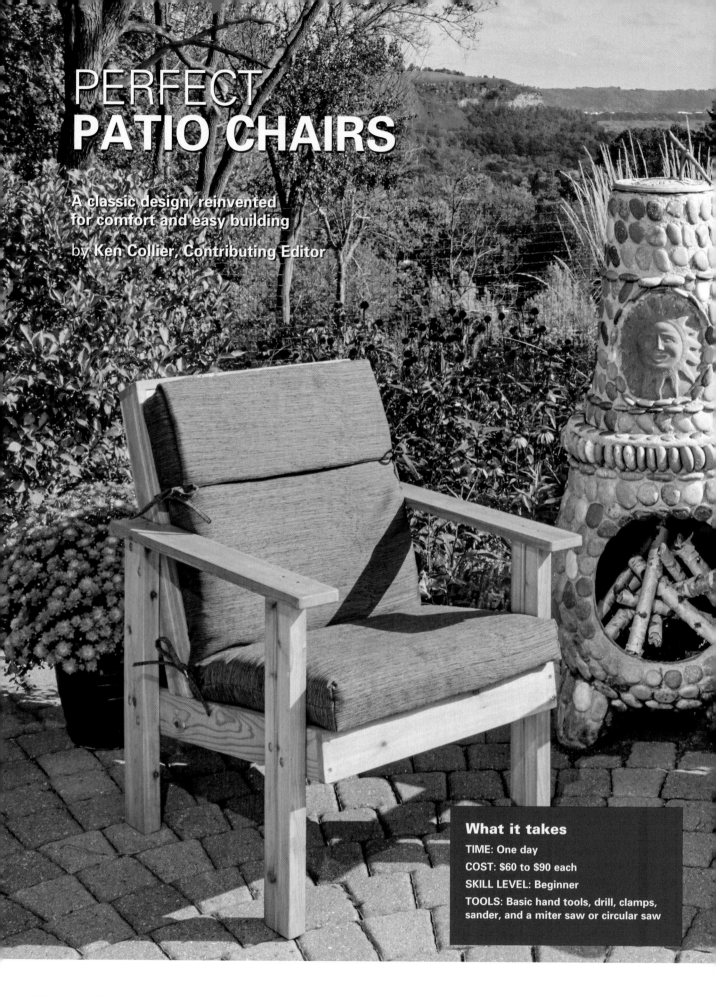

PERFECT
PATIO CHAIRS

A classic design, reinvented
for comfort and easy building

by Ken Collier, Contributing Editor

What it takes

TIME: One day
COST: $60 to $90 each
SKILL LEVEL: Beginner
TOOLS: Basic hand tools, drill, clamps,
sander, and a miter saw or circular saw

This chair is hard to beat for comfort, economy and ease of building. The design is based on a couple chairs I've had at the family cabin for more than a decade. Being a fiddle-with-it kind of guy, I modified the originals over the years, built others and eventually chose this design.

I think it's about as close to perfect as you can get: It's comfortable to sit in for hours at a time, the arms are wide enough to hold a drink, and you're reclined enough for relaxation, but not so much that you'll groan every time you get up (unlike with most Adirondack chairs). It will accept a common type of outdoor chair cushion, available at any home center, but doesn't require one. It's light enough to move around easily, and you can fit it through a doorway without contortions. Plus, it's inexpensive and easy to build.

Skills, tools & lumber

This is a beginner to intermediate level project. If you have just a little experience with tools, you can do it. You'll need an orbital or a random-orbit sander, a 7/16-in. wrench, six clamps and a drill. You can cut parts with a circular saw and drive nails with a hammer, but you'll get faster, nicer results with a miter saw, an air compressor and an 18-gauge brad nailer.

I've built this design from both pine and cedar. Each pine chair will cost you about $60, cedar about $90. Cedar is a better choice if your chairs are going to spend much time out in the rain. You may find it hard to buy 1x3 cedar, so you may have to rip a 1x6 in half. Also note that rough cedar is usually thicker than 3/4 in., while pine boards come in the standard 3/4-in. thickness. When building the seat and back, keep the different thicknesses in mind (see **Photos 2 and 3**).

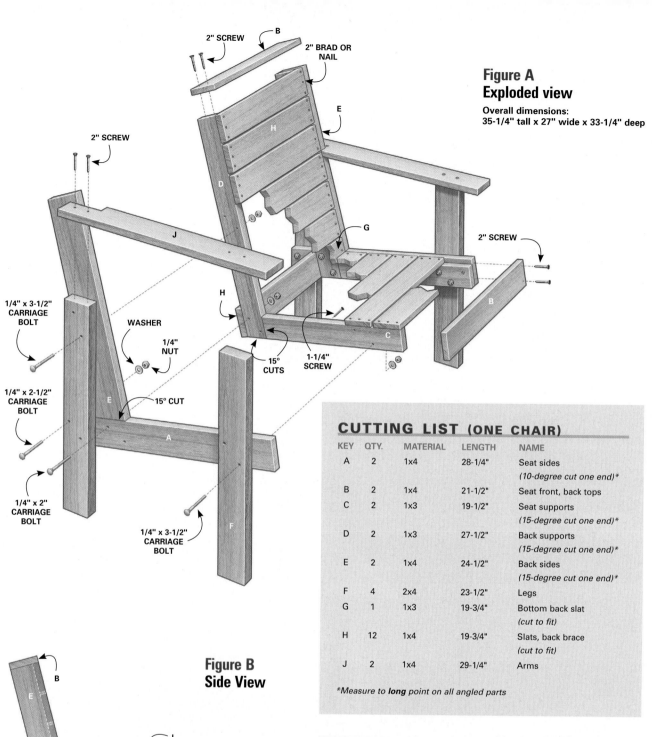

Figure A
Exploded view
Overall dimensions:
35-1/4" tall x 27" wide x 33-1/4" deep

CUTTING LIST (ONE CHAIR)

KEY	QTY.	MATERIAL	LENGTH	NAME
A	2	1x4	28-1/4"	Seat sides *(10-degree cut one end)**
B	2	1x4	21-1/2"	Seat front, back tops
C	2	1x3	19-1/2"	Seat supports *(15-degree cut one end)**
D	2	1x3	27-1/2"	Back supports *(15-degree cut one end)**
E	2	1x4	24-1/2"	Back sides *(15-degree cut one end)**
F	4	2x4	23-1/2"	Legs
G	1	1x3	19-3/4"	Bottom back slat *(cut to fit)*
H	12	1x4	19-3/4"	Slats, back brace *(cut to fit)*
J	2	1x4	29-1/4"	Arms

*Measure to **long** point on all angled parts

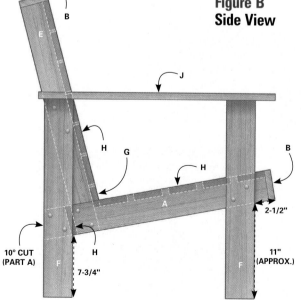

Figure B
Side View

MATERIALS LIST (ONE CHAIR)

ITEM	QTY.
8' 2x4	1
8' 1x4	5
8' 1x3	2
1/4" x 2" galv. carriage bolts	4
1/4" x 2-1/2" galv. carriage bolts	4
1/4" x 3-1/2" galv. carriage bolts	8
1/4" galv. washers	16
1/4" galv. nuts	16
2" deck screws	1 lb.
1-1/4" deck screws	1 lb.
18-gauge galv. 2" brads or 4d galv. finish nails	
Exterior glue and finish	

4" THICK
21" WIDE
44" LONG
SUGGESTED CUSHION SIZE

1 **Cut the parts.** Making more than one chair means cutting a lot of pieces to the same length. A stop block lets you cut a bunch without measuring and marking each board.

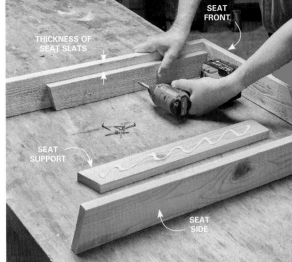

STOP
BLOCK

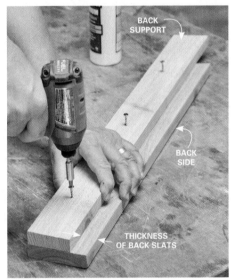

THICKNESS OF
SEAT SLATS

SEAT
FRONT

SEAT
SUPPORT

SEAT
SIDE

2 **Assemble the seat base.** Screw the front to the sides, then glue and screw the seat supports to the sides. If needed, raise or lower the seat supports slightly so that the space above them matches the thickness of the slats.

BACK
SUPPORT

BACK
SIDE

THICKNESS
OF BACK SLATS

3 **Build up the back supports.** Screw and glue the back supports to the back sides. Position the back supports to match the thickness of the back slats.

WOODWORKING & WORKSHOP
PROJECTS & TIPS

Build a prototype

Over decades of chair building, I've learned this: Every chair is a compromise, and no chair is right for everyone. This chair, for example, is midsized and may not be comfortable for large people. So I strongly recommend that you build a prototype before you settle on this or any other design. Use pine or plywood scrap, and don't bother sanding the parts.

The biggest advantage to a prototype is that you and your family can test it for comfort. You can also shop for cushions and actually try them out on the chair. Thicker cushions change the feel of a chair significantly. A prototype is also a building lesson: Once you've built one chair, you can churn out others faster, better and without mistakes.

First, cut and sand the parts

Begin by cutting all the parts except G and H (**Photo 1**). If you're using cedar that's rough on one side, you need to cut each part so that the smooth side will face out. That means you'll have left and right sides to parts A, D and E. In other words, for each pair of parts, make sure the angled cut goes one direction on one part, the other direction on the other. This will allow you to assemble the chair with the smooth face of the cedar facing out.

As you're cutting, label the parts with masking tape. Parts G and H are cut after the chair is assembled so you can get them to fit perfectly. In cedar,

BACK SUPPORT

SEAT SIDE

TEST THE BOLTS
A heavy buildup of zinc coating on galvanized bolts can make it nearly impossible to thread on the nut. So try a nut on each bolt first. Better to discover a stubborn bolt before you pound it into the hole.

4 **Bolt on the back.** Attach the back to the seat side with galvanized carriage bolts. Then screw the back brace to the back side supports.

LEVEL THE SEAT

PLUMB THE LEGS

5 **Attach the legs.** On a flat, level surface, clamp the legs to the seat and back. Check the legs for plumb and the seat for level, then bolt on the legs.

END SLATS

6 **Nail on the slats.** For both the seat and the back, position the end slats first. Then space the others between them (typically 3/8 in. apart).

Hide the ugly boards
If the seat and back will get covered by cushions, use up knotty or odd-colored stock for the slats. But check the slats before you use them: Big, loose knots can create a weak spot that will crack under stress.

---

the length is likely to be about 19-3/4 in. instead of 20 in. Once pieces are cut, sand them. Generally, you don't need to sand finer than 120 grit. For cedar parts, sand only the smooth face.

Build the frame

For pieces that are screwed together, you should drill a pilot hole. In pine, you should countersink a little so the screw head doesn't splinter the wood; cedar is so soft that it's better not to.

Build the seat frame on a flat surface so it stays flat (Photo 2). Begin by screwing the front (B) to the sides (A), then screw and glue the seat support (C) to the inside surface of A. Now glue and screw the back supports (D) to the back sides (E), keeping the square ends flush (Photo 3). The angles at the ends should be parallel. Put the sides in position and tack them on with one screw each at the bottom into the seat sides (A). Screw the back top (B) to the top of the back sides (E). With the back lightly screwed in place, drill two bolt holes each through the seat sides and the back supports (see **Figure A**). Install galvanized carriage bolts and tighten the nuts firmly (**Photo 4**).

Attach the legs

Mark two legs (F) at 7-3/4 in. from the end and mark the other two legs at 11 in. Turn the chair assembly on its side and clamp two legs into place (**Figure B**) so one leg is flush to the angled cut on the seat sides (A) and the other is 2-1/2 in. from the front edge of the seat. After clamping the legs to the seat sides and back, turn the chair over and clamp on the other

BACK SIDE

NOTCH

WIDTH OF
BACK SIDE

ARM

7 **Mark the arm for a notch.** Hold the arm in position and mark the angle of the back onto its edge.

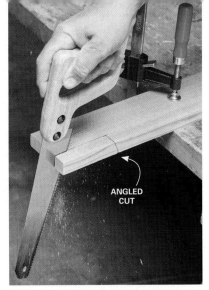

ANGLED
CUT

8 **Cut the notch with a handsaw.** When you reach the end of the long cut, angle the saw to match the angled cut. Any handsaw will do, but smaller is better.

9 **Mount the arms.** Screw on the arms. Round over corners and sharp edges with a file or sandpaper. Give everything a final sanding and you're ready for finish!

EXTERIOR
FINISH

Soak the legs

If the chair will sit on a wet patio or deck, the legs will wick up moisture and rot. To prevent that, soak each leg in a pan of finish for a few minutes. Set the leg on a nut or washer to expose the end of the leg. The finish will penetrate deep and lock out moisture.

two legs. Turn the chair right side up to adjust the legs (**Photo 5**).

Tweak the position of the chair seat so all four legs are on the work surface, the legs are plumb and the seat is level (assuming your work surface is too). Don't worry if the chair seat is not quite on the leg marks you made earlier. When all is well, drill the bolt holes and attach the bolts. Be careful drilling; your holes must go through the back and seat supports (C and D), well away from the edges where the slats will rest.

Seat slats and arms

Measure the inside width of the chair seat and cut a test slat. If it's a good fit, drill the ends and screw it to the bottom edge of the seat supports, in back (see **Figure A**). Cut part G and the rest of the slats (H).

Divide your slats into good and better, and use the better ones on the back, where they're more visible. Nail on the top slats of the back, the front slat of the seat, and the bottom back slat (G). Then space the other slats out and nail them on (**Photo 6**). It helps to tip the chair over to do the back slats.

Follow **Photos 7 – 9** to install the arms.

Sand and finish

Gently round the corners of the arms with a file or sandpaper. Then file a small round-over on all exposed edges, especially on the undersides of the arms, to prevent splinters.

You can cover the screw heads with exterior-grade wood filler or leave them exposed. Lightly sand the entire chair to 120 grit and it'll be ready for finish. I finished our chairs with transparent deck stain.

FOOLPROOF
DADOES & RABBETS

Expert tips for perfect, strong joints

by **Jeff Gorton, Associate Editor**

Dadoes, grooves and rabbets are the workhorses of cabinet and bookcase construction. They're used in woodworking projects to make stronger joints.

Dadoes and **grooves** are flat-bottomed recesses that strengthen supporting shelves and connecting panels. A dado runs perpendicular to the grain of the wood while a groove runs parallel to the grain. A **rabbet** is like a dado that's missing a side. It's essentially a notch cut into the edge of a board or piece of plywood.

You can cut dadoes, grooves and rabbets in many different ways. In this article, however, we're going to show you a simple, foolproof cutting method that requires only a router, a pattern bit and two straight guides.

RABBET

DADO

HOW A PATTERN BIT WORKS

The bit we're using is called a top-bearing pattern bit or top-bearing flush-trim bit. The bearing follows along the straight router guide as the cutters carve out the recess. Since the bearing and the cutters have the same diameter, you just line up the edge of the guide or pattern with the marks for the dado, groove or rabbet and run the router bit along the guide. Using two guides as we show here allows you to cut an exact size dado for any wood thickness that's greater than the bit diameter. The router bit can't go off track either, since it's trapped between the guides.

Most home centers and hardware stores don't stock top-bearing pattern bits, but they're readily available online and at woodworking stores. The bits come in different diameters and lengths. Make sure to buy a bit that's narrower than the thickness of the spacers (**Photo 4**). We're using a 1/2-in.-diameter bit with 1-in.-long cutters (Freud No. 50-102; $23).

CUTTER

GUIDE
BEARING

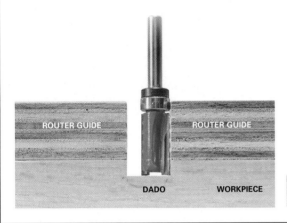

ROUTER GUIDE   ROUTER GUIDE   ROUTER GUIDE

DADO   WORKPIECE   RABBET   WORKPIECE

How to cut perfect dadoes

ROUTER
GUIDE

1 Make two straightedge guides. The dado cutting method we show here requires two perfectly straight guides. You can make your guides any length you want, and whatever thickness is required for your router bit. Since the bit we're using has relatively long cutters, we needed a 1-in.-thick guide to give the bearing something to ride against and the clearance necessary for the bit to reach the bottom of the dadoes.

To make guides like those shown here, cut four 6-in.-wide by 4-ft.-long strips of 1/2-in.-thick plywood. Glue pairs together to make two 1-in.-thick strips. When the glue is dry, use a table saw or circular saw and straightedge to trim the guides and create one perfectly straight edge. Draw an arrow toward the straight edge of each strip to remind you which edge you should use for the guide (**Photo 3**).

When you're done trimming the edges, check the straightness of the guides by placing them next to each other on your workbench, with the arrows facing, and press them together. The guides should fit tight with no gaps. If there is a gap, recut one or both pieces until they fit tightly together.

2 **Mark the location of the dado.** You only need to mark one edge of the dado. Then draw an "X" to indicate which side of the mark the dado goes on. A good tip is to make three, not just two, marks across the workpiece. Then when you line up your straightedge with the marks, if one of the marks doesn't line up, you'll know you've made a layout mistake.

3 **Clamp the first guide.** The method we're using requires two guides, one for each side of the dado. This allows you to cut a perfect-width dado regardless of the thickness of the material. Line up the guide with the marks and clamp it securely. Be careful to position the clamps where they won't interfere with the router base as you're cutting the dado.

4 **Add spacers.** When you're cutting out the parts for your cabinet or bookcase, save a few scraps of the material. Then use those scraps as spacers. This ensures that the thickness of the material you're using will match the dado widths perfectly.

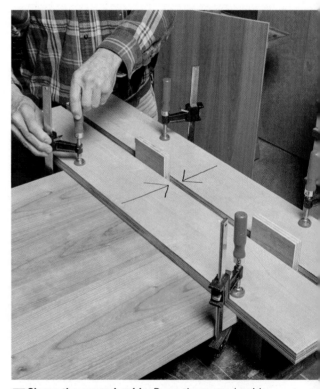

5 **Clamp the second guide.** Press the second guide against the spacer blocks and clamp it. Again, make sure the clamps won't interfere with the router base. Remove the spacers and you're ready to cut the dado.

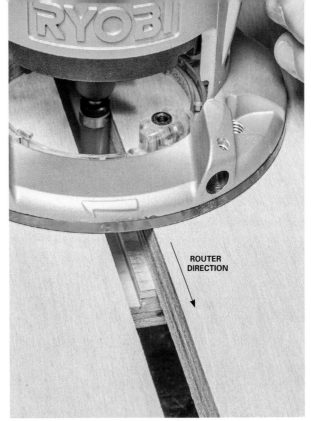

6 **Rout the first side of the dado.** Since the dado we're cutting is a little less than 3/4 in. wide, and we're using a 1/2-in. bit, it will take two passes, one along each router guide, to complete the dado. First adjust the router depth. This will be the thickness of the guides plus the desired depth of your dado. We set the router to cut a 1/4-in.-deep dado. If you're positioned as shown in this photo, start at the left side and move the router left to right, keeping the guide bearing pressed against the guide farthest from you. The rule of thumb is to rout inside cuts like this in a clockwise direction.

7 **Finish up with a second pass.** Complete the dado by moving the router right to left, keeping the guide bearing in contact with the guide closest to you. Before you remove the clamps and guides, inspect the dado to make sure both edges are straight and smooth. If you find any imperfections, run the router over that area again. That's all it takes to cut a perfect dado.

How to cut perfect rabbets

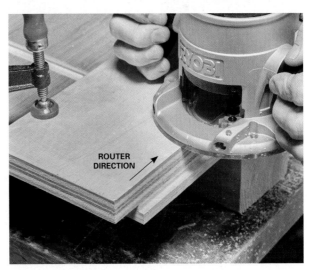

1 **Position the guide.** There's more than one way to cut a rabbet, including buying a special rabbeting bit. But since you already have the guide and a pattern bit, why not use them to cut rabbets, too? Here we're cutting a 1/4-in. x 1/4-in. rabbet in the back of a cabinet side to accept the 1/4-in. plywood back. Use a scrap of the same plywood to set the position of the guide, then clamp the guide into place.

2 **Rout the rabbet.** Starting at the left end, run the router left to right along the guide to cut the rabbet. You can use this same technique to cut wider rabbets like the one along the top edge of the cabinet (see photo on p. 164), but you'll have to make one pass along the guide, and then clean up the remaining wood using the router freehand. That just means holding the bearing a tad away from the straightedge to remove the rest of the wood. Be sure to keep the router base tight to the guide at all times.

CUSTOM PICTURE LEDGES

Make them any length, any color, for any wall

by **Travis Larson, Senior Editor**

ANYONE CAN BUILD!

Picture ledges are the perfect marriage of beauty and function. They elegantly display your picture collections, large or small, and they're ultra easy to use. You don't have to mess with positioning hooks. Your photos and artwork will never go crooked, and best of all, you can "redecorate" instantly just by swapping things around. There's no need to patch holes every time you move a picture.

These shelves are super-simple to build too. It's mostly a matter of gluing and nailing together two boards and a length of molding—no fancy cuts, tools or skills required. This is a great woodworking project for beginners.

Planning your shelves

Even though you'll likely be swapping out and rearranging pictures down the road, it's a good idea to lay out the initial arrangement of pictures on the floor. That way, you can sketch a plan for the length of your ledges and the spacing between them. The other advantage is that you'll be able to assemble a materials list to take to the home center.

You can build your ledges any length you wish. It takes two 1x3s for every ledge, one for the apron (back) and one for the shelf (**Photo 1**). A 1-1/4 x 1/4-in. molding nailed to the front (**Photo 2**) acts as a lip to hold picture frames in place.

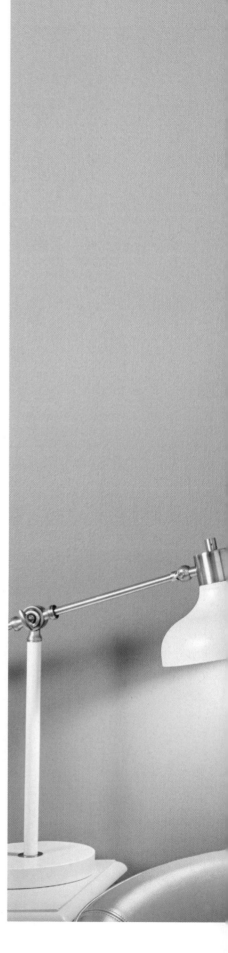

Just three parts, so they're fast and easy to build

- Even a beginner can build these picture ledges—no experience needed.
- You can do it with basic tools. If you don't have a brad nailer or miter saw, you can assemble the ledges using a hammer and nails, then cut them with a handsaw.
- Each ledge is made from just three parts. All you have to do is glue and tack them together.

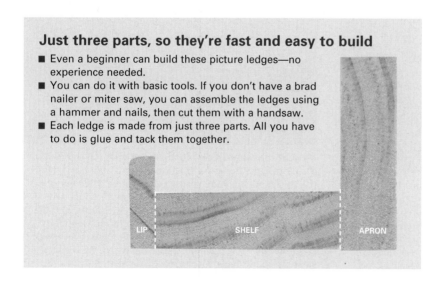

LIP   SHELF   APRON

1 Glue and nail the parts. Glue and nail the 1x3 apron onto the 1x3 shelf with 2-in. brads.

2 Add the lip. Use the benchtop to make the shelf and molding flush while you glue and nail them together with 1-in. brads.

3 Trim the ends. Cut to final length after the ledge has been assembled. Sand the freshly cut ends before painting.

We made our ledges from clear pine because we planned to paint them. If you prefer a natural wood look, oak is available at the home center along with the 1/4-in. matching molding. You can choose any wood you want if you're capable of making your own molding.

Remember to get wood glue along with the nails. Finish washers are a simple, elegant way to dress up screw heads. They'll largely be hidden behind the pictures, but you can paint them to help them blend in better if you wish. You'll need 2-1/2-in. screws, about one for every 8 in. of shelf plus a package of screw-in. anchors that accept conventional threaded wood screws. (E-Z Ancor is one brand.) You can use other drywall anchors if you wish.

Assembly takes minutes

You'll glue the pieces together and then nail them with an 18-gauge brad nailer (**Photo 1**). Fasten the apron to the shelf with 2-in. brads, and secure the 1/4-in. molding to the front with 1-in. brads. If you don't have an air nailer, you can certainly do it the old–fashioned way with finish nails and a hammer.

4 **Draw a guideline.** Scribe a line on the back of the apron 3/4 in. down from the top.

3/4"

5 **Drill pilot holes.** Mark for screw holes 2 to 3 in. from both ends. Then space holes evenly every 8 to 12 in. between them. Drill 1/8-in. holes.

6 **Sand and paint.** Fill the brad holes with filler, sand them flush, and prime and paint the ledges. (Or use a combination primer/paint product.)

LEDGE
LOCATION

MARK
ON TAPE

7 **Mark ledge locations on masking tape.** Stick a vertical strip of masking tape to the wall to position one end of the ledges. Mark the top of each ledge on the tape, and use those marks to draw level lines on the wall for each ledge.

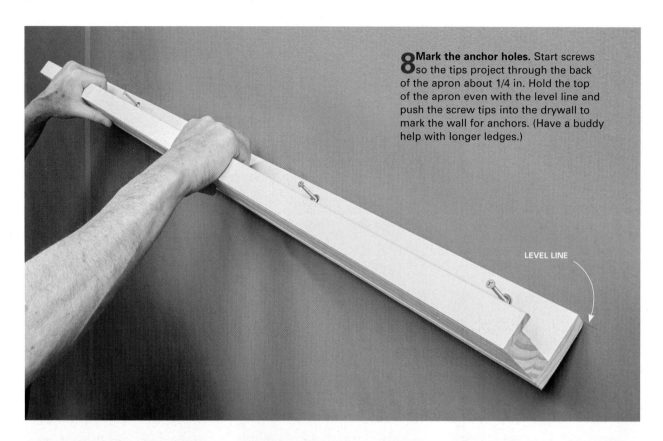

8 **Mark the anchor holes.** Start screws so the tips project through the back of the apron about 1/4 in. Hold the top of the apron even with the level line and push the screw tips into the drywall to mark the wall for anchors. (Have a buddy help with longer ledges.)

LEVEL LINE

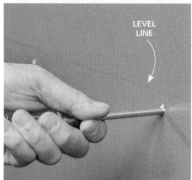

LEVEL LINE

9 **Drill anchor holes.** Twist and drive a Phillips screwdriver through the marks. Draw a circle around any holes that have studs behind them.

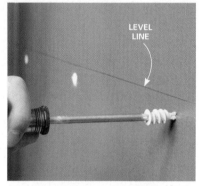

LEVEL LINE

10 **Sink the drywall anchors.** Screw a drywall anchor into each hole except the ones over studs.

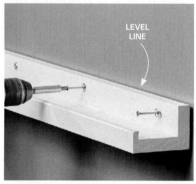

LEVEL LINE

11 **Screw the ledges to the wall.** Screw each shelf to the anchors or into the studs.

2-1/2"
SCREW

FINISH
WASHER

It's smart to assemble all three parts first and then cut the ends so they're perfectly flush. If you don't have a miter saw, make the cuts with a handsaw.

Finish after assembly

Whether you paint or stain and varnish for a natural wood finish, do it after the shelves are built but before they get mounted on the wall. If you

choose to paint, start with a coat of primer. The best topcoat to use is acrylic latex enamel. It's easy to apply and is much tougher than ordinary latex paint, so it resists scratches and wear—and it's easier to dust.

Hang the ledges

Use screws with finish washers along with drywall anchors to hang the ledges—no glue. That way if

you want to remove them later for repainting, you won't have to patch the walls. The screws will be mostly hidden by pictures, but if you want, you can paint them after installation. Some screws will fall over studs. You'll find them when you drill pilot holes with a Phillips screwdriver. You can skip the anchors and drive those screws directly into the wood.

SUPER-CAPACITY **TOOL CART**

Roll it to your work zone for instant access; park it in a corner for space-saving storage.

by **Jeff Gorton, Associate Editor**

This cart would make a great addition to any workspace, but it's especially perfect for a garage workshop. It brings your whole tool arsenal within easy reach during a project but takes up minimal floor space, leaving plenty of room for your car when the job is done. It's also adaptable—easy to build as shown and easy to alter. You can add or subtract drawers and shelves to meet your workshop needs.

WOODWORKING & WORKSHOP PROJECTS & TIPS

What it takes

TIME: **Two days**

COST: **$350-$450**

SKILL LEVEL: **Intermediate**

TOOLS: **Table saw, drill, drill bits, router, 1/4-in. straight-cutting router bit, basic hand tools**

The cart is open on both the front and the back—a design that combines easy access with maximum capacity.

FRONT

BACK

1 MEDIUM SHELVES are just right for most power tools.

2 HOMEMADE DRAWER PULLS are convenient, sturdy and good-looking.

3 SHALLOW DRAWERS are perfect for chisels and other hand tools.

6 ADJUSTABLE SLOTS house nail guns, drills or sandpaper.

7 ADJUSTABLE SHELVES adapt as your tool collection grows.

8 SHALLOW SHELVES are ideal for glue and finishes.

4 DEEP DRAWERS hold small power tools or screw containers.

5 DEEP SHELVES hold long tools like grinders and recip saws.

9 HEAVY-DUTY CASTERS provide smooth mobility.

It's a great weekend project

You could cut all the plywood parts with a circular saw, but we recommend using a table saw for greater accuracy and to speed things up. If you want to include the slots—grooved shelves with plywood dividers—you'll need a router and a 1/4-in. straight bit to make the dadoes. And a brad nailer is handy for tacking the parts before adding the screws.

We used birch plywood for this project, but you could choose MDF (medium-density fiberboard) or less expensive plywood to save money. We shopped around at local home centers and found nice-looking birch plywood with B-grade face veneer for about $40 per sheet. The entire project requires four sheets of 3/4-in. plywood and one sheet of 1/4-in. plywood.

Build the cabinet box

Start by cutting out the parts, using **Figure C** on p. 179 and the **Cutting List** on p. 175 as a guide. You'll notice that some of the dimensions in the Cutting List have an asterisk indicating that you may have to adjust the size. That's because plywood varies slightly in thickness. We used a table saw for ripping and a crosscut sled on the table saw to crosscut narrow parts. This allowed us to cut the parts accurately for tight-fitting joints.

Photos 1 – 3 show how to get started building the basic box. Drill pilot holes for the screws to avoid splitting the plywood. Use the shelves (**Photo 2**) or temporary spacers (**Photo 3**) to hold the interior dividers in place while you secure them with screws. There are a few spots where dividers are aligned with each other, making it impossible to drive screws straight in. In these situations, start the screws alongside the part that's in the way and drive the screws at a slight angle, being careful to keep the screw tips from going through the opposite side of the plywood.

When you're done with the box, attach the casters. Start by building up the base with two strips of plywood so you can use 1-1/2-in. lag screws to attach the casters (**Photo 4**). We found good-quality 4-in. casters with locking ball-bearing wheels for about $10 each at a home center. Buy good-quality casters because this cabinet could weigh hundreds of pounds fully loaded.

Table saw sled
For step-by-step instructions on how to build a table saw sled, go to **tfhmag.com/tablesawsled**.

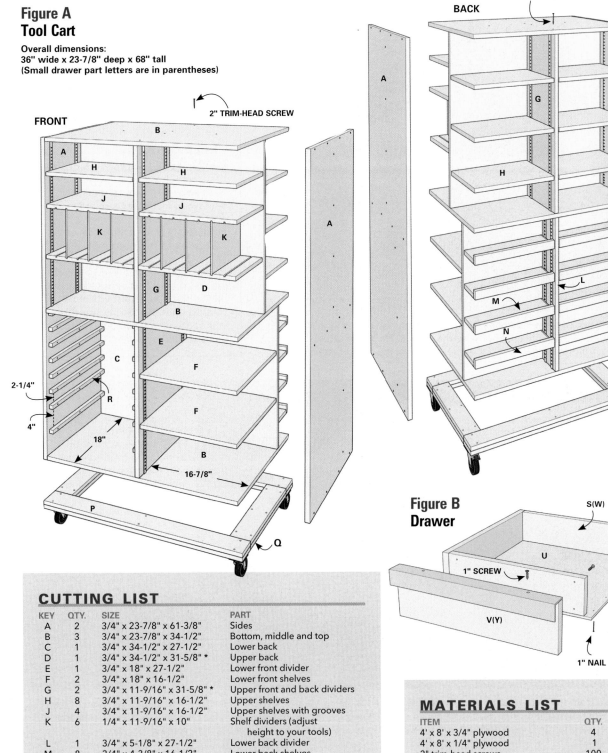

Figure A
Tool Cart

Overall dimensions:
36" wide x 23-7/8" deep x 68" tall
(Small drawer part letters are in parentheses)

FRONT

2" TRIM-HEAD SCREW

A
B
H
J
K
G
D
E
C
F
F
R
B
B
P
Q

2-1/4"

4"

18"

16-7/8"

2" TRIM-HEAD SCREW

BACK

A

G
H
L
M
N

Figure B
Drawer

S(W)
T(X)
U
V(Y)

1" SCREW

1-1/4" SCREW

1" NAIL

CUTTING LIST

KEY	QTY.	SIZE	PART
A	2	3/4" x 23-7/8" x 61-3/8"	Sides
B	3	3/4" x 23-7/8" x 34-1/2"	Bottom, middle and top
C	1	3/4" x 34-1/2" x 27-1/2"	Lower back
D	1	3/4" x 34-1/2" x 31-5/8" *	Upper back
E	1	3/4" x 18" x 27-1/2"	Lower front divider
F	2	3/4" x 18" x 16-1/2"	Lower front shelves
G	2	3/4" x 11-9/16" x 31-5/8" *	Upper front and back dividers
H	8	3/4" x 11-9/16" x 16-1/2"	Upper shelves
J	4	3/4" x 11-9/16" x 16-1/2"	Upper shelves with grooves
K	6	1/4" x 11-9/16" x 10"	Shelf dividers (adjust
			height to your tools)
L	1	3/4" x 5-1/8" x 27-1/2"	Lower back divider
M	8	3/4" x 4-3/8" x 16-1/2"	Lower back shelves
N	8	3/4" x 1-1/4" x 16-1/2"	Shelf nosing
P	4	3/4" x 3-1/2" x 36"	Caster supports
Q	4	3/4" x 3-1/2" x 16-7/8"	Caster support side fillers
R	16	3/4" x 3/4" x 17-1/4"	Drawer runners
S	4	3/4" x 3-5/8" x 15-1/4"	Large drawer back and front
T	4	3/4" x 3-5/8" x 17"	Large drawer sides
U	8	1/4" x 16-3/4" x 17"	Drawer bottoms
V	2	3/4" x 16-3/4" x 4-1/2"	Large drawer fronts
W	12	3/4" x 1-7/8" x 15-1/4"	Small drawer back and front
X	12	3/4" x 1-7/8" x 17"	Small drawer sides
Y	6	3/4" x 16-3/4" x 2-3/4"	Small drawer fronts

* Measure and cut to fit.

MATERIALS LIST

ITEM	QTY.
4' x 8' x 3/4" plywood	4
4' x 8' x 1/4" plywood	1
2" trim-head screws	100
1-1/4" screws	80
1-1/2" x 5/16" lag screws	16
No. 4 x 1" flat-head screws	16
1-1/2" finish nails	
1" finish nails	
3" casters	4
36" shelf standards	28
Shelf clips	88
Wood glue	
96" x 1-1/2" x 1-1/2" x 1/8"	
aluminum angle	1
24" x 1-1/2" x 1-1/2" x 1/8"	
aluminum angle	1

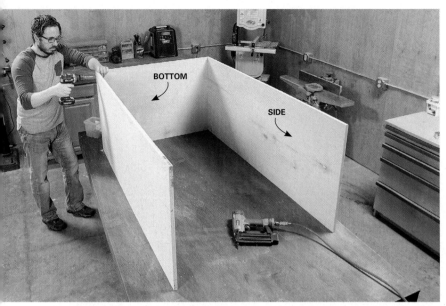

THREE OPTIONS:

CHOOSE YOUR FASTENING METHOD

We assembled the parts with trim-head screws and covered them with wood filler, but there are other options. You could use screws and finish washers for a more industrial look (**above left**) or assemble the entire storage unit with pocket screws (**above right**). Pocket screw assembly would leave a lot of exposed pockets on the inside, but most would be covered once the cabinet was filled with tools, or you could buy wood plugs to fill the pockets.

1 **Start with a three-sided box.** Nail or clamp the two sides (A) to the bottom (B) and drill pilot holes for the screws. Place two screws about 1-1/2 in. from the edges, and add three more evenly spaced between them.

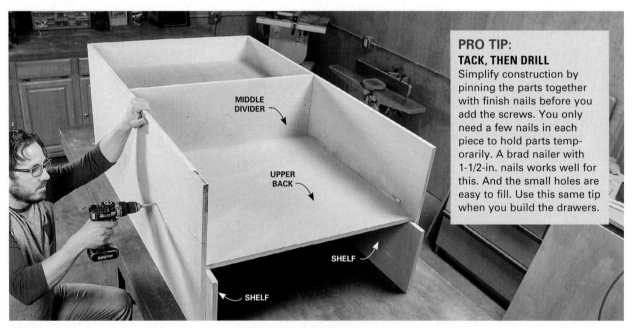

PRO TIP:

TACK, THEN DRILL

Simplify construction by pinning the parts together with finish nails before you add the screws. You only need a few nails in each piece to hold parts temporarily. A brad nailer with 1-1/2-in. nails works well for this. And the small holes are easy to fill. Use this same tip when you build the drawers.

2 **Build from the bottom up.** Screw in the lower back (C), using the divider (E) and a shelf (F) to support it. Then add the horizontal middle divider (B). Set the upper back (D) and the top (B) in place and check the fit. You may have to trim a little from the top of D for a good fit. Use shelves (H) to support part D as you attach it with screws.

Build the drawers

The drawers are simple boxes that slide on 3/4-in. square runners. The drawers are sized to allow about 1/16-in. clearance on the sides and 1/8 in. on top for easy movement. **Photos 5 and 6** show how to build the drawers. Cut the 1/4-in. plywood bottoms accurately and make sure they're square so you can use them to square the drawer frame. Finish the drawers by attaching the fronts with screws (**Photo 6**).

Mark the location of the drawer runners on the sides of

the cabinet (**Photo 7**). Then attach the runners with glue and 1-1/4-in. screws (**Photo 8**). We fabricated drawer pulls from 1/8-in.-thick aluminum angle (**Photos 9 and 10**). Attach the aluminum angles to the drawers with two screws through the top. If you've laid out your drawer runners correctly, there should be about 1/8 in. of space between all the drawers.

Add shelves

The plywood shelves rest on shelf clips attached to metal

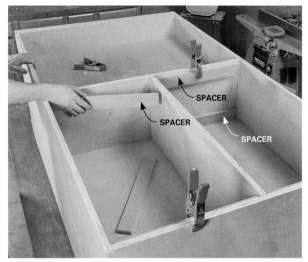

3 **Complete the cabinet assembly.** Add the four vertical dividers, Parts E, G and L. Use temporary spacers to hold the panels in the center as you attach them. You'll need eight spacers, 16-7/8 in. long.

SPACER
SPACER
SPACER

4 **Add the casters.** First glue and screw four strips of plywood (P) to the front and back edges of the box. Then mark the caster screw holes and drill 3/16-in. pilot holes for the 5/16-in. x 1-1/2-in. lag screws. Attach all four casters with the lag screws.

CASTER SUPPORTS
LAG SCREW
4" CASTER

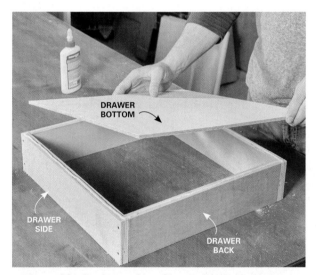

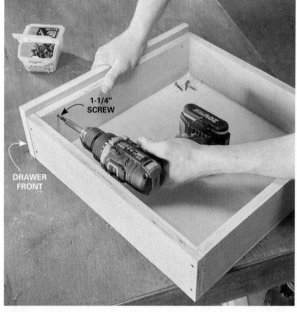

DRAWER BOTTOM
DRAWER SIDE
DRAWER BACK

5 **Assemble the drawer box.** Glue and tack the drawer sides to the front and back. Then add screws for more strength. Apply a bead of glue to the drawer and place the drawer bottom on the drawer box. Line up one edge of the drawer bottom with the drawer and nail it. Then square the drawer by lining up the remaining edges with the edges of the drawer bottom and nail the other three sides.

1-1/4" SCREW
DRAWER FRONT

6 **Add the drawer fronts.** The drawer fronts are the same width as the drawers, but a little taller. Line up the sides and bottom and attach the fronts with 1-1/4-in. screws.

shelf standards (**Photo 12**). This allows you to customize the shelf heights to accommodate your tools. Some of the shelves have dadoes cut into them to accept plywood dividers. **Photo 11** shows how to cut the dadoes with a router and router guide.

Build the guide by gluing a perfectly straight strip of 3/4-in. plywood (fence) to a strip of 1/4-in. plywood. Then mount a 1/4-in. straight bit in the router and run the router along the fence to cut off the excess 1/4-in. plywood. Now you can mark the dado locations on your shelves, line up the edge of the router guide to the marks and clamp it, and

rout the dadoes (**Photo 11**). It's easier to cut dadoes across a 16-1/2-in.-wide by 4-ft.-long piece of plywood first, and then cut the shelves to 11-9/16 in. deep after all the dadoes are cut (**Photo 11**).

To prevent stuff from falling off the narrow shelves, nail 3/4 x 1-1/4-in. plywood strips to the face of the shelves (**Figure A**).

We finished our rolling tool cabinet with two coats of satin polyurethane. If you plan to paint or finish your tool cabinet, you'll save time and get a better job by mounting the shelf standards and drawer pulls after you apply finish.

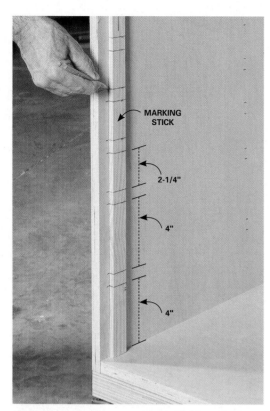

8 Install the runners. Drill pilot holes and attach the runners with glue and 1-1/4-in. screws. Use spacers to hold the runners. If necessary, make slight adjustments to keep the runners aligned with the marks.

7 Mark for the drawer runners. Make a marking stick using the measurements in Figure A. Then use the stick to mark the positions of the drawer runners. Make marks at the front and back.

SLICK TIP
SMOOTHER DRAWER RUNNERS
You can make your drawers slide easier by applying melamine tape to the tops of the drawer runners. You'll find rolls of melamine tape at home centers, woodworking stores or online. FastEdge, a self-adhesive version, is available at fastcap.com. If you buy iron-on tape, apply it before you mount the runners in the cabinet.

9 Cut aluminum with a miter saw. Make drawer pulls by cutting aluminum angle to length. Many carbide blades are designed to cut nonferrous metals as well as wood—check the fine print on the blade or packaging to make sure.

10 Drill and countersink the pulls. Drill two holes in each aluminum pull. Place the holes 3 in. from the ends and 3/8 in. from the edge. Use a countersink in your drill to create a recess for the screws. Line up the edges of the aluminum angles with the back edge of the drawer fronts and attach them with small screws.

Figure C
Cutting Diagrams

3/4" PLYWOOD

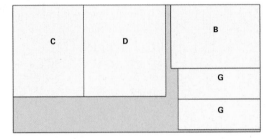

3/4" PLYWOOD

3/4" PLYWOOD

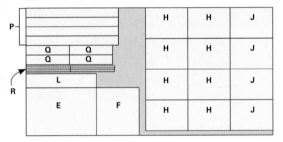

3/4" PLYWOOD

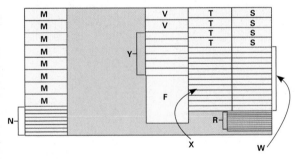

1/4" PLYWOOD

1/4" DADO
ROUTER GUIDE

11 **Cut slots for plywood dividers.** Four shelves require slots for plywood dividers. To save time, cut the dadoes across all four shelves before ripping them to the correct width. Make a straightedge jig as shown and clamp it at the marks indicating your slot location. Then use a router with a 1/4-in. straight bit to cut the slot.

SHELF STANDARD

12 **Mount the shelf standards.** Cut the metal shelf standards to fit with a hacksaw. Make sure to cut off the same end of every standard so the holes will line up correctly. Position the standards 1 in. from the front and back of every shelf side and attach them with small screws.

PAN-HEAD SCREW

SHELF CLIP

NO-SLIP TIP
ANCHOR THE SHELVES
Drive short pan-head screws into the bottom of the shelf, directly behind the shelf clips. This will prevent the shelf from slipping forward and falling off the supports. You only need two per shelf.

HOW TO BUY
ROUGH-SAWN LUMBER

Advice from a pro on how to choose the best boards

by **Tom Caspar, Contributing Editor**

If you're into woodworking even a little bit, you should consider buying rough-sawn lumber for your next project. And rough-sawn is the only way to go if you need really thick boards. Plus, you can save yourself a ton of money converting rough-sawn lumber to finished product; maybe enough to justify buying that planer you've always wanted. A lumberyard that specializes in rough-sawn lumber will have a much, much larger selection of species to choose from than a home center.

But there are a few things you should know before heading to the yard. That's why we took a field trip with a pro woodworker to Youngblood Lumber Company in Minneapolis. He clued us in on which tools you should take along to the yard and how to estimate what size lumber to buy. He showed us what to look for and warned us what to avoid. These great tips will help you choose your lumber carefully and spend your money wisely.

MEET AN EXPERT

Tom Caspar has been a professional cabinetmaker since 1978. He has designed dozens of projects for home woodworkers and is the former editor of *American Woodworker* magazine.

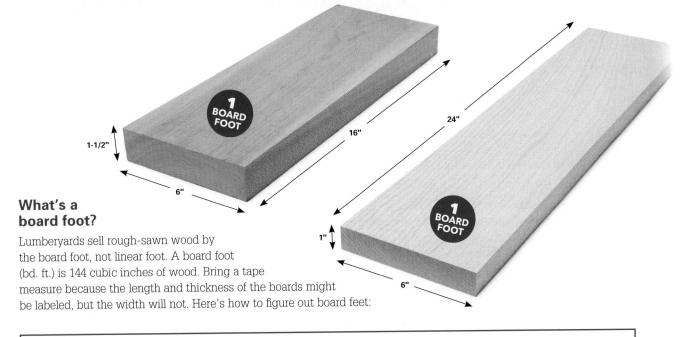

What's a board foot?

Lumberyards sell rough-sawn wood by the board foot, not linear foot. A board foot (bd. ft.) is 144 cubic inches of wood. Bring a tape measure because the length and thickness of the boards might be labeled, but the width will not. Here's how to figure out board feet:

$$\text{WIDTH (INCHES)} \times \text{LENGTH (INCHES)} \times \text{THICKNESS (INCHES)} \div 144 = \textbf{BOARD FEET}$$

Buy Extra

Picking out and hauling home rough-sawn lumber and then milling it into usable boards is time-consuming, so buy extra. You don't want to go through the whole process to mill one board to replace one that gets damaged. Also, the color and grain of the new board may not match the boards you bought on your first trip. Buying and milling at least one extra full board is a good idea.

Go Long

The ends of rough-sawn boards often contain checks (cracks). Some checks are obvious, but some you won't discover until you cut the board near the end. So plan on discarding several inches on each end of every board. That means that if you need two finished 4-ft. boards for your project, buy a 10-ft. rough-sawn.

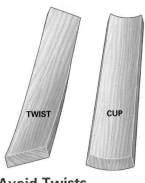
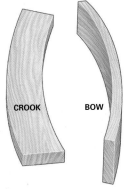

Avoid Twists

Steer clear of any board that looks like a banana, but minor warping can be removed in the milling process. The shorter the boards you need, the bigger the bend you can work with. However, avoid twisted boards. The internal forces that are causing the twist may never go away no matter how much material you remove. Our expert's motto: "Once twisted, always twisted."

Pick thicker boards

Hardwood lumberyards sell rough-sawn lumber in various thicknesses. Most yards label thicknesses in 1/4-in. fractions: 4/4 = 1 in., 5/4 = 1-1/4 in., 6/4 = 1-1/2 in., etc. Buy boards at least 1/4 in. thicker than your final dimension in order to account for the material that will be removed by the jointer and planer. Thicker boards cost more per board foot, so you won't save any money by buying a 2-in. board and resawing it into two 1-in. boards.

Check the color with water

These days, most rough-sawn lumber receives one pass through a planer or sander on each side before it reaches the yard. The process, called hit-and-miss, usually smooths the surface enough to see the character of the grain you're dealing with. But two similar-colored boards in the same bin may differ dramatically in color when finished with a clear topcoat. If it's important that all your boards be close to the same color, take along a spray bottle filled with water. A couple quick squirts should expose any surprises.

KNOTS

KNOTS

NO.1 COMMON   SELECT

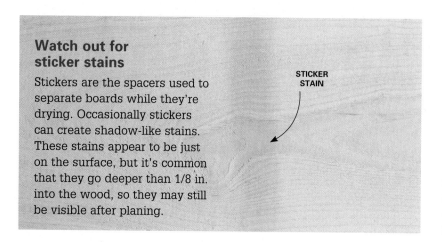

Watch out for sticker stains

Stickers are the spacers used to separate boards while they're drying. Occasionally stickers can create shadow-like stains. These stains appear to be just on the surface, but it's common that they go deeper than 1/8 in. into the wood, so they may still be visible after planing.

STICKER STAIN

Use lower-grade lumber and save

Lumber with more knots costs less, which makes sense. If your project contains a bunch of smaller pieces, you can save money by cutting out and around those defects. This lower-grade lumber is often called No. 1 Common (1C). Sometimes you can find a gem or two that may look good enough as is, or have long enough clear cuts between the knots for the boards you need.

Save money on rough-sawn

Buying rough-sawn lumber and planing your own wood definitely saves money; how much money depends on the species and on the size of the project. The larger the project, the more you save.

ROUGH-SAWN PRICE:
9 BD. FT. = $25
(BEFORE MILLING)

HOME CENTER PRICE:
5.5 BD. FT. = $60

RED OAK

Old boards need cleaning

Dirty boards will dull planer and jointer blades. If it looks like your board may have been kicking around the yard for quite a while, plan on scouring it with a wire brush before milling.

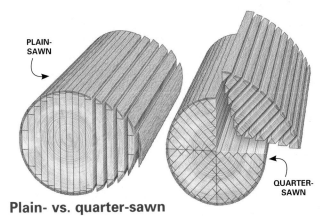

PLAIN-SAWN

QUARTER-SAWN

Plain- vs. quarter-sawn

Most rough-sawn wood these days has been plain (or flat) sawn. But you may come across a couple of species that have been quarter-sawn. Quarter-sawn wood is more stable and much less likely to warp, but it also costs a lot more.

Take a saw

Your perfect board may be 12 ft. long, which isn't likely to fit in the back of your Ford Fiesta. Take along a saw to cut long boards into manageable lengths. Pay for the boards before you cut them down.

Beautiful boards
To see great tips for turning rough lumber into beautiful boards, search for "planing wood" at **familyhandyman.com.**

Beware super-wide boards

You may come across a gorgeous slab that's wide enough for a tabletop. But building with wide boards is risky. If they're cut too near the center of the tree, they can cup dramatically. To guarantee a flat surface, you're better off gluing up boards that are 5 to 7 in. wide than ones that are 12 in. plus. Also, really wide boards may not fit in your planer.

Don't have a jointer?

Many yards will "straight-line" one edge for you so that you can rip the boards to the desired width on your table saw. Some can plane boards down in thickness, too, but there's no guarantee they'll come out flat.

Buy local

There may not be a commercial hardwood lumberyard near you, but it's likely that someone in your area has a small sawmill and sells various local species. Your state's DNR website might have a listing of these smaller sawmills. Hiring someone with a portable sawmill is a good option if you want to saw up wood harvested from your own property and are willing to go through the lengthy drying process.

Invest $30 in a moisture meter before buying rough-sawn lumber that has been air-dried. Check that the moisture level is between 12 and 15 percent before loading up your truck. And when you get your air-dried boards home, store them inside to dry them even further. Ideal moisture content is about 6 to 8 percent. The lumber you buy at a commercial yard should have been kiln-dried.

Buy online

A lot of furniture builders buy rough-sawn wood online, especially when working with hard-to-get exotic woods, extra-wide boards or boards with a live edge (bark still on). Shipping will be expensive and returns may not be an option, so make sure you see a photo of the exact boards you're buying. The best suppliers will have photos on their website.

HOT GLUE— A WOOD SHOP STAPLE!

You can't DIY without hot glue!

by **Travis Larson, Senior Editor**

I used to think hot glue guns were just for school projects and holiday decorations. But then I discovered just how useful hot glue can be in the workshop, and now my gun is one of my favorite tools.

Here are some of my favorite hot glue tips. They're mostly for woodworking since that's my passion. But with a little creativity, you'll find uses for a hot glue gun no matter what your hobby.

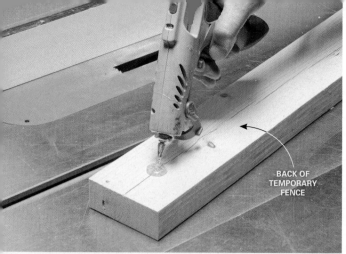

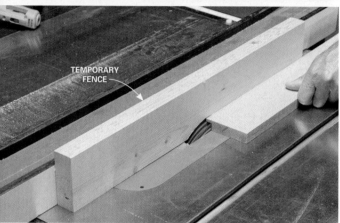

1 **Fasten a temporary fence.** When you're woodworking, you often need a temporary fence or stop on a table saw or router table or other power tools. Clamps aren't always an option because they can get in the way, and you probably don't want to drill holes in the machine's fence or table for bolts or screws. Instead, use a few dollops of hot glue to hold your temporary fence in place.

2 **Hot-glue parts together for shaping and sanding.** When you have several identical parts to make, hot-glue them together and work on them all at once. This will save you lots of time, and all the pieces will be exactly the same. Don't use too much glue—just a little dab will do. Use too much and it can be nearly impossible to separate the parts later. Apply glue near edges so you can easily cut it with a putty knife later.

3 **Cut and twist to separate.** Hot glue is a tenacious fastener. If you just pry apart the wood, you're very likely to tear out some of the grain along with the glue. Instead, cut through the glue blob at one end with a putty knife. Then twist the boards apart to free the other end. That'll break the bond without damaging the wood.

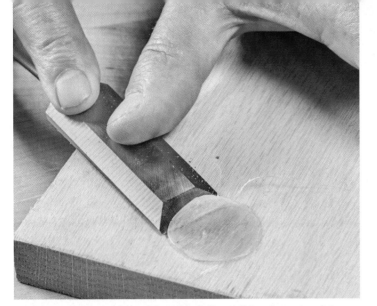

4 **Remove leftover glue with a chisel.** If possible, place glue dabs where they'll be trimmed off later, such as along edges or on ends. Then you won't have to deal with glue residue. But if you do have glue dabs to remove, shave them off with a sharp chisel held flat to the board. Get as much as you can without gouging the wood, and then sand off the residue. Be sure to get it all—leftover glue won't accept finishes.

5 **Glue small parts to a pedestal.** Sometimes it's impossible, impractical or downright dangerous to hold small pieces in your hand while you shape or sand them. So just hot-glue them to a temporary pedestal and clamp that in a vise while you work on them.

6 **Hard-to-clamp repairs call for hot glue.** When you need to glue parts that can't be clamped together, hot glue is the answer. Hot glue will set in just a few seconds while you hold the pieces together.

FAST
FEMUR FIX

7 **Hot glue for pattern routing.** The best way to make multiple identical parts is to first create a perfect pattern from 1/2-in. MDF. Then cut out the parts slightly oversize, and final-shape them by using a router and a pattern bit to transfer the shape to the part. The best way to temporarily attach the pattern is with hot glue.

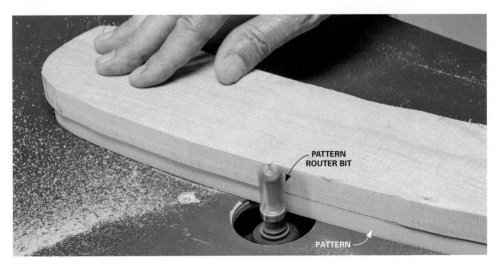

PATTERN
ROUTER BIT

PATTERN

HOT GLUE—A WOOD SHOP STAPLE!

8 **Stick stock to your workbench.** If you need your workpiece to be stationary but clamps would be in the way, use a few dabs of hot glue to hold it in place.

DABS OF
HOT GLUE

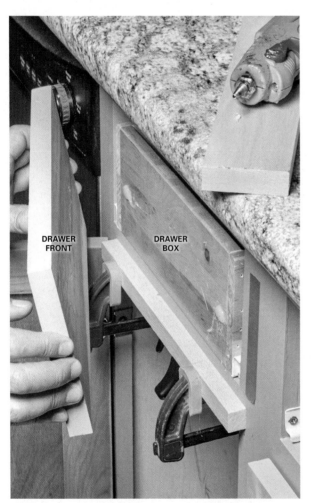

DRAWER
FRONT

DRAWER
BOX

9 **Position drawer fronts.** When you're installing new cabinet drawer fronts, apply hot glue, align the fronts perfectly in the cabinet opening and hold them against the drawer box until the glue sets. Then pull out the drawer and fasten them permanently with screws from the back.

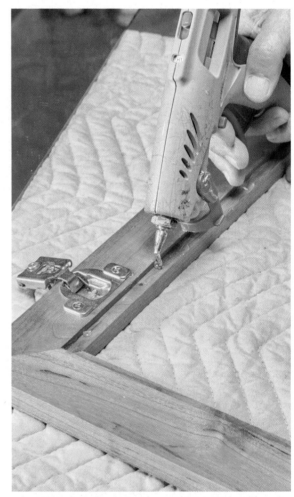

10 **Secure mirrors or glass in cabinet doors.** Swivel clamps are typically used to hold glass in cabinet door rabbets. But hot glue is a quick, rattle-free alternative. Just don't skimp on the glue or the glass may fall out. If you ever need to remove the glass, just heat the back with a heat gun to soften the glue.

BENCHTOP **ORGANIZER**

Combine plastic bins with a simple plywood cabinet to super-organize small stuff.

by **David Munkittrick, Contributing Editor**

1-HOUR PROJECT

A stack of plastic bins can organize thousands of small items. But it's not very convenient when the bin you need is at the bottom of the stack. That's the point of this cabinet: You can slide out any bin—no stacking and unstacking.

You can easily build a cabinet identical to this one. Or you can customize it, using larger or smaller bins, more bins or fewer. Whatever configuration you choose, this project is a great clutter solution for the garage, workshop or craft room.

Shop before you build

Our cabinet is built for Husky 11-in. Parts Bin Organizers ($4) from The Home Depot. Most discount stores and home centers carry similar bins. Be sure the bins you choose have a sturdy rim that can rest on the runners.

You'll also need a 2 x 4-ft. sheet of 1/2-in. plywood for the cabinet box. If you have a table saw, you can cut runners from any 3/4-in.-thick board. If not, check the millwork aisle at your home center. You'll find 1/4 x 3/4-in. stock like we used or other moldings that will work. When you're done shopping, just follow **Photos 1 – 3** and **Figure A** to build the cabinet.

What it takes

TIME: One hour
COST: $50
SKILL LEVEL: Beginner
TOOLS: Basic hand tool, drill, saw

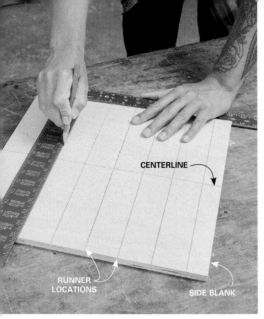

CENTERLINE

RUNNER
LOCATIONS

SIDE BLANK

1 **Mark both cabinet sides at once.** Mark the centerline and the runner locations onto a single plywood blank. In Step 3, you'll cut the blank in half to make two identical cabinet sides.

RUNNER

2 **Attach the runners.** You can use brads, staples, nails or screws. Just be sure to keep the fasteners at least 1/2 in. away from the centerline so you don't hit them with your saw in Step 3.

3 **Cut the blank in half.** Set the table saw fence at 7-1/2 in. and cut the blank. Since the blank is slightly oversized, also trim the offcut side to 7-1/2 in. If you don't have a table saw, make the cuts with a circular saw or jigsaw. Join the two sides to the top, bottom and back as shown in **Figure A**.

Figure A
Benchtop Organizer

Overall dimensions: 15-1/4" tall x 11-3/4" wide x 8" deep

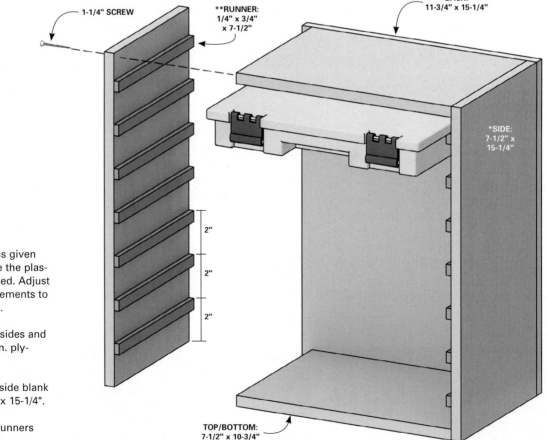

1-1/4" SCREW

**RUNNER:
1/4" x 3/4"
x 7-1/2"

BACK:
11-3/4" x 15-1/4"

*SIDE:
7-1/2" x
15-1/4"

2"

2"

2"

Notes:

All dimensions given accommodate the plastic bins we used. Adjust these measurements to suit your bins.

Top, bottom, sides and back are 1/2-in. plywood.

*Start with a side blank that's 15-1/4" x 15-1/4".

**Start with runners 15-1/4" long.

TOP/BOTTOM:
7-1/2" x 10-3/4"

SAWTOOTH
PICTURE HANGER

PICTURE HANGER TAPE HOLDER

I use my tape measure a lot in the workshop, so I like knowing where it is at all times. Sick of digging through piles of stuff to find it, I screwed a "sawtooth" picture hanger on the edge of my workbench, and that's where the tape measure lives—always

— Ryan Sorensen

EYEGLASS-CASE HARDWARE STORAGE

My wife has a drawer full of old eyeglass cases that she doesn't use anymore, so I re-purposed them to store small things like drill bits and screws. I stick a case in my shirt pocket when I'm working and toss it into a toolbox when I'm done. It's much easier than digging around for small stuff in the bottom of my tool apron.

— Norm Smith

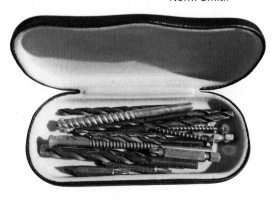

SANDPAPER SHEETS

NEAT SHEET ORGANIZER

An expanding file from an office supply store was all I needed to keep my sandpaper organized by grit. It also has given me plenty of room to stash my instruction manuals, warranties and other paperwork.

— Bruce Hinnenkamp

DRILL DOCK

by **David Munkittrick, Contributing Editor**

Cordless drills and drivers are our most-used tools. We couldn't work without them. But with their chargers and spare batteries, they're also a prime source of workbench clutter. What they need is a dedicated space that allows for easy organization and instant access—like this drill dock.

2-HOUR PROJECT

1 Measure drill with a clamp. To determine the width of the pipe slot, use a clamp to measure the width of the tool handle.

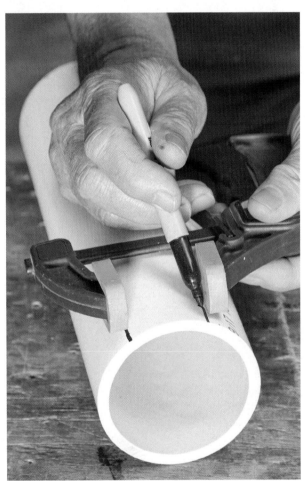

2 Mark the slot. Transfer the handle width to the pipe and mark out the slot. Make the slot about 1/8 in. wider than the tool handle. The length of the slot isn't critical; 5 in. is about right for most drills.

What it takes

TIME: 2 hours

COST: $50

SKILL: Beginner

TOOLS: Clamp, jigsaw, circular saw, basic hand tools

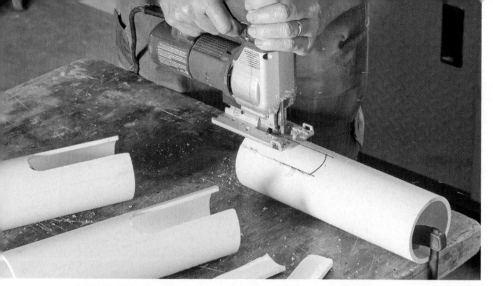

3 **Cut the slot.** A fine-tooth jigsaw blade, such as a metal-cutting blade, is best. After cutting, ease the sharp edges with a file or sandpaper.

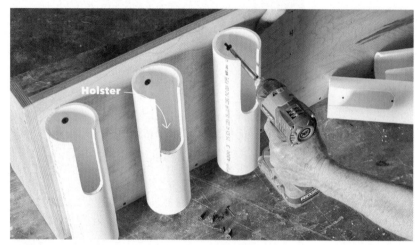

Holster

4 **Mount the holsters.** Drill holes in the pipes and fasten each with at least two screws. You can mount the holsters on an existing shelf or build the drill dock as shown below in **Figure A**.

Customize it!

If the drill dock shown here suits your needs perfectly, just build it as detailed in **Figure A**. If not, you can easily alter it. Here are some suggestions:

■ Three-inch PVC pipe is best for the holsters and accommodates most tools. A 10-ft. pipe costs less than $20. Many home centers also sell shorter lengths.

■ We made our holsters 12 in. long. Shorter is fine, but don't go so short that you'll have to remove bits in order to stow the tools. Cut the pipe with a miter saw or a handsaw.

■ Leave enough space between holsters so you can comfortably grab the tool. We centered our holsters 6-1/2 in. apart.

■ Adjusting the width of the dock to suit your tools is easy; just change the length of the shelves and the back. But don't skimp. Leave space for future tools.

■ Get a power strip ($10) and park it on the bottom shelf so you can plug in all your chargers. Drill a hole in the side of the dock to accommodate the power strip cord.

■ Tools and batteries are heavy, so build the dock from 3/4-in. plywood. Ours required a 4 x 4-ft. sheet ($20).

Figure A
Drill Dock

Overall dimensions: 37-1/2" wide x 14" deep x 12-1/4" tall

TOP SHELF: 6" x 37-1/2"

6"

2" SCREW

BACK: 7-1/4" x 36"

8"

2-1/2"

BOTTOM SHELF: 14" x 36"

14"

SLOT

BACK, SIDES AND SHELVES ARE 3/4" PLYWOOD

12"

3/4" SCREW

3"-DIA. PVC PIPE

DRILL BIT SAVERS

Sometimes I carry Forstner drill bits in my toolbox. To protect the cutting edges, I customize plastic pill bottles by drilling holes in the lids for the shank to poke through. Works great for router bits too!

— Earl Hagen

RECIPROCATING SAW BLADE BINDER

I used to keep all my reciprocating saw blades inside my saw's case, but they were a mess and it was hard to find just the right one. I got a binder ring at an office supply store to keep the blades together.

— Andrew Wolf

CIRCULAR SAW LUGGAGE

An old bowling ball bag makes a great portable home for your circular saw. The saw easily slides in and out of the zippered opening, so there's no more coaxing it into that molded plastic case and fumbling with those stubborn plastic snaps. And there's plenty of room for spare blades, a rip guide and the blade-changing wrench. So, if you're spending more time building frames than bowling them, nab a secondhand bag for a couple of bucks at a yard sale or secondhand store.

Handy Hints®

ROBIN HOOD CURVES

When I build woodworking projects with curves, I often turn to my trusty homemade curve tracer. It's made from a long, 1/4-in.-thick strip of straight-grained, knot-free wood with a 1/4-in. hole drilled in one end and a narrow V-notch cut into the other end. I tie mason's string to the drilled end and bend the strip to whatever size curve I need, tying a knot in the string that I slide into the V-notch. Then I just hold the bowed wood on top of my workpiece and trace the curve. Leave it unstrung between projects or it'll become permanently bowed.

— Bruce Philbrook

TRIM SCREWS TIGHTEN A WOBBLY CHAIR

Got a chair with a wobbly leg? This usually happens because the glue holding the legs and "stretchers" together no longer holds. The best fix is to take the chair apart and glue it back together, but that's a lot of work.

If it's an old chair and there's nothing particularly special about it, you can fix it with trim head screws. Just drill pilot holes and "toe-screw" into the loose joints. Be sure to drive the screws in from the bottom so you won't see them when the chair is upright. If a joint is really loose, you might need to force some epoxy into it to fill the gaps and make the joint stronger.

ARE FACTORY-RECONDITIONED TOOLS ANY GOOD?

If you're looking to save money on power tools, consider going the "factory-reconditioned" route. Most of the time they're good-quality tools that somebody just changed their mind about after they opened the box, or they returned it because of a defect. These tools are sent back to the manufacturers, who fix whatever's wrong with them and then sell them again at a discount.

"The product is good and often comes with a warranty," says Jason Swanson of Techtronic Industries, makers of Ryobi and Ridgid power tools. "All of our refurbished tools are inspected and rebuilt as needed by trained technicians."

You'll find factory-reconditioned tools online at sites like cpooutlets.com, acmetools.com and directtoolsoutlet.com.

INSPECTION STICKER

RECONDITIONED STAMP

MEET AN EXPERT

Jason Swanson is vice president of communications for Techtronic Industries. He's been in the tool business for more than 20 years.

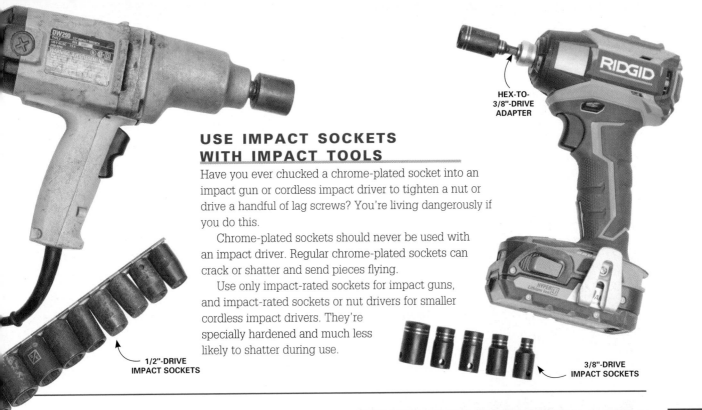

USE IMPACT SOCKETS WITH IMPACT TOOLS

Have you ever chucked a chrome-plated socket into an impact gun or cordless impact driver to tighten a nut or drive a handful of lag screws? You're living dangerously if you do this.

Chrome-plated sockets should never be used with an impact driver. Regular chrome-plated sockets can crack or shatter and send pieces flying.

Use only impact-rated sockets for impact guns, and impact-rated sockets or nut drivers for smaller cordless impact drivers. They're specially hardened and much less likely to shatter during use.

HEX-TO-3/8"-DRIVE ADAPTER

1/2"-DRIVE IMPACT SOCKETS

3/8"-DRIVE IMPACT SOCKETS

DUSTLESS DRILLING AND DRUM SANDING

Whenever I have curves to sand, I chuck a sanding drum into my drill press. The only problem is that the sawdust flies everywhere. I wanted to catch the dust with my shop vacuum, so I made a bracket to hold the nozzle. I glued together two 3/4-in.-thick pieces of medium-density fiberboard (MDF) and cut out the curved shape with my jigsaw. When I want to use it, I just clamp it to my drill press table. I made the hole just big enough so that the tip of the nozzle fits snugly.

— Doug Kaczmarek

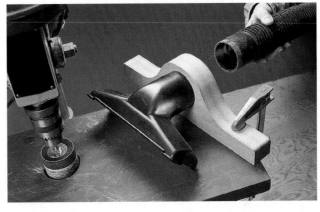

LONG-REACH MAGNET

Here's a simple tool that saves my old back whenever I drop screws, nuts or bolts on my garage floor. I just glued a magnet onto the end of a stick and use that to pick them up.

— Robert Wilson

MAGNET STICK

MAGNET

CARDBOARD SAWHORSES

I use cardboard appliance boxes as collapsible sawhorses. They're lightweight and plenty strong for many tasks. They hold heavy workpieces like doors without wobbling and fold up flat in seconds. You can cut them to a comfortable working height with a utility knife.

— Guy Lautard

Quick & Simple
Gift Projects

NO NEED TO SHOP!

'Tis the season for woodworkers. While others are slogging through crowded malls and spending hundreds on manufactured gifts, you can slip away to your shop and create handmade heirlooms. And if you have an ample pile of scrapwood, you won't have to spend a dime! Here are some projects you can complete in a few hours.

by **Gary Wentz, Editor-in-Chief**

TOOL TOTE

It's not just for tools: A portable organizer can be used for gardening gear, craft materials or cleaning supplies. To build it, you can use our dimensions or customize it to suit the person on your gift list. We cut our slats and partitions from 2x4 scraps with a table saw. Then we glued the partitions in place before adding the slats.

■ Drill the 3/8-in. storage holes in the top edges of the sides before assembly.
■ Screw together the sides and ends with the ends protruding 1 in. beyond the sides. Drill holes in the top of the ends for a 3/4-in. dowel handle and tap it in the holes before assembling the ends and sides.
■ Cut and screw on the 1/4-in. plywood bottom.
■ Cut partitions and screw them to the slats to create custom-width pockets for tools.
■ Saw 1/4-in. x 1-1/2-in. x 16-in. pine strips for the side slats and screw them to the protruding ends.

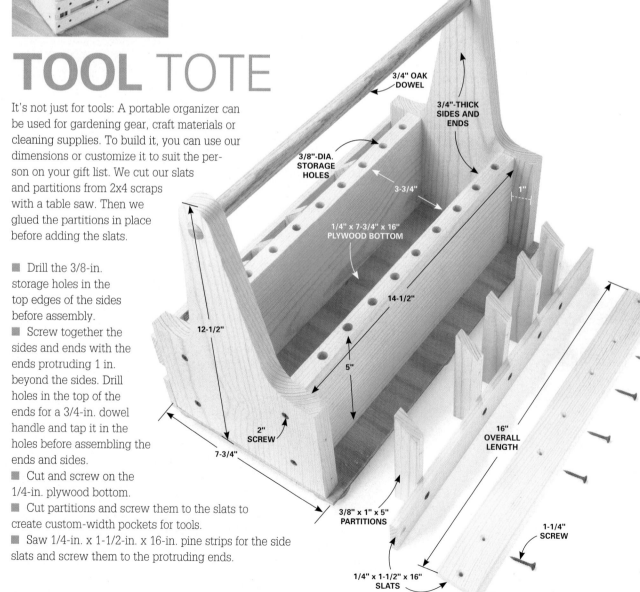

3/4" OAK DOWEL

3/4"-THICK SIDES AND ENDS

3/8"-DIA. STORAGE HOLES

3-3/4"

1"

1/4" x 7-3/4" x 16" PLYWOOD BOTTOM

14-1/2"

12-1/2"

5"

2" SCREW

7-3/4"

16" OVERALL LENGTH

3/8" x 1" x 5" PARTITIONS

1-1/4" SCREW

1/4" x 1-1/2" x 16" SLATS

SPACE-SAVING KNIFE RACK

BUILD A BUNCH IN 1 DAY!

Most people use one or two knives more often than all their others combined. So it makes sense to keep those favorite knives handy with a small block that doesn't take up much counter space. Ours is made from walnut and maple. Start by gluing two 9-in.-long 1x4s together. (To hold four knives, just glue three 1x4s together.) **Photos 1 – 3** show the rest!

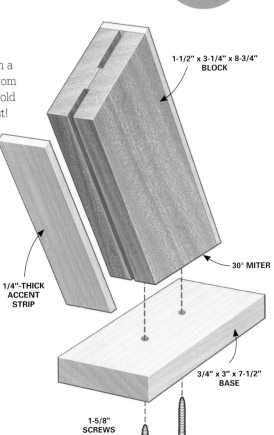

1-1/2" x 3-1/4" x 8-3/4" BLOCK

1/4"-THICK ACCENT STRIP

30° MITER

3/4" x 3" x 7-1/2" BASE

1-5/8" SCREWS

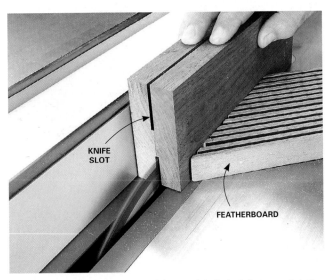

KNIFE SLOT

FEATHERBOARD

1 **Cut knife slots.** Set your table saw blade height to match the width of the knife blades, plus 1/8 in. Then cut slots in the block. A featherboard helps to keep the block tight against the fence. You have to remove the blade guard for these cuts—be extra careful!

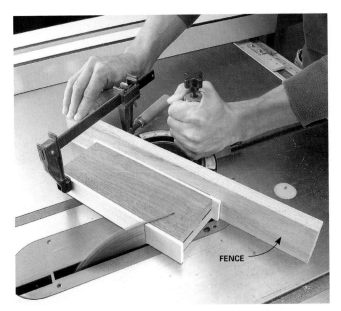

FENCE

2 **Cut the block.** Glue strips to the block, covering the slots. Then cut a miter on one end of the block and square off the other end. Make these cuts with a miter saw or table saw. We removed the blade guard for photo clarity. Use yours!

3 **Mount the block.** Mark the position of the block with masking tape and glue it to the base. Then add screws for extra strength.

TWO-WAY SERVING TRAY

GREAT FOR VALENTINE'S DAY, TOO!

The perfect gift for your spouse? How about breakfast in bed—along with the tray it's served on. This simple folding tray can be used as shown for the royal treatment or, with the legs folded up, as an everyday serving tray. We used cherry wood, dowels and plywood; you can use any wood to build yours.

Begin by cutting the four 3/4-in. x 1-1/2-in. frame parts an inch longer than the final dimensions, then use your table saw or router table to cut a 1/4-in.-wide x 3/8-in.-deep groove exactly 3/4 in. away from the bottom edge

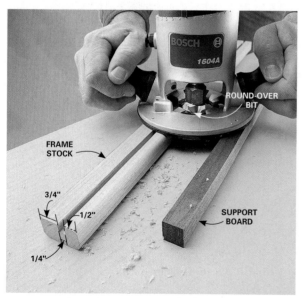

FRAME STOCK

ROUND-OVER BIT

3/4"

1/2"

1/4"

SUPPORT BOARD

1 Prep the frame parts. Groove and rout the frame pieces. First cut the 1/4-in. x 3/8-in. groove in the frame stock, then round over all four edges. The support board helps keep the router base flat.

2 Frame the tray. Glue or epoxy the mitered corners together, then add nails or brads for extra strength. Don't glue the 1/4-in. plywood bottom to the sides—it should "float" in the grooves.

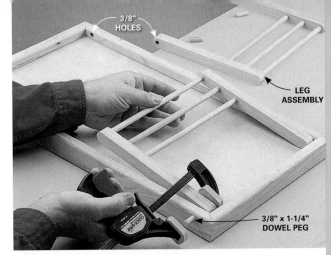

(see **Figure A** below). Use a router and 1/4-in. round-over bit (**Photo 1**) to shape all four edges. Use a miter saw to cut the frame pieces to final length with 45-degree angles on both ends. Predrill, glue and nail three of the frame pieces to one another. Slip the 1/4-in. plywood into the groove (don't glue it), and install the final side of the tray (**Photo 2**).

Build the two leg assemblies from 3/4 x 3/4-in. strips of wood and 3/8-in. dowels , as shown in **Figure A**. Round both ends of the legs to a 3/8-in. radius. Drill 3/8-in. holes halfway through the top, outside surface of each leg and completely through both ends of the tray. Use a clamp (**Photo 3**) to install the 1-1/4-in. length of 3/8-in. dowel for connecting the legs and tray, then use a 3d finish nail to secure the dowel to the frame portion of the tray.

To create the leg-lock block (J), turn the tray upside down and measure the distance between the bottom dowels on each leg when the legs are folded; make the ears of the lock 1/8 in. wider than this measurement. Secure the block with carpenter's glue and clamps.

Finish all components with three coats of tung oil, letting it dry then lightly sanding between coats. Now you're really ready to start cooking!

3 Add the legs. Build and install the leg assemblies. Use a clamp to squeeze the dowels that join the legs to the tray into place, then secure the dowel to the tray frame using a 3d finish nail.

CUTTING LIST

KEY	QTY.	DIMENSIONS	NAME
A	2	3/4" x 1-1/2" x 23-1/8"	Tray front/back
B	2	3/4" x 1-1/2" x 13"	Tray sides
C	1	1/4" x 12" x 22-1/8"	Plywood bottom
D	4	3/4" x 3/4" x 9-1/2"	Tray legs
E	6	3/8" x 10-3/8" dowels	Leg spacers
F	4	3/8" x 1-1/4" dowels	Leg swivels
G	4	3/8" x 2-5/8" dowels	Handle uprights
H	2	1" x 7" dowels	Handles
J	1	3/4" x 3/4" x 2-1/4"	Leg-lock block

Figure A
Serving Tray
Overall dimensions: 13" wide x 23-1/8" long

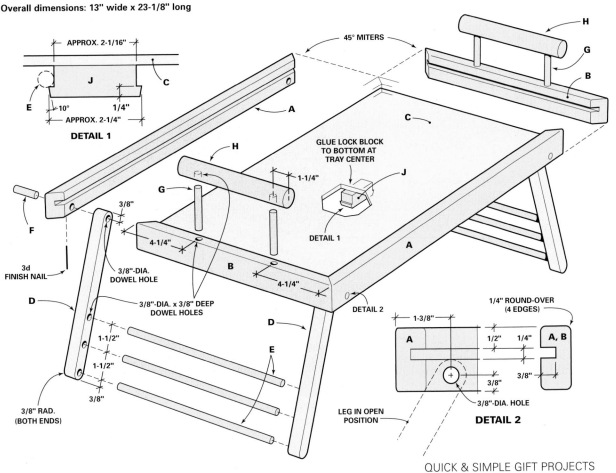

Quick & Simple Gift Projects
CLEVER KEEPSAKE BOXES

USE THE CENTER CUTOUT TO MAKE SMALLER BOXES

1 CUT FIRST SIDE

2 CUT SECOND SIDE

3 CUT LID

4 CUT OUT CENTER

USE UP YOUR SCRAP WOOD!

If you have thick blocks of wood (such as 4x4s) lying around, you're ready to make handsome boxes with your band saw. If not, you can glue up thinner boards to make blocks; contrasting woods yield a nice two-tone effect. We started with a 3 x 4 x 18-in. block and made three boxes. Here's how:

■ For smooth cuts and nearly invisible glue joints later, install a fine band saw blade (10 teeth per inch or more).
■ Set your band saw fence 3/8 in. from the blade and slice off both sides.
■ Flip the block on its side and cut another 3/8-in.-thick part for the lid.
■ Remove the fence, sketch the cutout for the inside of the box on the side of the block and cut it freehand.
■ Sand the cutout, then glue the sides back onto the block. Round the box and lid edges with a file, sand the parts and add a lid handle if you like.

You can make more boxes and lid handles from the leftover cutout.

Just four cuts
Make these cuts and you'll have all the box parts in minutes.

CUTTING BOARD & SERVING TRAY

Use it as a cutting board or a serving tray for breads or cheeses. Either way, it's an elegant piece that's surprisingly simple to build using scrap wood. The size and design are up to you. Here are the parts we used:

- Three 3-1/2-in. x 20-in. maple boards (3/4 in. thick).
- Two 23-1/2-in. x 1/2-in. x 3/4-in. walnut strips.
- Two 5-in. x 1/2-in. dowels (handles).

MAKE IT ANY SIZE YOU LIKE!

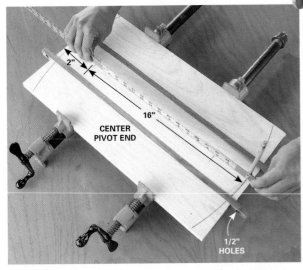

2"

16"

CENTER PIVOT END

1/2" HOLES

1 Mark the curves. Clamp the parts together (without glue!) and mark the curves as shown using a yardstick. Unclamp the boards and cut the curves using a jigsaw. Then sand the cut ends.

2 Glue it up. Apply exterior glue (such as Titebond III) and clamp the parts together. A snug fit is typically enough to secure the handles. If not, use only a tiny dab of glue. Sand the entire assembly and apply a food-safe finish such as mineral oil or butcher block finish.

TAKE-ALONG
TIC-TAC-TOE
BOARD

Even in this age of techno-toys, kids still like a game they can play with anyone, anywhere. This version is made from a 1-in.-thick block (4-3/8 in. x 4-3/8 in.), but other dimensions will work. The door is a 1/8-in.-thick strip, fastened with a brass screw and washer. Make a dozen of them in one afternoon!

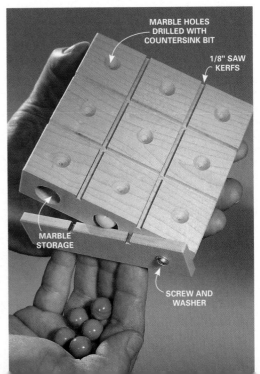

MARBLE HOLES DRILLED WITH COUNTERSINK BIT

1/8" SAW KERFS

MARBLE STORAGE

SCREW AND WASHER

203

1-HOUR PROJECT

SPACE-SAVING WINE RACK

It's easy to build with just three boards!

by Travis Larson, Senior Editor

There's a lot of usable space below many upper kitchen cabinets, and it's the perfect place to store your favorite vintages. This easy-to-build wine rack requires just two 1x4s the length of the under-cabinet bay (**Photo 1**) and a strip of 3/4-in. plywood that same length and 8 in. wide (**Photo 8**). If you have painted cabinets, poplar is a good choice for the 1x4s. Prime it and paint it to match the cabinets. If you have natural wood cabinets, select and finish the wood to match.

What it takes

TIME: 1 hour
COST: $10–$20
SKILL: Beginner
TOOLS: Drill, 3-1/8-in. hole saw, any type of saw, 1-1/2-in. drum sander, clamps

1 **Measure the cabinet bay.** Measure the bay opening on the underside of the cabinet. Subtract 1/8 in. and cut two 1x4s to that length. Also cut an 8-in.-wide piece of 3/4-in. plywood to the same length.

2 **Locate the holes.** Mark a line 1-5/8 in. from the top edge of each board. Place the boards next to each other and mark the center of each hole. The centers should be at least 3-3/4 in. apart.

Modify the wine rack to fit your cabinets

You can use any of the bays under the upper cabinets you wish. The wider the bay, the more wine you can store. Our instructions will work for any size cabinet bay. Most cabinets have a 3/4-in.-deep lip surrounding each bay so the plywood will be hidden. If you have lips that are deeper than 3/4 in., shim down the plywood. If your lips are shallower, use thinner plywood.

This wine rack will hold the most common bottle diameters, but not all. If you're a serious wine collector, measure the diameters of the bottles in your collection. Select a hole saw at least 1/8 in. larger than the largest bottle. If you need to drill holes larger than 3-1/8 in., substitute 1x6s for the 1x4s.

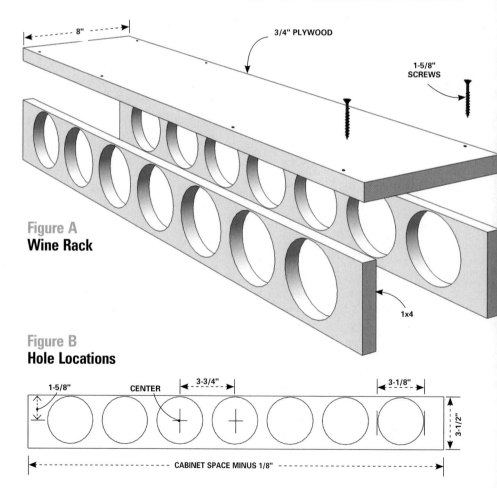

Figure A
Wine Rack

Figure B
Hole Locations

3 **Start the bottle holes.** Clamp the wood over a 2x6 scrap or wider to protect your work surface from the hole saw. Then score each hole with the hole saw about 1/4 in. deep.

AUXILIARY HANDLE

4 **Drill clearance holes.** Using a spade bit, drill 1/2- to 3/4-in. clearance holes adjoining each hole-saw kerf.

CLEARANCE HOLE

2x10 SCRAP

5 **Complete the holes.** Finish cutting the wine bottle holes. Rock the drill slightly as you cut. That enlarges the kerf, reducing friction on the hole saw and speeding up cutting.

HAMMER TIP: Tap or pry out plugs after each hole.

CAUTION

Drill with the slow speed and use the auxiliary handle if you have one (**Photo 3**). Don't force the cut, and *never* use the trigger lock. Hole saws can catch and cause bodily harm.

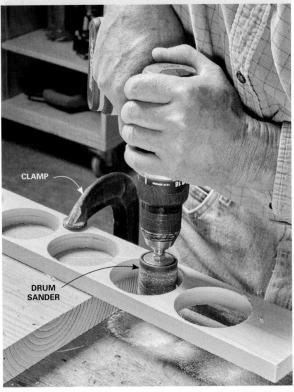

CLAMP

DRUM SANDER

6 **Sand before finishing.** Smooth the holes with a drum sander and ease the edges around the holes by hand-sanding with 100-grit paper. Finish the boards before screwing them to the plywood.

Quick & Simple Gift Projects

7 **Assemble the rack.** Drill pilot holes and fasten both boards to the plywood backer with 1-5/8-in. screws. Be sure to place the screws between the holes.

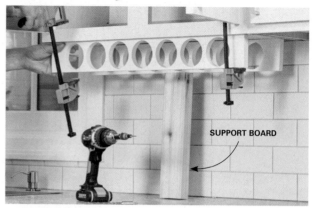

SUPPORT BOARD

8 **Install the rack.** Clamp the rack to the cabinet and prop up the back with a support board. Drive 1-5/8-in. screws through the cabinet bottom into the 1x4s. Position the screws between the holes so the screw tips won't show.

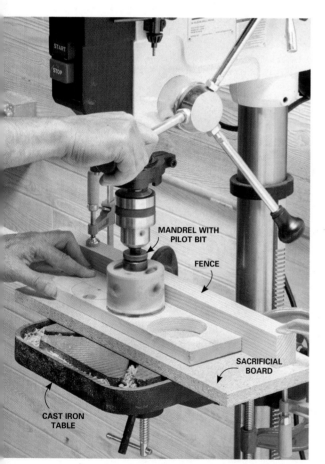

MANDREL WITH PILOT BIT

FENCE

SACRIFICIAL BOARD

CAST IRON TABLE

Got a drill press? Use it!

Protect your hole saw from damage by clamping or bolting a sacrificial board over the cast iron drill press table. Then clamp a fence to the board, positioned to exactly locate each hole from the edge without any guesswork. A speed of about 600 rpm is good for drilling the holes.

Hole-saw smarts

■ Running a 3-1/8-in. hole saw will tax all but the most powerful drills. If you have a drill press, use it instead of drilling by hand.

■ For handheld hole-saw work, use a corded drill instead of a battery-powered one if you have one.

■ Feel the motor housing as you drill. If it starts getting hot, let it cool down before continuing. Excess heat will destroy the motor whether the drill is corded or battery-powered.

■ Space the board up from the workbench on 2-by scraps to eliminate tear-out and anchor it with two clamps or the board will spin free (Photo 5).

■ After you score each hole about 1/4 in. deep, drill a 1/2- to 3/4-in. clearance hole adjoining each score (Photo 4). This will provide a place for sawdust to exit, which will keep the hole saw cooler and speed up drilling.

■ Take your time and let the hole saw cool off after about 15 seconds of cutting or you'll scorch the wood.

Tools & materials

■ **1x4s:** Choose straight, knot-free boards.

■ **3/4-in. plywood:** You'll find 2x4 partial sheets at the home center, enough to do a few wine racks. Any type of plywood will work.

■ **3-1/8-in. hole saw:** The hole saw itself will run you about $15. If you already have other hole saws, buy the same brand so your mandrel will work in the new one. Otherwise, you'll need to spend another $15 for a mandrel/pilot bit to operate it.

■ If you don't have spade bits, pick up a 3/4-in. bit for drilling the clearance holes.

■ A small box of 1-5/8-in. No. 8 screws will take care of all fastening needs.

■ **1-1/2-in. drum sander:** For less than $10, you can get a drum sander kit that comes with several sandpaper sleeves of different grits.

DRUM SANDER AND SLEEVE

5 Exterior Repairs & Improvements

IN THIS CHAPTER

Home Care & Repair 210
Stay-dry generator, caulking concrete, consider storm windows and more

Build a Long-Lasting Retaining Wall 213

Better Than Wood! 218

5 Solutions for a Shabby Deck 223

Working With Bagged Concrete 228

Pour a Perfect Slab 232

Handy Hints 237
Ladder-borrow, vinyl siding helper, caulk caddy

MIXING TUB

STAY-DRY GENERATOR

If you're using a generator, chances are a storm just rolled through and you're likely to get more rain. Here's an easy way to add a roof to keep some of the water off your generator. Cut four lengths of 1/2-in. EMT (electrical metallic tubing) and secure them to each corner of the generator using hose clamps. Next, invert a concrete mixing tub and secure it to the tubing with self-tapping screws. Drill holes into the inverted lip of the tub so the water can drain.

BACKER ROD

CAULKING CONCRETE

The best caulks for concrete are usually labeled "urethane" or "polyurethane," and most can fill cracks 1/2 in. wide or more (check the label). For any crack wider than 1/4 in., stuff in foam backer rod first. Using backer rod saves expensive caulk and results in a stronger joint. And since it seals off the crack, it allows you to use runny "self-leveling" caulk, which provides a much neater look on flat surfaces.

KEEP YOUR GENERATOR AWAY FROM THE HOUSE

A backup generator can be a lifesaver in a blackout. But it can also make you black out (or die). Hurricane Katrina led to more than 50 cases of carbon monoxide poisoning. A generator engine exhausts carbon monoxide gas, which can give you a headache, knock you out or even kill you. Don't run a generator in your garage or porch, and keep it at least 10 ft. away from your house.

PVC PIPE CEMENT FOR PVC TRIM?

A reader asked whether you can use PVC plumbing cement to glue PVC trim boards together. You certainly can, but for some situations, there's a better option. The cement used for plastic plumbing pipes sets up in seconds, while PVC cement made specifically for trim takes several minutes to fuse—a major plus if you have a complicated glue-up and need more "open time" to get all your parts aligned and assembled. You probably won't find PVC trim cement at a local home center, but AZEK and Kleer are among the brands available at professional lumberyards and online.

CONSIDER STORM WINDOWS

If you want windows that look great and open smoothly, complete replacement is definitely the way to go. But if your main concern is air leakage and energy costs, consider storm windows. Quality storm windows can stop air leaks almost as well as full replacements but cost half as much—or even less. Plus, the labor savings are huge; a DIYer can install 10 storm windows in the time it takes to replace one window. You might find storm windows for less than $50 each, but shop around. Chances are, you'll discover that spending $75 to $150 is smarter.

BUILD A **LONG-LASTING RETAINING WALL**

by **Mark Peterson, Senior Editor**

Anyone with a strong back can stack up a bunch of blocks and build a pretty retaining wall. But it takes skill and planning to construct an attractive wall that can also handle immense pressure, shrug off the forces of gravity, stand for decades and laugh in the face of Mother Nature.

That's the kind of wall we wanted to learn how to build, so we went to work with some hardworking hardscaping pros. They showed us that it's all about a solid base, proper drainage and the right materials for the job. They also shared a few handy tips they've picked up over the years.

MEET THE EXPERTS

Joe Blakeborough (right) owns and operates Blakeborough Hardscapes in Prior Lake, MN, with the assistance of his younger brother, Jake (left). They run multiple crews that specialize in block and boulder retaining walls, paver projects, outdoor living spaces and other services.

Make the trench wide, deep and level

Size the trench so there's enough room for the block and at least 8 in. of space behind it. Excavate deep enough to completely bury at least one full course, including space for 6 to 8 in. of base material.

Establish a level trench to ensure an even layer of base material. That will help prevent the wall from tipping after freeze/thaw cycles. Our experts use a laser level and a story pole to determine the depth of the trench.

Compact the trench

Compact the soil in the trench bottom with a hand tamper or vibrating plate compactor. This step is often neglected. The excavator, and even hand shovels, can disturb and loosen the top inch or two of soil, and that's enough to make your wall settle—settling is bad!

Lay a crushed stone base

Our experts prefer crushed stone for the base rather than naturally occurring gravel dug from a pit. Crushed stone is a little more expensive. However, it provides better drainage, and because of the sharper angles on the stone, it requires less compacting, and once it's compacted, it stays that way.

Joe and Jake have found that crushed stone sized between 1/2 in. and 3/4 in. is best suited to handle the heaving forces created by the harsh freeze/thaw cycles here in Minnesota. Avoid rounded stones like pea gravel or river rock; they don't form strong interlocking bonds like angular stone.

Leave the stone no more than 1/2 in. higher than you want the final height to be, and then make a couple passes with a hand tamper or plate compactor. You'll notice the stone is almost 100 percent compacted as soon as it's laid in the trench. The same type of stone will be used for backfilling, which also eliminates the need for hauling in multiple materials.

Sweep before stacking

Even a pebble on the surface of a block will throw the one above it out of alignment. And that crooked block will affect the one above it, and so on. That little stone will eventually create an unattractive hump in the top course.

Get the first course right

Use a torpedo level to level each block front to back and a 4- or 6-ft. level to keep each course level and even. Set the blocks with a heavy rubber or plastic mallet. Getting the first course flat and level is extremely important, so take your time. Try to lay the course as close to the center of the trench as possible.

Provide plenty of drainage

Once a few rows have been stacked, backfill the wall with rock so it matches the grade height in front of the wall, and then lay down perforated drain tile on top of the rock. Install drain tee fittings and a drain grate every 25 ft. to 50 ft., depending on how much rainwater is expected to run down to the wall. Cut one block down to accommodate the drain grate. Screw the drain tile parts together so they won't come apart when they get covered with more rock. Also, drain the tile to daylight at the ends of the walls whenever possible.

Step up after two full courses are below grade

If the wall runs up a hill, continue each base course into the hill until the top of the second course is level with the grade, and then start your second base course at that point. If you have the option, it can be easier to excavate and lay the lowest course before excavating the trench for the next step, especially if you have to step up several times. Save yourself some money and install the cheapest style/color that matches the wall style (usually the gray ones) on the bottom course since it won't be seen.

WHICH BLOCKS ARE BEST?

These solid blocks are heavy. Lighter, hollow blocks are available, but they can't be split because cutting will expose the voids. Also, some hollow blocks require individual backfilling, which is time consuming. Many pros prefer blocks that are held together with pins rather than a lip on the bottom because pinned blocks work better on tighter curves, and the flat bottom makes them easier to stack. Also, the small lip on some lipped blocks can be prone to cracking, which will weaken the wall.

Mark cuts with a soapstone pencil

These pros like soapstone because the lines created by grease pencils and markers can stay visible for a long time, whereas soapstone washes off in the rain. The downside is that soapstone doesn't work as well on wet blocks. You can find these pencils at online retailers for as little as 25¢ each.

KEEP SPACE BETWEEN TIERS

If you're building tiered retaining walls, set each tier back far enough to prevent the weight and pressure of the wall above from destroying the one below it. The rule of thumb is to separate wall tiers by a distance that's no less than twice the height of the wall below. So if the bottom wall is 4 ft. tall, the wall above it should be built at least 8 ft. behind it.

Split blocks for a rough finish

If the end of a block will be visible, and you'd like it to match the other rough surfaces, use a block splitter. You can rent one like this for about $85 per day.

Make smooth cuts with a saw

Use a gas-powered cutoff saw like this one for a smooth cut. This saw can cut with or without water. Water eliminates the dust but creates a messy slurry that can permanently stain surfaces like driveways and sidewalks. You can rent a saw like this for about $80 per day.

LOCKING PIN

Keep the joints tight

Stagger the overlaps (at least 4 in. for this Versa-Lok product) and try to keep the butt joint between the blocks as tight as possible. Large gaps can create a pathway for water and sediment. Whichever type of block you use, make sure you follow the manufacturer's instructions.

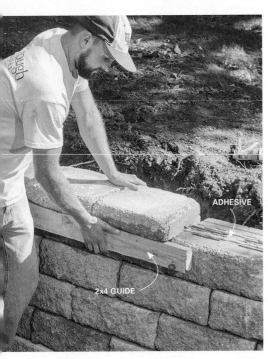

ADHESIVE

2x4 GUIDE

Keep the capstones even

Secure the capstones with a specialty landscape block adhesive, which stays flexible over time. Make sure the blocks are dry before applying the adhesive. Overhang the capstones about 1 to 1-1/2 in. Joe and Jake use a scrap 2x4 as a guide.

TALL WALLS NEED ENGINEERING

Walls more than 4 ft. tall will likely require a building permit and a plan made by a licensed engineer. The engineer will specify the base's width and depth, how far down the base course should be buried, and whether or not a geogrid (soil reinforcement system) should be used.

Backfill with stone

Versa-Lok recommends compacting the angular stone as you backfill, but check the installation instructions for the type of block you're using. Backfill about 8 to 10 in. below the top of the capstones. This will allow enough room for the topsoil and turf.

EXTERIOR REPAIRS & IMPROVEMENTS

BETTER THAN
WOOD!

**Manufactured exterior trim beats wood
in every way**

by **Jason White, Associate Editor**

Wood is a troublesome material for exterior trim. It shrinks
and swells, rots, warps and feeds insects. Years ago,
builders used wood because that was their only
option. But today, you have better choices. So skip the real
wood—and all the headaches—and go for something that
looks just as good!

Wood moves, paint peels

Wood trim expands and contracts with changes in humidity. Paint can flex with that movement for a while. But eventually, tiny cracks develop. Those cracks let in moisture, which causes more movement, which leads to larger cracks and peeling, rot... you get the idea.

One of the big advantages of manufactured products is that they remain stable when exposed to moisture. That means the paint lasts longer. Like all materials, they move with temperature changes, but that movement is less extreme and easier on the paint than moisture movement. A related advantage of manufactured products is that they don't warp or split like wood. So you don't have to hunt for straight, good-looking boards.

The bucket test

We soaked five types of trim in a bucket of water for about a month. That's not a scientific simulation of real-world conditions, and most of these products aren't intended for that kind of punishment. Still, we think the results are worth sharing.

■ **Cellular PVC** and **poly ash** were completely unaffected—just what you'd expect from products rated for ground contact.
■ **Fiber cement** seemed unaffected by the water, which surprised us because it's not approved for ground contact.
But don't try this at home!
■ **Composite** swelled near the edges but didn't blister or blow apart.
■ **Engineered wood** also swelled a little bit but didn't blister or blow apart.

Again, this isn't a fair test. But we were very impressed by how well all five products held up. Bottom line, any of these five trim options is likely a great choice for your home as long as you carefully follow the manufacturers' installation instructions, which are available on their websites.

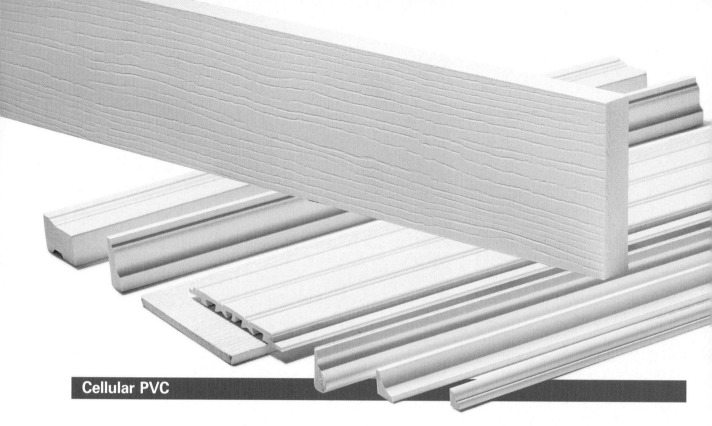

Cellular PVC

Because it's plastic, cellular PVC trim will probably last longer than the rest of your house. It's rot- and insect-proof and doesn't absorb water, which makes it a great option for trim that'll get wet a lot. It's also the most expensive—about twice as much as other manufactured options.

Cellular PVC looks and cuts just like wood and comes in traditional widths and thicknesses. You can work it with regular power tools, blades and router bits. It expands quite a bit along its length when it's hot out or the sun hits it, so it's important to fasten it well with nails or screws, being sure to drive them through the sheathing and into framing members. You'll need to leave 1/8 in. of space for heat expansion per 18 ft. of trim (skip this if it's already hot outside).

Dark paint colors absorb heat and can make expansion problems worse. Some manufacturers recommend using paint with a light reflective value (LRV) of 55 or higher to minimize expansion of the trim when the sun hits it. Detailed installation guides are available on manufacturers' websites.

HANDYMAN RECOMMENDS: If maintenance-free sounds good to you, especially if you'd like to avoid painting it, spend the extra money and go with cellular PVC.

COST: A 1x4 costs about $1.75 to $2.50 per foot at home centers.
PROS: Extremely long life expectancy.
CONS: Expensive. Expands and contracts a lot as temperature changes.
WORKING WITH IT: Can be installed with ordinary woodworking tools using carbide-tipped cutters. Painting is optional. Joints should be glued with PVC cement.
BRANDS: AZEK, Kleer, KOMA, Veranda and others.
PERFORMANCE: Very long lasting and holds paint well. Expands along its length on hot days; fasten securely to framing and paint a light color to minimize expansion.
AVAILABLE AS: Trim boards, tongue-and-groove bead board, premade corner boards, moldings and sheets. Smooth and rough textures.

MEET AN EXPERT

I replaced a lot of rotted wood trim on my house a few years ago with cellular PVC. It cuts and routs just like wood—I even replicated some moldings with it using my router table. It smells bad when you cut or rout it, and the shavings stick to your skin. The edges are a bit rough after you rout profiles, but they smooth easily with a little hand-sanding. Really long lengths get floppy and are hard to move around. I didn't experience a lot of the expansion problems that others have reported, most likely because I used lots of screws. Because it's white, you don't have to paint it if you use white hole filler, but I think it looks much better painted. Scuff-sanding the trim with fine-grit sandpaper helps paint stick better.

–Jason White

PVC trim
Learn more about working with PVC trim by visiting **familyhandyman.com** and searching for "PVC trim."

Composite

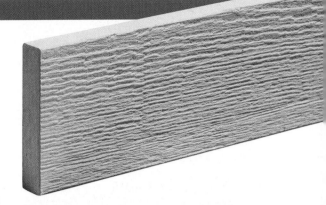

This kind of trim looks like medium-density fiberboard (MDF), but it's made to handle weather extremes. It's basically wood fibers mixed with resins with chemicals added for insect and rot resistance. You can cut and rout it just like wood. It comes primed and holds paint very well.

HANDYMAN RECOMMENDS: If you're looking for affordable trim that'll look great for decades, MiraTEC is hard to beat and easy to find at home centers.

COST: A 1x4 costs about $1 per foot at home centers.
PROS: Inexpensive. Rot and insect resistant. Minimal expansion in humid conditions.
CONS: Can be damaged by water; must be protected by paint and caulk. Not recommended for ground contact.
WORKING WITH IT: Cuts and routs with regular woodworking tools. Prime cut edges before installation.
BRANDS: MiraTEC
PERFORMANCE: Holds paint well. Can swell and blister when in direct contact with water for too long.
AVAILABLE AS: Trim boards. Primed and prefinished, smooth on one side, textured on the other.

MEET AN EXPERT

Fifteen years ago, I replaced my trim with MiraTEC. It has held the paint remarkably well and looks almost as good as new. Just one trouble spot: Some sloppy flashing work allowed water to puddle against the MiraTEC, which swelled and blistered. Since I was the sloppy flashing installer, I guess I can't complain.

–Gary Wentz

Engineered wood

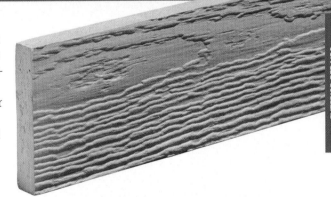

This trim looks much like oriented strand board (OSB) on the back side but has far better weather resistance. It's basically compressed wood fibers and resins with a textured shell, giving it the appearance of solid wood. It comes primed, and the boards stay nice and straight during and after installation. It's treated for rot and termite resistance.

HANDYMAN RECOMMENDS: If you like being able to find manufactured trim at home centers and not having to pay too much for a good-looking, long-lasting product, this is a great choice.

COST: A 1x4 costs about $1 per foot at home centers.
PROS: Rot and insect resistant. Nice, straight boards.
CONS: Mitering of corner and edges is not recommended. Can't rout profiles in it.
WORKING WITH IT: Must be installed a minimum of 6 in. above grade and 1 in. above rooflines and decks. Cut ends and edges must be primed and painted.
BRANDS: LP SmartSide
PERFORMANCE: Minimal expansion and contraction with changes in humidity. Engineered wood takes and holds paint well.
AVAILABLE AS: Trim and fascia boards, cedar shakes, lap siding, soffit and panels.

MEET AN EXPERT

As good-quality, paintable wood for exterior use has gotten harder to find and super expensive, I've switched to engineered wood for exterior trim. I really like the fact that all the boards are long and of consistent quality. No more searching for a straight board with a good-looking face. They're all straight with a surface that's perfect for painting.

–Jeff Gorton

EXTERIOR REPAIRS & IMPROVEMENTS

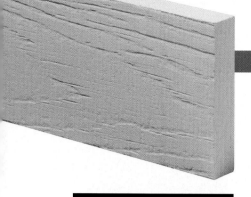

Fiber cement

This is a masonry-like product containing mostly cement, cellulose fibers and sand. Unlike wood, it resists cracking, splitting, rotting and swelling. It doesn't expand and contract a lot, so paint jobs can last for decades. You can't rout it, however, and dust collection is highly recommended when cutting it. You can cut it with regular carbide blades, but they'll dull quickly because fiber cement is very abrasive. Use blades made for fiber cement instead. Hot-dipped galvanized or stainless steel nails are recommended and must be set flush. Field-cut edges must be painted. You can get fiber cement trim primed or prefinished in many colors. You won't find this trim in stock at every home center, but you can special-order it.

HANDYMAN RECOMMENDS: If you want moderately priced trim that won't need a new paint job for many years, fiber cement is a terrific option.

MEET AN EXPERT

Fiber cement trim is relatively easy to work with. The boards cut easily with a regular circular saw blade, but fiber cement blades last longer. Cutting fiber cement is very dusty, so I always do it outside and use a cheap circular saw because it will eventually ruin the saw—at least in my experience. Be sure to blow off all the dust before caulking or painting.
–Tom Dvorak

COST: Varies by region because of product differences, but a 1x4 or 5/4x4 usually costs about $1.20 per foot at home centers.
PROS: Minimal expansion from heat and humidity. Takes and holds paint well.
CONS: Dusty when cutting and special saw blades are needed. Must be painted. Can be damaged by water.
WORKING WITH IT: It's extremely dusty, so wear a dust mask and always cut it outside. Use saw blades made for fiber cement.
BRANDS: Plycem, James Hardie and others.
PERFORMANCE: Excellent as long as trim is never in contact with standing water.
AVAILABLE AS: Trim, molding, soffits, siding, shakes and sheets. Smooth or rough textures. Primed and prefinished.

Poly ash

This is an interesting product because it's made from coal ash left behind by power plants. Referred to as "poly ash" because it's made of polymers mixed with ash, this trim doesn't expand or contract with changes in humidity or in hot weather, and it's suitable for ground contact. You can cut and rout it with regular blades and router bits and install it just like wood. It's rot resistant and you can even nail near the end of a board and not split it. You don't have to prime the ends of cuts before installing, and you can paint the trim any color you like without worrying about heat expansion issues.

HANDYMAN RECOMMENDS: If you like using building materials that contain recycled products and want trim that'll last a lifetime, poly ash trim might be just the answer.

COST: A 1x4 costs about $1.55 per foot at pro lumberyards.
PROS: Water doesn't hurt it; suitable for ground contact. Cut and rout with regular blades and router bits.
CONS: More expensive than other options (but less than PVC). Can be hard to find locally.
WORKING WITH IT: Dusty. Use dedicated carbide-tipped blades made for wood cutting. Support long boards so they won't break.
BRANDS: Boral
PERFORMANCE: Virtually no expansion and contraction with changes in heat or humidity.
AVAILABLE AS: Trim, bead board panels, and bevel and lap siding.

MEET AN EXPERT

We used Boral trim when we needed something that could withstand splashing water. Unlike PVC, it doesn't expand and contract a lot in hot weather, so you can paint it any color. Trim nails and screws work great without blowout, and you can cut curves with a jigsaw and get a clean edge. Long lengths can be a bit floppy if you're moving them around, so support them to keep them from snapping.
–Nathan Christenson

5 SOLUTIONS FOR A
SHABBY DECK

Pick the one that's best for you

by **Jason White, Associate Editor**

Nothing beats the natural appeal of a real wood deck. But after just a few years of weather and foot traffic, wood can become an eyesore. To revive it, there are five main directions you can go, and we'll guide you through them all. This article will also help you decide whether to refinish your old decking or step up to a lower-maintenance option so you can spend more time enjoying your deck and less time taking care of it.

Is your deck dangerous?
Before you take steps to make your deck look better, make sure it's structurally sound. You don't want it falling down after all that hard work! To identify and fix the most common deck problems, go to **familyhandyman.com** and search "deck inspection."

① Clean and refinish

The basics of refinishing a deck are pretty straightforward: Strip, clean, stain … repeat! It's a tough chore that might take you several days to complete, one you'll have to do every few years to keep your deck looking great. But all that hard work has a huge payoff! When you're finished, your all-wood deck will look almost as good as it did the day it was built. Here are some things to think about before tackling the job yourself.

Pressure washers make refinishing easier

A pressure washer does a great job of cleaning your deck and stripping old finishes. They're available as gas or electric models and vary widely in price—anywhere from $70 to $1,000 at home centers. You can also rent one for about $80 per day. You can get the job done without a pressure washer, but it's a real time and labor saver. For more information about choosing and using pressure washers, visit tfhmag.com/pressurewasher

More info
To find step-by-step instructions for refinishing your deck, visit **tfhmag.com/deckrefinish.**

Cost:
About $300 total for tools, materials and pressure washer rental.

Life Span:
Lasts 1 to 6 years.

Pros:
- Makes old deck look almost like new.
- Much less expensive than most other options.
- Far less work than tearing off your old deck boards and replacing them.
- Maintains the natural beauty of real wood.

Cons:
- You'll have to refinish your deck every few years.
- You'll have to scrape or blast off any old flaking finish, and you might be left with a little sanding to do.
- You'll need to replace any rotted wood before refinishing.
- You'll still have to deal with bigger problems like rot or worn, damaged wood.

Other considerations:
- You'll need to do the job on a cool, dry day.
- Be prepared to spend a couple of weekends refinishing your deck.

2 Deck Restoration Coatings

Deck restoration coatings are acrylic based and go on like really thick paint. You'll need to apply two coats. Once dry, they form a coating similar in appearance to composite decking.

A word of caution about these products: We found many online complaints and even some reports of lawsuits related to peeling of deck coating products not long after application. It's very important to follow preparation instructions from the manufacturer, which might include power washing and application of a prime coat. Bottom line: Read the manufacturer's instructions before use and contact the company directly if you have questions or concerns about whether it'll work for your particular situation.

Cost:
About $35 per gallon, which covers up to 75 sq. ft. in two coats.

Life Span:
Some manufacturers claim 12 years or more, but it's hard to gauge since these products have been around for only a few years.

Pros:
- Fills in small holes and cracks.
- Textured for slip resistance.
- Excellent UV protection.
- Lots of color options (tintable).
- Goes on easily with a roller and paintbrush.
- Much cheaper than replacing all old decking.
- Can be recoated if you follow manufacturer's prep instructions carefully.

Cons:
- Wood can look like plastic after coating.
- Lots of careful prep involved.
- Two coats required.
- Susceptible to scratches from pets, furniture, etc.
- Prone to peeling if you don't carefully follow prep instructions.
- If it ever starts peeling, you'll have lots of scraping to do.

More info
To see how we applied one of these products to an old, worn deck, visit tfhmag.com/deckrestore.

3 Replace the Deck Boards

It's not the easiest option, but replacing your wooden deck boards with synthetic decking (composite or PVC) might be your best investment, in both time and money. In just a few weekends and with basic carpentry tools, you can have a stunning deck that looks brand new and will look great for many years.

Costs vary widely for synthetic decking, but expect to pay anywhere from $5 to $10 per square foot. Be warned, however, that synthetic decking requires closer spacing of joists and stair stringers (maximum 16 in. apart), so you might have lots of framing to do.

Cost:
Varies widely, but generally $5 to $10 per sq. ft.

Life Span:
Can easily last 20 years or more.

Pros:
- Low maintenance—just needs occasional cleaning.
- Stands up well to heavy traffic.
- Lasts for decades.
- Can use screws or hidden fasteners.
- Wood grain patterns available with many brands.
- Lots of color choices.

Cons:
- You'll have to tear off the old decking first—a huge job.
- Expensive.
- Gets very hot when the sun hits it (especially dark colors and dense boards).
- Doesn't look like real wood (but some brands come close).
- Can be slippery when wet.

Other considerations:
- You'll need a building permit and inspection.
- It's a lot of work to install.
- You'll need a dumpster for all the old material.

More info
For more tips on replacing your old wood decking with synthetic materials, visit tfhmag.com/deckrebuild.

SYNTHETIC DECKING OPTIONS
There are three types:
Composite. Lowest cost but the surface isn't as tough or stain resistant.
Capped composite. Composite capped in hard plastic for extra durability and stain and fade resistance.
Solid PVC. Lighter weight than composite, making it easier to handle. Good for wet areas like docks because there's no organic content that could promote mold. Most expensive option.

COMPOSITE

CAPPED COMPOSITE

SOLID PVC

4 Deck Tiles

Think of this option as a slipcover for your deck. Instead of ripping out or recoating your old deck boards, you place new wood or synthetic decking right over your old deck. Several companies make tiles out of composite or exotic woods like ipe that you just lay down and snap together. Plastic grids underneath the tiles allow for airflow, which helps prevent wood rot.

Cost:

Varies depending on manufacturer and material, but generally $4 to $12 per 12 x 12-in. tile.

Life Span:

Decades, depending on material selected.

Pros:

- Super easy to install.
- No fasteners required.
- Tiles snap together in any direction, allowing you to be creative with patterns and layout.

Cons:

- It will create height changes with steps and at door thresholds.
- You might see old decking in the gaps of the new deck tiles.

5 Exterior Floor Coverings

DeckRite is a sheet material that comes on a roll, much like sheet vinyl flooring. It basically turns your old deck into an outdoor floor with no gaps in it and creates a watertight roof for the area beneath your deck. As long as your old deck boards are at least 5/4 thick and structurally sound, you can screw 1/2-in. pressure-treated plywood right over it and stick the flooring membrane on top. If the deck is really big, it might require multiple sheets, and you'll need to rent a hot air welder from DeckRite to deal with the overlapped seams. Cost is about $6 per sq. ft. for all the materials you'll need. Visit deckrite.com for more information.

WORKING WITH BAGGED CONCRETE

Expert advice for working with this DIY-friendly product

by **Travis Larson, Senior Editor**

Large jobs that require several yards of concrete—like patios and driveways—always call for ready-mixed concrete trucked to your site. But if you need just a few cubic feet of concrete for a stoop, deck stair landing or fence-post setting, you'll use bagged concrete mix. We'll show you the proper mixing technique plus a few tips to help you get the most from this affordable, DIY-friendly product.

1 Mixing made easy. Stab the bag in the center with a shovel. Then open the bag like a clamshell and dump it into a wheelbarrow or plastic mortar pan.

2 **Don't add too much water!** Read the directions on the bag for the proper amount of water to add. Use that exact amount and resist the temptation to pour in more. Too much water makes for weaker concrete.

3 **Mix from both directions.** Use a hoe to pull portions of the dry mix through the water. When you've moved all the concrete to one end, start over from the other direction. Keep reversing direction until no more dry powder remains.

4 **Test the consistency.** When concrete is properly mixed, it looks surprisingly dry and crumbly. You can tell whether it has enough water by patting it with the flat part of the hoe. If you pack it a half dozen times and the surface becomes creamy, you'll know it's just right.

REBEL WITH A RAKE

Everyone I know mixes concrete with a hoe. But I don't care what they say—a rake gives me a faster, more thorough mix. And since many jobs require a rake anyway (for spreading the concrete), it means one less tool to clean up. My friends are wrong about another thing too: They mix it in a wheelbarrow. A plastic mortar pan like the one shown in **Photo 2** is much better. You can get one at a home center for about $10.

— Gary Wentz

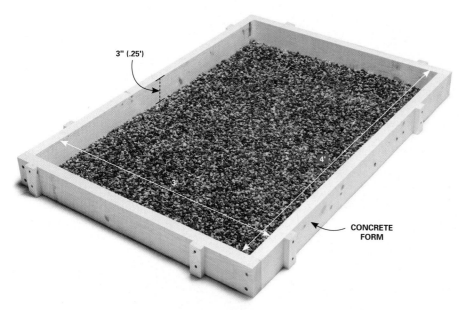

3" (.25')

4'

3'

CONCRETE
FORM

5 **How many bags should you buy?** When you mix up a 60-lb. bag of concrete, you'll have a volume of .5 cubic feet; an 80-lb. bag yields 0.66 cubic feet. (The volume is listed on each bag.) To determine how many bags you need, measure the length, width and depth of the form. Then go online and find a "concrete calculator." One example is at sakrete.com/products/calculators.cfm.

6 **Rent a mixer for big batches.** Hand-mixing a few bags is one thing. Mixing 20 bags will wear you out. Plus, you'll have a much stronger chunk of concrete if all of it is mixed and placed as quickly as possible. Don't hesitate to rent a mixer. You can find small electric ones that fit in the back of your hatchback and cost you about $50 per day. For about $10 more, you can get a much larger electric or gas unit that you tow home.

7 **Don't forget specialty mixes.** There are several mixes formulated for special purposes. Two of our favorites are fast-setting and countertop mixes.

Fast-setting mix is great because there's no mixing involved. You just pour water into the hole and add the concrete mix.

If you'd like to cast custom concrete countertops, tabletops or bench tops, choose countertop mix. It's formulated for high strength and low shrinkage. This mix also has special additives and aggregates to make it flow well. Best of all, you can polish it. But if you use melamine forms, it'll be very smooth and need little polishing.

8 **Keep it dry.** Bags of concrete will absorb moisture from damp concrete floors and the air. And before long you'll have rock-hard bags out in the garage. Never store bags on concrete surfaces, and for long-term storage, keep them in giant sealed bags.

Can concrete burn your skin?

Yes! Portland cement is the glue that binds concrete together. You'll also find it in building materials like mortar, plaster, stucco and grout. When it's wet, Portland cement becomes caustic and can damage sensitive skin. Burns from Portland cement can cause blisters, dermatitis and hardened skin. And in severe cases, it can burn you to the bone and result in disfiguring scars or even disability.

Be sure to wear protective gloves—butyl or nitrile gloves are best—and wash your hands before and after using them. A long-sleeve shirt duct-taped to your gloves is also a good idea, as are long pants and boots. And don't skip the knee pads, especially if you're on your hands and knees hand-floating and troweling.

9 **Want some color?** You'll find several earth-tone dyes at the home center. So if you'd like a terra cotta, buff or other color besides basic gray, it's simple. But don't throw the dye into the mix and start working it in or you'll have uneven color distribution. Instead, stir it into the water before you add the water to the dry concrete.

DYE

POUR A **PERFECT SLAB**

Tips from the pros for a long-lasting slab

by **Mark Petersen, Senior Editor**

A concrete driveway makes a beautiful gateway to your home that can last for decades if it's installed correctly. But if you don't follow the proper procedures, it could turn into a pile of rubble in half the time. The good news: Installing it the right way doesn't take extra time or money. We tagged along with a longtime professional mason, who showed us the best ways to prevent water from pooling and stop unsightly cracking, spalling and scaling. We'll feature the actual pour in this story. For great tips on prepping the ground before the pour, visit constructionprotips.com.

MEET AN EXPERT

Glenn Anderson is the owner/operator of Above Quality in Prior Lake, MN. He's been finishing slabs, laying block and stacking stone for 25 years.

Protect adjoining concrete

Our expert uses duct tape to protect adjacent slabs and sidewalks. Concrete can splash when it runs from the chute onto the ground, so you'll also want to lay plastic over doors, siding, brick, windows or anything else you want to keep clean. Smearing wet concrete into porous surfaces creates an even bigger mess, so if you do get a couple globs where you don't want them, wait until they dry and then scrape them off.

Dampen the base to lengthen finish time

To extend your finish time on hot, sunny days, spray bone-dry ground with water to keep the base from sucking the water out of the concrete. A water spray also slows down curing, which makes for a stronger slab. If there's no hose bib nearby, you can use the water and hose that are onboard the truck. If you don't have water on site, also use the truck hose to fill a couple buckets of water for cleaning your tools after the truck leaves.

HAND SIGNALS
Here are some basic hand signals to help you communicate with the truck driver. Make sure you can see the driver's face in the side-view mirror—if you can't see him, he can't see you.

| BACK UP THE TRUCK | STOP THE TRUCK | START POURING | STOP POURING |

Pour the concrete in small sections

Spread the concrete by moving the chute back and forth and by having the driver pull forward as you go. Once the truck has reached the end of a section, spread the concrete out evenly, and a touch higher than the form, with a concrete placer/rake. Don't fill the whole form or giant sections because the mound of extra concrete you'll drag back with the screed board will get too heavy.

This rebar grid is sitting on chairs, a setup that keeps it suspended at the proper height. You won't be able to use chairs if you have to distribute the concrete throughout the form with a wheelbarrow. If that's the case, use the hook on the edge of the concrete placer to pull the rebar up into the center of the concrete as you pour. Rebar should be placed near the center of the slab for maximum strength, not near the ground or the surface.

MR. MUCKER

NICE GUY! (DRIVERS USUALLY DON'T HELP)

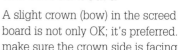

SCREED BOARD

Slide the screed board back and forth as you pull

Pull back the excess concrete with the screed board. As you pull, slide the screed board back and forth to help you prevent voids in the surface. Have a mucker (that's what they're really called) pull the excess back and fill in low spots during the screeding process.

Crown side up on the screed board

A slight crown (bow) in the screed board is not only OK; it's preferred. Just make sure the crown side is facing up. That will create a slight hump down the middle of the slab, so water will drain off. If the crown faces down, you'll end up creating a trough in the slab where water can pool.

Push the rocks down

Larger aggregate (chunks of gravel) near the surface may cause spalling (chipping). Our expert pushes the larger rocks deeper into the mix. He does this by making small stabbing motions with the float on the first return pass. Start floating the slab immediately after the pour is complete.

Start floating right away

In addition to pushing the aggregate down under the surface, a bull float helps level the slab, so start floating right after you screed, while the concrete is still wet enough to shape.

Whenever possible, run the bull float perpendicular to the direction you pulled the concrete with the screed board (this slab was too long to do that). That will help to smooth out the ridges, troughs and valleys created by screeding. Our expert likes to float in both directions when he can.

BULL FLOAT

More tips online
For more great information, search for "pouring concrete" at **familyhandyman.com**

Clean your tools as you go

Don't wait until the end of the day to clean your tools. Clean them immediately after use.

FRESNO
TROWEL

Don't over-trowel concrete

Actually, exterior concrete surfaces don't need to be troweled at all. But if you want to use a trowel to knock down the ridges left by the bull float, make as few passes as possible and wait until all the surface "bleed water" is gone. Overworking and troweling wet concrete can trap water just under the surface, making it weak and more prone to spalling and scaling (pitting and peeling), especially on slabs poured in cold climates.

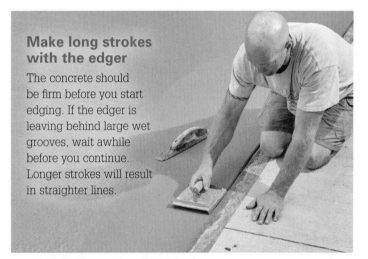

Make long strokes with the edger

The concrete should be firm before you start edging. If the edger is leaving behind large wet grooves, wait awhile before you continue. Longer strokes will result in straighter lines.

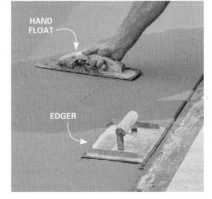

HAND
FLOAT

EDGER

Keep a hand float nearby when edging

Run a hand float over the ridges left behind by the edger. A hand float is also a good tool for dragging small amounts of material or moisture (cream) into any voids or dry spots near the edge.

GROOVER

Cut in control joints

A 100-ft. run of concrete can shrink as much as 1/2 in. as it hardens. Shrinking causes cracks. You can't stop your slab from cracking, but you can control where it cracks. Cut in control joints to create individual sections no larger than 8 x 8 ft. for a 3-1/2-in.-thick slab, and no larger than 10 x 10 ft. for a 5-1/2-in.-thick slab. Cut the control joints at least one-fourth the depth of the concrete. You could use a groover like this one, which works similar to an edger, but many pros prefer to cut the control joints with a diamond blade saw the day after pouring.

Spray on a sealer

Concrete will become significantly weaker if the water in the mix evaporates before the chemical curing process is complete. Spray down the slab with water every day for at least a week to slow down the curing process. Another option is to spray on an acrylic cure and seal product. Sealing the surface protects the concrete from scaling and spalling in cold climates. Apply sealer right after you broom.

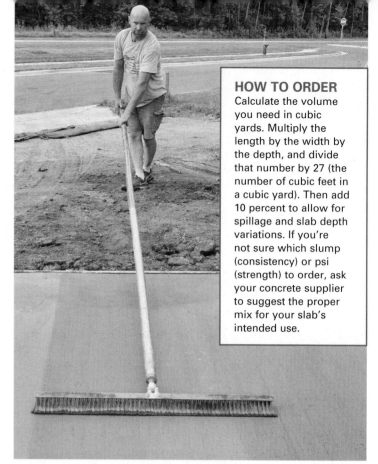

HOW TO ORDER
Calculate the volume you need in cubic yards. Multiply the length by the width by the depth, and divide that number by 27 (the number of cubic feet in a cubic yard). Then add 10 percent to allow for spillage and slab depth variations. If you're not sure which slump (consistency) or psi (strength) to order, ask your concrete supplier to suggest the proper mix for your slab's intended use.

Create traction with a broom

A broom finish creates a nonslip surface for wet conditions. The harder the concrete, the less rough the broom will leave the surface. Try to achieve a surface rough enough for traction but not so rough that it hurts to walk on barefoot. If the broom starts to bounce as you pull, lower the angle of the handle. If possible, broom perpendicular to the direction that the slab is most visible. Wavy, crooked broom lines are less noticeable that way.

Finishing up

The slab can be walked on and the forms pulled in 24 hours. Wait at least 10 days to drive on it, and avoid spreading any ice melting chemicals for the first two years. Ask your neighbors to keep an eye on their pets before you pour, and use caution tape around the area to warn the pesky neighbor kids.

HandyHints®

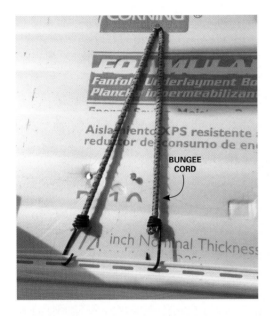

VINYL SIDING HELPER

Long lengths of vinyl siding can be tough to install by yourself, so I came up with this trick. I hung a bungee cord on the wall above the siding and used it to hold the siding in place while I nailed it off. The elasticity of the bungee cord made it easy to pull the siding down to snap it into place before nailing.

— Michael Winter

BUNGEE CORD

C-CLAMP

CAULK CADDY

Finding a place to hang a caulk gun on some ladders can be tough. And if you move the ladder a teeny bit, the caulk gun starts to swing and falls to the floor. I had a C-clamp handy, so I attached it to my ladder—now I have the perfect spot for my caulk gun.

— Doug Whiting

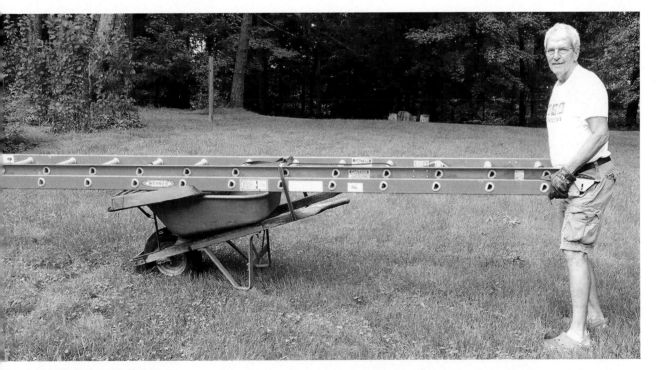

LADDER-BARROW

The older I get, the heavier my extension ladder gets. Instead of lugging it around, I just strap it to my wheelbarrow! A rubber mat on the front lip of the wheelbarrow and a ratcheting cargo strap around the handles keep it from sliding as I wheel the ladder around the yard.

— Ken Apacki

EXTERIOR REPAIRS & IMPROVEMENTS

Storage Hodgepodge

SCREW

DRIP TRAYS

STAY-PUT BALLS
Screw flowerpot saucers to shelves so balls can't roll off. Cheap plastic trays come in sizes to suit all kinds of balls.

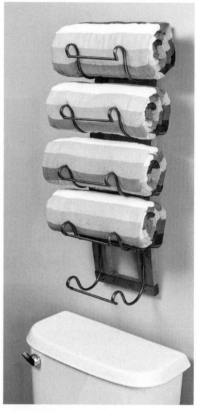

WINE RACK TOWEL HOLDER
I have very little space to store fresh towels in my bathroom, so I used a wine rack. The wall over my toilet was pretty much wasted space, and the wine rack fits there perfectly. Plus, it looks really cool!

— Christy Beling

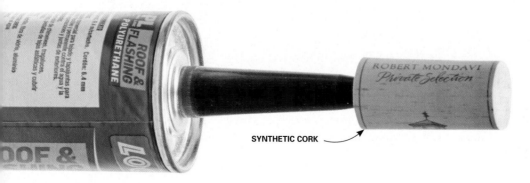

SYNTHETIC CORK

WINE CORK CAULK SAVER
Synthetic wine corks are great for sealing partially used tubes of caulk. Drill a 5/16-in. hole into the cork about 1 in. deep. The cork fits perfectly and makes an airtight seal.

— Susan Claussen

COFFEE BAG TIE

COFFEE BAG TIES

Small bags of fancy coffee have heavy-duty ties to keep them airtight. The ties are handy for securing small coils of electrical cable and rope. They're usually fastened to the bag with just a dab of glue, making them pretty easy to pull off.

— Joe Gemmill

SIX-PACK SHOP ORGANIZER

Six-pack cartons are useful for storing and transporting items like spray paint, lubricants and caulk.

— Gerald Fitzgibbon

DON'T DRINK IT!

Storage Hodgepodge

ORNAMENT HO-HO-HOLDER

I found a nifty way to store my Christmas ornaments using clear plastic tubs (with lids), some wooden dowels, and rubber leg tips that I got from the home center. I drilled two holes in each end of the tubs, inserted the dowels through them, and then capped the dowels with the rubber tips to keep the dowels in place. I store things like Christmas tree skirts in the bottom and hang ornaments from the dowels. Now it's really easy to see which ornaments are in each tub!

— Carol Pierce

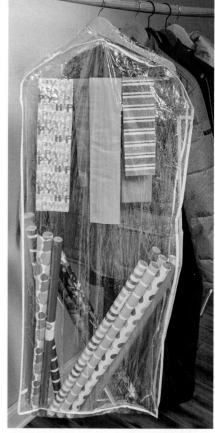

GIFT WRAP ORGANIZER

I used to keep rolls of wrapping paper under a bed or in the corner of a closet, making them hard to get at and covering them with dust. And then I'd go hunting for scissors and tape.

To make wrapping presents easier, I now use a clear garment bag as a portable gift wrap organizer. It's great for storing all my ribbons, bows, tape and scissors—all clearly visible and grouped together. I just hang it in the closet until I need it, and I can carry the whole she-bang to the dining room table whenever I have a big wrapping project.

— Sue Rosenkranz

UNDER-SINK STORAGE ROD

I keep so much stuff in the cabinet under my kitchen sink that it gets cluttered beyond belief. I could never find what I needed quickly, so I bought an inexpensive spring-tension curtain rod and installed it under the sink. Now I have a place to hang things like towels, spray bottles and rubber gloves. I put the items I can't hang in a couple of plastic baskets, which are easy to pull out.

— Gabi Perez

STRETCH WRAP IS ESSENTIAL

Keep a roll of stretch wrap handy and we promise you'll use it. Wrap unruly items for storage, tie box lids down or bind assorted items together for transport. A roll costs $8 at home centers, and you'll have enough to last for years.

13 TOP SPRING STORAGE TIPS

Ingenious ideas to help you prep for a no-clutter summer

1 Garden tool hideaway

A mailbox hidden behind shrubs near your garden provides a convenient home for tools. A small mailbox like this one costs less than $20 at hardware stores and home centers. King-size models cost about $35.

— Lynn Samples

2 PVC tool holder

Build this rack to store your tools on the wall. Use a jig-saw to cut a 1-1/4-in.-wide notch the length of a 2-in.-diameter PVC pipe. Cut several 3-1/2-in.-long, 1/8-in.-wide holes behind the notch. Use 1-1/4-in. drywall screws to attach these pieces to a 2x4 screwed to the wall.

—John Schorling

5 Hang-it-high helper

With this extension pole, you can hang objects in high, hard-to-reach areas. Attach a spring clamp to the end of an ABS or PVC drainpipe, and use the end of the clamp as a hook to lift items on or off a hook or nail.

— Joseph and Debra Wronkowski

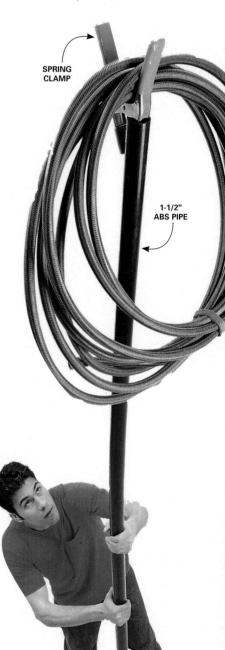

SPRING
CLAMP

1-1/2"
ABS PIPE

WOOD
BLOCK

3 Garage storage

Cardboard concrete-forming tubes are inexpensive ($10 at any home center) and provide a great place to store baseball bats, long-handled tools and rolls of just about anything. Rest the tubes on a piece of 2x4 to keep them high and dry. Secure each tube to a garage stud with a plumbing strap.

— David S. Mallinak

4 Tool bucket

A 5-gallon bucket comes in handy in the garden—and not just for collecting weeds. You can load it with all your gardening tools and carry them easily from place to place. If it starts to rain, protect the tools with the lid. But here's the best part—it doubles as a portable stool when you need to rest or do some pruning. The only problem is that the lid can be hard to pry off. Solve that by cutting off all but two of the plastic tabs. The lid will go on and off in a snap.

— Julie Abbott

6 Hang-it-all hooks

Those plastic hooks that plumbers use to support pipes make convenient hangers for almost anything. They're strong and cheap and come in a range of sizes. Find them in the plumbing aisle at home centers and hardware stores.

— Lori Callister

7 Save your lawn products

Leave a bag of fertilizer or weed killer open for long and it'll soak up moisture from the air and won't go through a spreader. Even grass seed could use an extra layer of protection from a moisture-wicking concrete floor. Place opened bags of lawn products in large resealable plastic bags ($1 at discount stores). The products will be free of clumps or pests when you need them.

— James A. Hanna

8 Garden gear caddy

An old golf bag, especially one on a cart, is perfect for storing and hauling garden tools. Get them all to the garden in one trip and park them in the caddy shack when you're done. Fore!

— Randy Roush

9 Wheelbarrow rack

Hang up your wheelbarrow to free up floor space. Center a 2-ft. 1x4 across two studs, 2 ft. above the floor. Tack it into place, then drive 3-in. screws through metal mending plates and the 1x4 and into the studs. Leave about 3/4 in. of the plate above the 1x4 to catch the rim. Rest the wheelbarrow on the 1x4 as shown, and mark the studs 1 in. above the wheelbarrow bucket. Drill pilot holes and screw ceiling hooks into the studs. Twist the hooks so they catch on the wheelbarrow lip and hold it in place.

— Bryan Turnbo

MENDING PLATE

CEILING HOOK

Storage Hodgepodge
13 TOP SPRING STORAGE TIPS continued

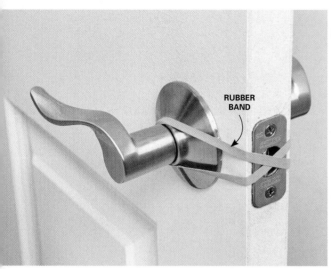

10 Hands-free door trick

As the temps warm up, we run in and out of our house more often. To keep the door from latching shut, I loop a rubber band around one doorknob or handle, then twist it once and loop it around the other knob. The rubber band holds the latch in. Now if the door closes, I can push it back open with my body whenever my hands are full.

— Nick Paone

RUBBER BAND

11 Simple spiral hose storage

Here's a handy tip for storing your spiral hoses so they don't end up tangled. Just wrap them around the handle of a rake or shovel. The long-handled tool does double duty!

— Bill Aloi

2" HOLE

12 Yard tool organizer

Create a simple long-handled tool hanger out of two 1x4s. On the first one, drill a series of 2-in. holes along the edge of the board. Center each hole about 1 in. from the edge. That leaves a 1-1/2-in. slot in the front that you can slip handles through. Space the holes to accommodate whatever it is you're hanging. Screw that board to another 1x4 for the back and add 45-degree brackets to keep it from sagging. If you wish, pound nails into the vertical board to hang even more stuff. No more tripping over the shovels to get to the rakes!

— Robert Johnson

13 Storage hooks

Get ladders, tree pruners, kids' bikes and other unwieldy items off your garage floor with these inexpensive PVC hooks. For heavy items, you could make the hook out of steel pipe.

— Fred Kendle

6 Outdoor Structures, Landscaping & Gardening

IN THIS CHAPTER

Home Care & Repair 246
  *Fixing dog spots in your lawn, buying
  carburetors online and got wasps?*

Fabulous Fire Table 248

Double-Duty Pub Shed 257

Patio Planter 266

Handy Hints 272
  *No more smelly lawn clippings, mud
  ladle, extension cord tamer, pinecone
  scooper and a better way to replant*

FIXING DOG SPOTS IN YOUR YARD

If you have a dog, it goes with the territory!

by **Jason White,**
Associate Editor

Burn spots caused by dogs relieving themselves on the lawn are usually about 4 to 8 in. wide with dead grass in the middle and a ring of dark green grass around them. Dog urine contains high concentrations of acids, salts and nitrogen, which kill the grass. The only way to fix the burn spots is to plant new grass.

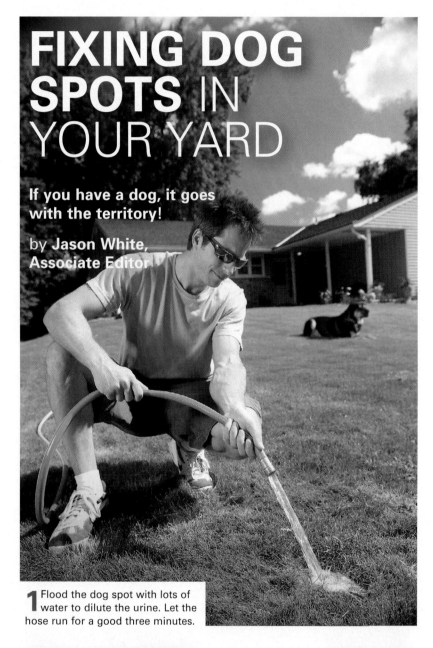

1 Flood the dog spot with lots of water to dilute the urine. Let the hose run for a good three minutes.

2 Scrape up the dead grass with a hand rake and loosen the soil about 1/2 in. deep. Seeds germinate and take root better in loose soil.

3 Add a 1/2-in. layer of new topsoil over the spot and sprinkle on grass seed. Cover with a thin layer of soil and keep the area moist (don't overwater) until the grass grows about 3 in. tall.

WATER DEEPLY BUT LESS OFTEN

Heavy watering every few days develops deep roots that tap into subsurface nutrients. Frequent, light watering does just the opposite, encouraging grass to stay healthy under only ideal conditions. To give your lawn the right amount of water, start with this test: Water for 30 minutes, then dig into the soil with a spade. If the soil is wet to a depth of less than 6 in., you need to water longer. If the moisture depth is more than 6 in., you can water for a shorter period. How often you water depends entirely on your soil and climate. In most areas, two to four times per week is best.

GOT WASPS?

If you have a nest of yellow jackets or paper wasps near your house and they're not bothering you, just leave them alone and let them eat the caterpillars and spiders in your yard. These types of wasps die off after a couple of hard frosts, anyway.

According to the "bee lab" at the University of Minnesota—beelab.umn.edu—only the new queens survive winter. They hibernate underground and establish new nests in the spring and don't reuse the old nest, whether it's underground or inside an exterior wall of a house.

If you're really worried about getting stung, and the nest is visible, you can kill the entire nest with an aerosol spray product available at hardware stores and home centers. You just spray the product directly into the nest at sunset or sunrise (follow the directions on the can). Just make sure you're standing far away from the nest while you're spraying in case all the wasps decide to fly out and try to sting you.

BUYING CARBURETORS ONLINE

Tom Dvorak, one of our field editors, says to skip trying to rebuild carburetors for gas-powered string trimmers and lawn mowers and just order new carburetors online. "My string trimmer was running poorly and needed a new carburetor," says Tom. "I've tried rebuilding them in the past, but I don't have the talent or patience. Now I just order new ones online. They cost about $20. All it took was two bolts and about 15 minutes to replace the one in my string trimmer, and now it runs like new."

NEW CARBURETOR

CARBURETOR

LAWN MOWER

MEET AN EXPERT

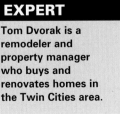

Tom Dvorak is a remodeler and property manager who buys and renovates homes in the Twin Cities area.

FABULOUS **FIRE TABLE**

Create an outdoor gathering space for family & friends

by **Mark Petersen, Senior Editor**

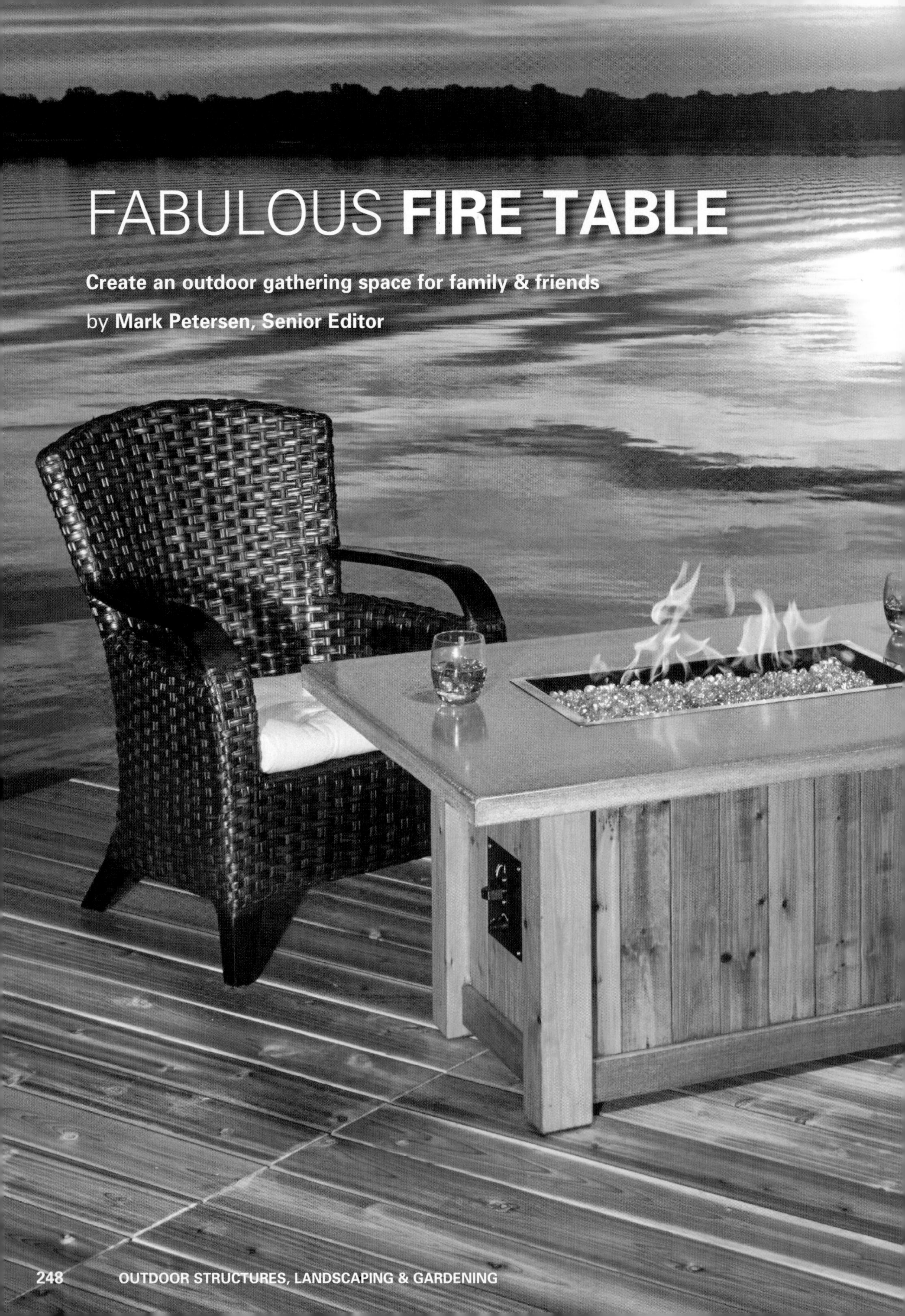

A fire table is a beautiful addition to your outdoor living space—and an invitation to gather around, enjoy a drink and shoot the breeze. It's also a stylish centerpiece that gives you a great opportunity to showcase your DIY prowess. And this is a fun build because it entails a variety of skills: woodworking, masonry, metal work and a little mechanical. It does require a few more-advanced tools, and at $825 it's not the cheapest DIY project, but if you shop for one, you could easily spend a couple thousand dollars.

Tools and materials

This table is made from cedar, but you can use pressure-treated wood, which would save you about $30, or whatever exterior-grade lumber is available in your area. The concrete tabletop is formed from Quikrete Countertop Mix. I dyed the top charcoal gray, but many other colors are available. All the materials (besides the burner kit) are available at home centers. The biggest cost by far is the burner kit (see p. 256). You could save about $100 by buying a kit that doesn't have a control panel or a piezo starter.

I built this project with basic hand tools and a miter saw, table saw and trim gun. You could make all the cuts with a circular saw and fasten all the panels with a hammer and trim nails, but it would take a lot longer and the end product probably wouldn't turn out as polished.

How it works

The burner runs on propane and will last six to 12 hours on a 20-lb. tank (that's about $2 to $3 per hour). The fire it produces will warm your hands and take the chill off, but it doesn't throw off enough heat to keep you warm on a cold night the way a bonfire would. The propane tank is stored under the table, but you can bury a line and hook it up to your home's natural gas if you wish.

What it takes

TIME: Two days

COST: $700 to $825

SKILL LEVEL: Intermediate

TOOLS: Basic hand tools, drill, table saw, miter saw, trim nailer/compressor, concrete trowel, large wire cutters or small bolt cutters, and wheelborrow or mixing tub

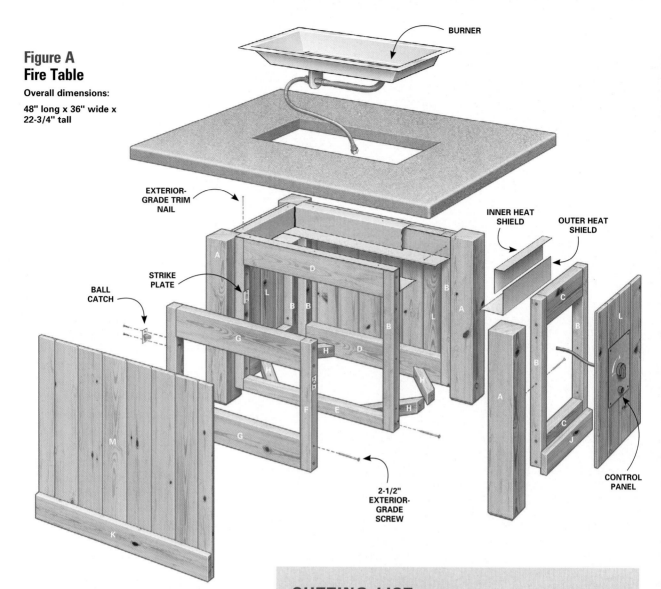

Figure A
Fire Table

Overall dimensions:

48" long x 36" wide x
22-3/4" tall

BURNER

EXTERIOR-
GRADE TRIM
NAIL

INNER HEAT
SHIELD

OUTER HEAT
SHIELD

STRIKE
PLATE

BALL
CATCH

CONTROL
PANEL

2-1/2"
EXTERIOR-
GRADE
SCREW

MATERIALS LIST

ITEM	QTY.
4x4 x 8' cedar post	1
2x4 x 8' cedar	4
1/4" x 3-1/2" x 96" planks, package of 6	1
42" x 84" wire remesh	1
4' x 8' x 3/4" melamine	1
3/4" x 48" wood dowel	1
3-1/2" x 5" x 10' galv. steel deck ledger flashing	1
Quikrete Countertop Mix, 80-lb. bags	3
2-1/2" exterior-grade screws, 100 pack	1
2" 18-gauge brads, sm. pack	1
1-1/4" ext. trim nails, sm. pack	1
1" 18-gauge brads, sm. pack	1
Construction adhesive	1 tube
Black silicone caulk	1 tube
High-temp RTV silicone	1 tube
Ball catches	2
Exterior-grade wood sealant	1 qt.
1-1/4" ext. trim nails, sm. pack	1
Concrete sealer	1 gal.
Burner kit	1

CUTTING LIST

KEY	QTY.	DIMENSIONS	NAME
Table box			
A	4	3-1/2" x 3-1/2" x 22"	Corner posts
B	8	1-1/2" x 1-1/2" x 20-1/2"	Frame sides
C	4	1-1/2" x 3-1/½" x 11"	Side frames, top/bottom
D	3	1-1/2" x 3-1/2" x 23"	Front and back frames top and back frame bottom
E	1	1-1/2" x 1-1/2" x 23"	Front frame bottom
F	2	1-1/2" x 1-1/2" x 15"	Door frame sides
G	2	1-1/2" x 3-1/2" x 19-5/8"	Door frame top and bottom
H	4	1-1/2" x 1-1/2" x 9"	Angle braces *(45-degree ends)*
J	2	3/4" x 2-1/2"	Side trim boards *(bevel top, cut to fit)*
K	1	3/4" x 2-1/2"	Back and front trim boards *(5-degree bevel top, cut to fit)*
L	16	1/4" x 3-1/2" x 18-1/4"	Back and side planks
M	8	1/4" x 3-1/2" x 20-3/4"	Door planks
Tabletop form (cut from a 3/4"-thick 4' x 8' melamine sheet)			
N	1	3/4" x 49" x 56"	Form base
P	2	3/4" x 1-3/4" x 49"	Perimeter side walls
Q	2	3/4" x 1-3/4" x 44"	Perimeter end walls
R	2	3/4" x 1-3/4" x 12"	Interior side walls
S	2	3/4" x 1-3/4" x 22-1/2"	Interior end walls

1 Taper the feet. Cut the posts (A) to length on a miter saw (see Cutting List on p. 250). Taper the bottom edges about 1/2 in. up with a miter saw. The tapered edges won't tear out when the table is slid around, and they'll look better when it's sitting on uneven ground.

2 Cut and assemble the frames. Cut three 8-ft. 2x4s in half to create six 4-footers. Rip down five of the six into 1-1/2-in. x 1-1/2-in. boards. From these, cut the frame sides (B) and the front frame bottom (E). The other frame parts (C and D) are cut from full 2x4s.

Secure the frame sides to the tops and bottoms with two 2-1/2-in. screws. Connect the smaller front frame bottom with one screw in each side. Drill 1/8-in. holes through the frame sides before you install the screws.

3 Attach the side frames to the posts. Drill three holes through the sides of the side frames. Lay the frames flat on your work surface. Align the frames and posts flush at the top, and secure the frames to the posts with three 2-1/2-in. screws. Take note of the wood grain on the posts and place the most attractive sides facing out.

4 Attach the front and back frames. Set the side frames and posts upside down. Line up the inside corner of the front and back frames with the inside corner of the posts and secure them with three 2-1/2-in. screws driven through predrilled holes.

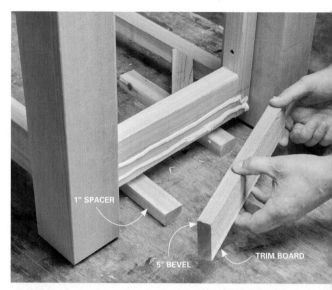

5 Install the angle braces. Cut the angle braces (**H**) from 1-1/2-in. x 1-1/2-in. stock. The total length (9 in.) is from the long point of the 45-degree angles. Use a framing square to check that all the posts are at right angles from the work surface. Then check that the box itself is square by measuring the diagonal distance from the outside of one corner post to another—the two measurements should be the same.

Once everything is square, install the brackets with a 2-1/2-in. screw on each side through a predrilled hole.

6 Fasten the trim boards. Set your table saw to a 5-degree angle and rip the 1x4 down to 2-1/2 in. That will create a beveled edge to help shed water. Cut the side trim boards (**J**) and the back trim board (**K**) to length, but hold off cutting the front. Apply construction adhesive to the frame and set the trim board on two 1-in. spacers. Drive 2-1/2-in. screws through the frame and into the back side of the trim board. Angle the screws a bit to prevent them from poking through the face of the trim board.

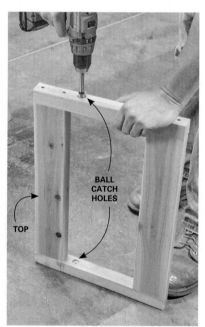

8 Build the door frame and install the ball catches. Cut the door frame sides (**F**) and door frame top and bottom (**G**). Assemble the door frame with two 2-1/2-in. screws driven through predrilled holes in the sides into the top and bottom. Dry-fit the door frame in the opening; there should be about a 3/16-in. gap on each side and a 3/8-in. gap above the top.

Predrill a 1/8-in. hole through the sides of the frame 1 in. below the bottom of the top frame board. Using that hole as a guide, drill a 3/4-in. hole (confirm this size with the installation instructions). Either a Forstner or a spade bit will work, but drill in from both sides to avoid a nasty tear-out.

Slide the ball catch into the hole and hold it in place with the retaining plate. The plate can sit on the surface of the wood; no need to cut in a mortise.

7 Fasten the planks. Cut the back and side tongue-and-groove planks (**L**) to length. On the back, rip 1 in. off the first plank; that way you'll end up cutting about 1 in. off the last one as well. I started the first one by removing the groove side. Apply adhesive, and fasten the planks with 1-in. brads, two at the very top of each plank and two near the bottom. Dry-fit the last two planks on the sides before applying adhesive.

9 **Attach the strike plates.** Set the door frame into place with the bottom of it resting on the bottom frame of the table. Mark the top and bottom locations of the strike plate using the ball catch retainer plate on the door frame as a guide. Bore out space with your 3/4-in. bit to make room for the recess in the strike plate.

Install the strike plates backward so the curved part of the plate faces in. If the plate protrudes toward the front, it will bump up against the door planks. Hold the strike plate in place, and mark the screw holes with a pencil.

10 **Fasten the door planks and trim board.** Adjust the ball catches so there's an even gap on both sides. Cut the door planks (M) to length and rip 1-1/8 in. off the first panel. Apply adhesive to the frame and set down 1-in. spacers for the planks to rest on. Start the first plank 1/8 in. short of the corner post, and leave the last plank short 1/8 in. Fasten the planks with two 1-in. brads as low and as high as you can (into the door frame, not the table!). Fasten the trim board with adhesive and 1-in. brads through the back of the door panel.

11 **Caulk and apply finish.** Apply caulk (that matches the finish) on the sides and the back where the tongue-and-groove planks meet the corner posts. Apply caulk to the top side of the trim board on the door. Don't caulk the tops of the other three trim boards. That way, if water does get behind the planks it can escape at the bottom.

A couple coats of an exterior-grade stain/sealer will add some color to your project and protect it from damaging UV rays.

12 **Install the outer heat shield.** Cut the 3-1/2-in. x 5-in. x 10-ft. galvanized steel dormer flashing (available at home centers) to length with tin snips. Install the flashing, keeping the top flush with the top of the box. Secure the pieces with 1-1/4-in. exterior-grade trim nails or small screws. Seal the corners with RTV high-temperature silicone (sometimes called "gasket maker"). **Caution:** The bottom of the pan gets hotter without stones in it, so don't ever run the burner without stones in the pan!

13 **Install the inner heat shield.** Cut the galvanized steel deck ledger flashing (sometimes called "drip edge") to length with tin snips. Pound the bottom lip of the flashing flat with a hammer. Install each side so the bottom of the flashing is facing up, and the lip (that was bent flat) is even with the outside of the box frame but short of the planks. This will create a small air gap between the two pieces of flashing.

BACK OF FLASHING

FRONT OF FLASHING

Figure B
Tabletop Form

Table Dimensions:
48" long x 36" wide x 1-3/4" thick

Hole Dimensions:
24" long x 12" wide

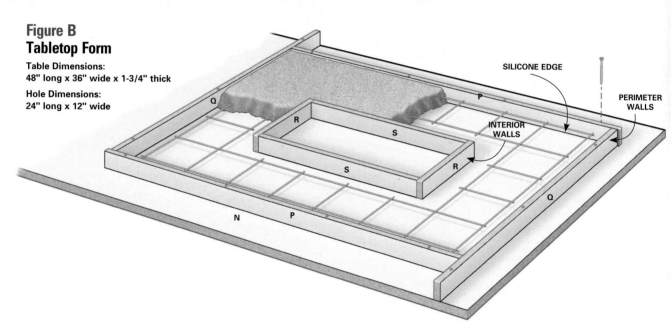

SILICONE EDGE

PERIMETER WALLS

INTERIOR WALLS

14 **Build the form.** Cut the melamine base (N) to size with a circular saw. Rip down the form walls on a table saw. Use a straightedge to mark the outline of the form. The inside dimensions of the perimeter walls (P and Q) should be 36 in. x 48 in. Let the perimeter walls run long; that way you'll have a surface to whack with a hammer when it's time to dismantle the form. The outside dimensions of the interior walls (R and S) are 12 in. x 24 in. Measure the actual burner ahead of time and check that it will fit before you cut

and assemble the inner form walls.

Fasten the form walls with 2-1/2-in. screws placed about 10 in. apart. Melamine splits easily; be sure to predrill holes for the screws. The screw heads need to sit flush, so create a hole for them with a countersink bit. Because the walls can split even if you predrill the holes, drive in the screws slowly so you can stop before they split and create a noticeable bump in the side of the tabletop. Secure the corners with 2-in. brads.

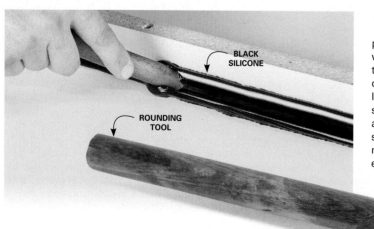

BLACK SILICONE

ROUNDING TOOL

15 **Create a rounded edge with silicone.** Run a healthy bead of silicone around the perimeter. Tool it into shape using a 3/4-in. dowel with the end cut at 90 degrees. While you're tooling, let the excess spill over onto each side of the bead. After the silicone dries, those two lines can easily be pulled and scraped off. Black silicone works best because you can clearly see any excess that needs to be removed. Don't use silicone on the inside edges. The silicone would make the form walls harder to remove, and those edges will be covered by the burner anyway.

16 **Mix the concrete.** Mix the concrete in a wheelbarrow or mixing tub ($15 at home centers), using a rake or garden hoe. I decided to darken my top by mixing in two bottles of Quikrete Liquid Cement Color dye. It's important to get exactly the same amount of dye into every bag of mix. If you mix each bag individually, stir the dye into some water first, and separate it into three equal amounts, one for each bag.

I used Quikrete Counter-top Mix. Some home centers stock it, but most can order it for you. Countertop mix works great because it can be poured a little wetter (like thick pancake batter) but still retain its strength. That helps prevent voids caused by air bubbles. Follow the directions for whatever product you use.

17 **Fill the form.** Set the form on a few 2x4s resting on sawhorses so you can beat the underside of it with a hammer to remove air bubbles. The form should sit fairly level. Spread out the concrete with a concrete trowel or taping knife. Pour in one of the mixed bags and beat the bottom and sides of the form to remove voids and air bubbles. Repeat the process with the second mixed bag before adding the wire mesh.

18 **Set in the wire mesh.** Wire mesh will strengthen the top. I cut down a 42-in. x 84-in. sheet (not roll) of remesh. The grid size worked out perfectly. Whatever size mesh you buy, keep it at least 2 in. away from the edges. I cut mine with a pair of small bolt cutters, but you could also use large wire cutters.

Once the mesh is laid in place, spread the last mixed bag of concrete over the top of it. Tap only the sides with a hammer to remove any voids; do not vibrate the rest of the form. This is very important: Vibrating the form will cause the remesh to sink. You'll get shadow lines if the remesh comes within 1/2 in. of the table's surface.

19 **Screed off the excess concrete.** Slide a 2x4 across the surface to scrape off the excess concrete. Wiggle it back and forth as you go, but try not to shake the whole form too much. That could also cause the remesh wire to sink and create shadow lines. Let the concrete harden a bit before you smooth it out with a trowel or taping knife. It doesn't have to be perfectly smooth because nobody will ever see it.

20 **The burner kit.** I bought my 12-in. x 24-in. burner kit (No. CF-1224-DIY) at The Outdoor GreatRoom Company (outdoorrooms.com). It cost about $500 and included the gas lines, the control panel, the fire gems and the burner with electronic piezo starter. Hooked to a propane tank, it cranks out about 55,000 Btu set on high. A natural gas orifice is included as well. The burner pan has drain holes, so a little rain won't hurt it, but it should be covered when not in use. And fire is inherently dangerous, so always follow the manufacturer's directions!

21 **Finish up.** Take out the form screws, and remove the form walls with a hammer and a pry bar or sturdy scraper. Have a strong buddy (or two) help you flip the top upside down. Seal the tabletop with an exterior-grade concrete sealer.

Install the control panel (if your kit has one), and set your table base exactly where you want it before setting the top into place. Apply the leftover black and high-temp silicone to the top edge of the table. The top is heavy enough that it shouldn't budge with normal use, but the silicone will create a stronger bond in case your burly, intoxicated brother-in-law falls down on it.

Insert the burner and make the gas line connections according to the manufacturer's directions. Fill the burner with the recommended amount of rocks. Too few rocks and the pan will overheat; too many rocks and the flame will sit too high and be blown out by the wind.

All that's left is to invite your friends and family (sans your brother-in-law) for a relaxing conversation around the fire.

MEET AN EXPERT

Mark Petersen is a senior editor at *The Family Handyman.* **He spent 20 years in the construction industry, 10 years as a siding contractor and 10 as a general contractor.**

DOUBLE-DUTY **PUB SHED**

The perfect party spot, plus tons of storage

by **Jeff Gorton, Associate Editor**

This year's shed is one of the most versatile we've ever built. The bar and covered patio area make it a perfect place to entertain or just hang out. The steep roof and sturdy lofts provide tons of extra storage space. And the high-tech materials, including reflective roof sheathing and prefinished floor panels, add to the shed's comfort and convenience. Of couse, if you don't want a bar, you can install a bank of windows in its place. In fact, without too much more work, you could eliminate the front porch and build one big shed for even more storage.

Shaded patio & bar
The built-in bar with swing-up bar door (shown on p. 265) provides plenty of seating and counter space for your next backyard party.

What it takes

TIME: 10-12 days

COST: $6,500

SKILL: Intermediate to advanced

TOOLS: Standard DIY tools, circular saw, miter saw, table saw, nail gun and compressor

Inexpensive windows that you build yourself
Barn sash mounted in easy-to-assemble pine frames provides abundant light and ventilation for a fraction of the cost of factory windows.

Tons of loft storage
Two huge loft areas supported by strong 2x8 joists provide lots of storage space.

Modern materials for a better shed

Our shed includes several Louisiana-Pacific (LP) engineered wood products that are favorites of shed builders. These materials come primed or you can order them with a factory paint finish. For more info, visit LPShed.com

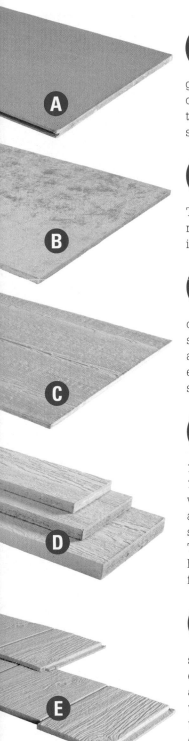

A LP ProStruct Flooring with SmartFinish

These 4 x 8-ft. tongue-and-groove floor panels come prefinished on one side with a tough, textured overlay that results in a great-looking, durable shed floor.

B LP ProStruct Roof Sheathing with SilverTech

The reflective SilverTech finish on this roof sheathing brightens the shed's interior while reducing heat buildup.

C LP SmartSide Primed Panel Siding

We used the no-groove version of the 4 x 8-ft. Cedar Texture textured siding panels, but grooved versions are also available. The panels come in different thicknesses as well as your choice of shiplap or square edges.

D LP SmartSide Trim and Fascia

Trim boards are available in 16-ft. lengths and widths from 2-1/2 in. to 11-1/4 in. You can even get the boards in various thicknesses from about 1/2 in. to about 1 in. thick. There are two varieties, stranded like we used, and fiber core. The fiber version is reversible so you can have either the rough or the smooth side facing out.

E LP SmartSide Cedar Texture Shakes

If you want the look of cedar shakes without all the extra work or expense of the real thing, these panels are perfect. Each panel is about 12 in. wide and 4 ft. long and can be installed with either the straight or the staggered edge exposed, depending on the look you're after.

Tools, time and materials

In addition to common building materials that you'll find at most home centers and lumberyards, we used some special products from Louisiana-Pacific (shown at left) that you may have to order if you want to duplicate our shed exactly. The windows are shop built using plastic utility window sash that we found at a local home center. Search for "barn sash" online if you can't find it locally. The swing-up bar door is site built. The entry door on the side is a standard prehung exterior door that's readily available at most home centers (about $220). The materials for the shed cost us about $6,500.

You'll need standard DIY tools including a circular saw and drill to build this shed. A framing nail gun and compressor will speed up the framing. Since there's a lot of trim and siding to nail up, we used a coil siding nailer loaded with galvanized ring-shank siding nails. You can rent a coil siding nail gun like this for about $30 a day. A miter saw and table saw aren't required but will make your cuts more accurate.

This is a big shed, but it's no more complicated than a small one. If you have experience with deck building or other small carpentry projects, you shouldn't have any trouble finishing this shed. There are a lot of materials to cut and hoist, though, so you'll want to round up a few helpers. Expect to spend five or six weekends completing the shed.

Getting started

Check with your local building department to see whether a permit is required. Also find out if there are rules about where your shed can be located on the lot.

Take the **Materials List** (online) with you to your favorite lumberyard or home center and go over the list with the salesperson to see what items you may have to order. Then set up a delivery so you'll be ready to build when your help arrives. A few days before you plan to dig, call 811 for instructions on how to locate buried utility lines.

Products were installed by *The Family Handyman* independent of LP Building Products installation instructions.

Figure A
Double-Duty Pub Shed

Overall dimensions (*including overhangs*):
14' 6" wide x 15' tall x 18' 1" deep

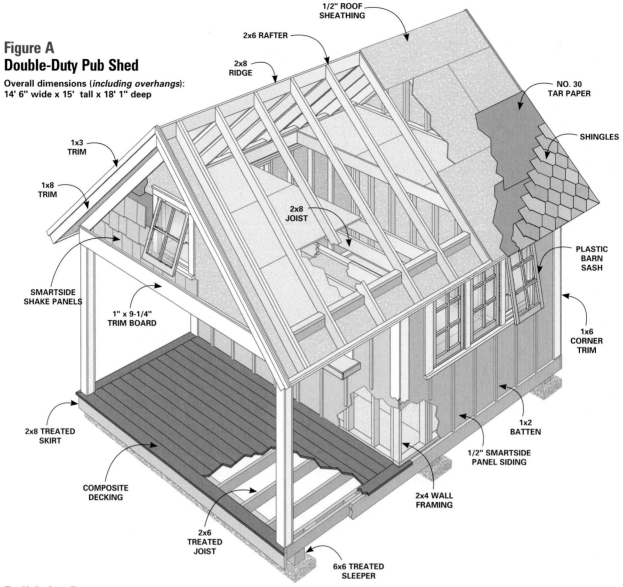

1/2" ROOF
SHEATHING

2x6 RAFTER

2x8
RIDGE

NO. 30
TAR PAPER

SHINGLES

1x3
TRIM

1x8
TRIM

2x8
JOIST

PLASTIC
BARN
SASH

SMARTSIDE
SHAKE PANELS

1x6
CORNER
TRIM

1" x 9-1/4"
TRIM BOARD

1x2
BATTEN

2x8 TREATED
SKIRT

1/2" SMARTSIDE
PANEL SIDING

COMPOSITE
DECKING

2x4 WALL
FRAMING

2x6
TREATED
JOIST

6x6 TREATED
SLEEPER

Build the floor

As we've done with many of our recent sheds, we built this shed on a wood floor supported by treated 6x6s. But you could substitute a concrete slab or provide footings or another type of support for the floor joists.

Start by laying out the perimeter of the shed, either with stakes and a string line, or with a rectangle built with 2x4s to represent the outside edges of the 12 x 16-ft. floor. Now measure in 8-3/4 in. from the short sides and drive stakes to mark the center of the trenches. Drive a third pair of stakes to mark the center beam.

Dig trenches about 12 in. wide and about 10 in. below where you want the bottom edge of the joists to end up. Pour 4 in. of gravel into

the trenches and level it off. Make sure the gravel in all three trenches is at the same height. Then cut the 6x6s to 12 ft. long and set them in the trenches. Measure to make sure the 6x6s are parallel. Then measure diagonally from the ends of the outside 6x6s to make certain they're square. The diagonal measurements should be equal. Finally, level the 6x6s (**Photo 1 and Figure B** online).

Next, frame the floor with 2x6s. Start by cutting the 12-ft.-long rim joists for the front and back and marking the joist locations. Cut the joists and nail them to the rim joists. When you're done, square the joists (**Photo 2**). Then use a taut string line or sight down the 12-ft. rim joist to make sure it's straight. Then drive toenails through the joists into the 6x6s to hold the joists in place.

We're using tongue-and-groove LP ProStruct Flooring with SmartFinish for the shed floor. **Photo 3** shows how to install the flooring.

Build the walls

Using **Figure C** (online) as a guide, chalk lines on the floor to indicate the inside edges of the walls. These lines provide a reference for straightening the bottom plate of the walls after the walls are standing. Cut the top and bottom wall plates and mark the stud locations on them (**Figures D – G** online). Build the side walls (**Photo 4**). Stand them up and brace them temporarily. Then build and stand the front and back walls. After nailing the walls together at the corners, install temporary diagonal braces on the inside to hold the walls plumb (**Photo 5**).

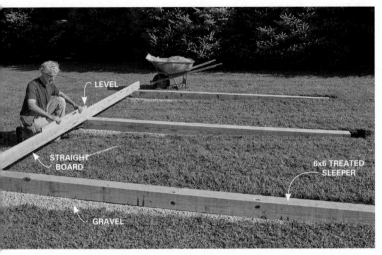

1 **Lay the foundation.** Rest treated 6x6 sleepers on beds of gravel. Use a long, straight board and a level to make sure the 6x6s are level from end to end, and level with each other. Pound the tops with a sledgehammer or heavy board to adjust the height of the 6x6s.

2 **Square the floor frame.** Build the 2x6 frame on top of the 6x6s. Then measure diagonally to make sure the frame is square. Diagonal measurements from opposite corners should be equal. If not, rack the frame until they are. Then nail or screw the four corners to the 6x6s to hold the frame square.

3 **Install the flooring.** Fasten the first sheet in the back corner with construction adhesive and deck screws. Finish the row with a half sheet. Then start with a full sheet from the opposite end so the seams between sheets are staggered.

More info online

■ Take a video tour

■ Check out the time-lapse video of the entire build

■ Go inside with 360 video

■ Get detailed plans and a materials list

PubShed.familyhandyman.com

There are two 4x4 posts at the front of the shed that support the front half of the roof. Secure the bottom of the posts to the deck frame with metal post anchors. Tie the top of the posts together with the second (top) 2x4 plates that run over the top of the walls. Miter the ends of the 2x4 plates over the posts and attach them with screws (**Photo 6**).

Add ceiling joists and attic flooring

The next step after installing deck boards on the front porch (**Figure M** online and **Photo 7**) is to build the attic floor. The 2x8 joists covered with sheets of flooring material provide storage space in the attic. We left a 4-ft.-wide opening for easy access to the front and back loft areas, but you could also cover the entire area with a floor and provide an access door or pull-down ladder instead.

Start by marking joist locations on the two side joists using **Figure H** (online) as a guide. Then cut and install the joists (**Photo 8**). Before you cover the joists with the 4 x 8-ft. sheets of flooring, plumb and brace the 4x4 posts with diagonal 2x4s. Also stretch a string or mason's line from front to back along the top edge of the outside joist to make sure walls and joists are

4 **Build the walls.** Cut the plates and mark the stud locations on them. Build and stand the side walls. Then build and stand the front and back walls.

5 **Plumb and brace the walls.** Make sure the walls are firmly nailed together at the corners. Then use a level to plumb the corners while you attach temporary diagonal bracing to the inside of the walls. Brace all four walls. You can remove the bracing after you install the siding panels.

6 **Fasten the plates over the posts.** Run the second top plate on each side of the shed out over the posts. Cut miters on the plates where they join over the posts. Connect the plates to the posts with screws.

7 **Install the decking.** Start by cutting and installing the perimeter boards. Leave a 1-in. overhang. Notch and miter the perimeter boards to fit around the post. Then space the remaining deck boards with a 16d nail and screw them to the joists. We used the Cortex hidden fastener system.

8 **Set the ceiling joists.** Mark the joist locations on two rim joists and nail the rims to the top plate. Make sure they are set in 1-1/2 in. from the outside edge of the wall to allow space for the second rim joist. Attach the joists with screws or nails driven through the rim joists. Then add the second rim joist and install joist hangers on every joist.

straight. The attic floor needs to be square and have straight sides. If not, the rafters won't fit correctly.

Install the siding

Double-check corners and front posts to make sure they're plumb. Then cut and install the 4 x 8-ft. sheets of siding (**Photo 9**). Follow the siding manufacturer's instructions for spacing and nailing the siding. Remember to install metal drip cap flashing (visible in **Photo 9**) over the 2x8 skirt board before installing the siding.

Frame the roof

Start by cutting the 2x8 ridge board to length and marking the rafter locations on both sides using **Figure K** (online) as a guide. Also mark the rafter locations on the floor along both sides of the shed. Next, set the ridge on temporary 2x4 posts and brace it with diagonal 2x4s (**Photo 10**). The top of the ridge should be 76 in. from the floor. Cut a pair of rafters (**Figure J** online) and set them in place to test the fit. Make any needed adjustments, and when you have a pair of rafters that fit perfectly, mark one of them as a pattern. Use the pattern to trace the rafter cuts on the remaining 2x6s and cut out the rafters.

Stretch a string along the top of the ridge as a guide to keep the ridge straight as you install the pairs of rafters (**Photo 10**). The 2x4 blocks nailed to the floor between the rafters help position the rafters and make them easier to secure. Add the 2x6 subfascias before you install the four overhang rafters at the front and back of the shed.

When the roof frame is done, you can build the front and back gable walls (**Figure L** online). The front wall requires an opening for the gable-end window (**Photo 11**). Finish the roof construction by covering the rafters with sheathing (**Figure N** online and **Photo 12**).

Trim out the exterior

Start by nailing the soffit boards to the underside of

SIDING

1/2" SPACER

DRIP CAP FLASHING

9 **Side the walls.** Measure and cut the siding so the seams align over wall studs. Rest the bottom on a temporary 1/2-in. spacer to provide space between the siding and drip cap. Nail the siding to the studs.

the rafters. Then add the 1x8 fascia boards that cover the 2x6 subfascias and overhanging rafters. Finish the overhang trim by installing the 1x3 roof molding over the 1x8 fascias (**Photo 13**).

The next step is to install the 1-in. x 9-1/4-in. trim board that fits against the soffit and runs around the perimeter of the shed and porch. This wide trim board forms one side of the false beam that runs around the porch ceiling. Add a 2x4 frame to the underside of the porch ceiling to create the false beam. Then nail the grooved panels to the porch ceiling and cover the 2x4 false beam with trim (**Photo 14**). You can install the corner boards at this stage, but the battens will have to wait until after you've built and installed the windows. **Figures S – V** (online) show details for the siding and trim installation.

Assemble the windows

We built inexpensive windows for the shed using plastic barn sash mounted in 1x4 pine frames (**Photo 15** and **Figures Q and R** online). Start by measuring the sash and building a 1x4 frame that's 1/4 in. wider and taller than the sash. Cut 10-degree angles on the bottom of the sides to provide a sloping sill. Cut 1x2 stops to fit in the frame and position them to hold the sash flush with the outside edge of the 1x4 frame. Then attach galvanized screen door hinges to the frame, set the sash in place and drill holes for the fasteners. Since the plastic isn't strong enough to hold wood screws, we drilled holes through the sash and attached the hinges with machine screws, washers and nuts.

Connect three windows to form the window assembly for the side wall (**Figures R and U** online). Use a pair of 2x4s as spacers between each window. Screw through the window frames into the spacers to hold the windows together. Tip the triple window assembly into the window opening. Shim under the windows until about 3/8 in. of the top frame is

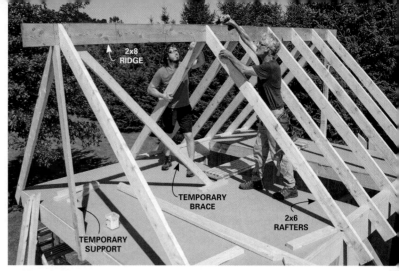

2x8 RIDGE

TEMPORARY BRACE

2x6 RAFTERS

TEMPORARY SUPPORT

10 **Frame the roof.** Mark the rafter locations on the ridge and set the ridge in place on temporary posts. Cut the rafters and install them in pairs, making sure the ridge stays straight as you screw or nail the rafters to the ridge.

STUD LOCATION

11 **Fill in the gable framing.** Mark the stud locations on the bottom plate. Then use a level to transfer the stud locations to the top plate. Measure to find the stud lengths.

TEMPORARY BLOCK

12 **Install the sheathing.** Screw blocks to the subfascia to support the first row of roof sheathing while you nail it to the rafters. Space the sheathing about 1/8 in. between sheets to allow for expansion. Stagger the seams between rows.

OUTDOOR STRUCTURES, LANDSCAPING & GARDENING

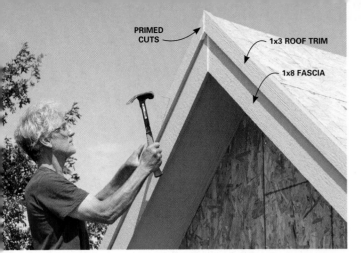

13 **Install the soffit and fascia.** Nail the soffits to the under-side of the rafters. Then nail the 1x8 fascia boards to the subfascia and gable-end rafters. Add 1x3 roof molding flush to the top of the sheathing.

14 **Build the false beams.** Frame down with 2x4s to create a false beam. After covering the ceiling with siding sheets, wrap the side and bottom of the false beam and add 1x2 trim around the ceiling.

15 **Assemble the windows.** Cut the 1x4s, including a 10-degree angle on the bottoms of the side pieces, and screw them together. Add 1x2 stops. Screw a pair of hinges to the frame. Set the sash into place and use the hinges as a guide to drill holes for the machine screws that you'll use to attach the sash.

16 **Trim the windows.** Rip 10-degree angles on the sill piece and screw it to the wall under the windows. Then cut 1x4s to fit between the top trim and the sill and nail them on.

exposed on the outside. Shim between the studs and the window frame to level and plumb the window unit and to adjust the frame until there's a consistent space between the window frame and the sash. Make sure the window frames are flush to the siding. Then screw through the window frames into the studs to hold the windows in place. We added Stanley Storm Window Adjuster hardware to the windows to hold them open and to lock them.

Rip a 2x4 to 2 in. wide with a 10-degree bevel on each side to form the sill piece. Cut the sill to extend 3-1/4 in. past the window frame on each end and attach it to the wall under the windows with long screws. Then cut and install the 1x4 trim pieces that fit between the top trim and the sill (Photo 16).

The front window is similar, except it's smaller and contains only one sash. Use the same process to build and install the front window.

Install the door and finish the trim

If your prehung door has exterior trim, pry it off. The wide trim board running around the shed, under the soffit, will take the place of the top door trim. Place the door in the opening to check the fit. The top doorjamb should rest against the wide trim board. Use wooden or composite shims between the side jambs and the 2x4 framing to square the door frame. Place shims behind each hinge and at the top, middle and bottom of the latch side. Adjust the shims until there's an even space between the door and the doorjambs on the top and sides. Then drive screws through the doorjambs into the framing at the shim locations to secure the door. Finish the door installation by adding 1x4 trim boards to each side.

Finish the exterior trim by nailing 1x2 battens over the stud locations and installing the corner boards.

Add the shake panels

The front and back gable ends are covered with panels that resemble cedar shakes. After installing a metal drip cap over the 1x2 that caps the wide trim board, install the shakes according to the manufacturer's instructions (Photo 17).

17 **Cover the gables with shakes.** Follow the manufacturer's instructions for installing shake panels. Provide space for caulk at the ends, and stagger joints according to the instructions.

Follow the manufacturer's instructions for details about panel placement and how much caulk space to leave between the panels and the trim.

Build the bar and the bar door

The bar consists of a frame of 2x2s and 2x4s covered on the top and bottom with plywood and finished with a wood edge (**Photo 18 and Figure P** online). For extra strength, use screws to attach the frame. Shim under the 2x4s if needed to level the bar top before installing the plywood.

When you're done building the bar, add jambs to the sides and top and install exterior trim. Cut the jamb material to fit and nail the pieces to the sides and top of the bar opening. Then add 1x6 trim to both sides of the bar opening to finish it off.

The bar door attaches to the inside of the shed with hinges and swings up to open. To build the door, simply cut a piece of siding material to the right size. Then attach frame and batten boards with glue and screws (**Photo 19 and Figure P** online).

To install the bar door, rest it on blocks so that the bottom is 2-1/4 in. below the bar top. Add a 1-1/4-in.-thick strip of wood along the top of the door to provide a hinge attachment point. Then screw strap hinges to the wood strip and to the door (**Photo 20**). Remove the temporary support blocks when you're done attaching the hinges.

We mounted a pair of locking hasps on the interior side of the bar door to secure it when it's closed. Then we added eye bolts to the door edges and to the ceiling above the door to provide a way to hang the door when it's open.

Finishing up

Before you shingle the roof, install metal drip edge. Then nail a row of starter shingles along the bottom of the roof. Install the rest of the shingles according to the package instructions.

Before painting, we filled spaces on the exterior with acrylic caulk. Then we rolled and brushed two coats of top-quality acrylic exterior paint onto the trim and siding.

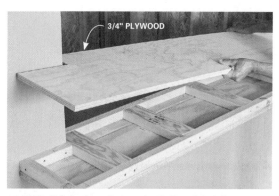

18 **Build the bar.** Screw the 2x2 and 2x4 frame to the framing. Then cover the top and bottom with plywood. Finish the bar by covering the face with trim, mitered at the corners.

19 **Assemble the bar door.** Cut a sheet of siding according to the dimensions given in Figure P online. Glue and screw 1x6s and 1x4s to the siding to create the bar door.

20 **Mount the bar door.** Rip a strip of 2x4 to 1-1/4 in. thick and nail it along the top of the opening to provide a fastening location for the hinges. Support the door on temp-orary blocks while you attach the strap hinges to the door.

PATIO **PLANTER**

A mini garden with fresh veggies—steps from your kitchen

by **Spike Carlsen, Contributing Editor**

A raised planter "beets" traditional gardening in a bunch of ways. And our planter is tops for easy construction, sturdiness and convenience. Plus, the curves and trim make it a pretty addition to your deck or patio. You'll get about 8 sq. ft. of planting area. If you need more, you could make a larger planter, but consider building two instead: A bigger planter filled with soil is tough to move.

A better design

1 The optional trellis supports climbing plants like tomatoes and peas.

2 Side tables are convenient work surfaces and handles when you need to move the planter.

3 Boards protrude at the ends or corners. Those "reveals" hide mistakes. If your measurements or cuts are a little off, no one will notice.

4 Notched joinery is super sturdy and easy enough for a beginner.

5 Lower shelf provides about 8 sq. ft. of storage space.

What it takes

TIME: One day
COST: $175
SKILL LEVEL: Beginner
TOOLS: Standard woodworking tools, framing square, drill, jigsaw, circular saw

9 advantages of a raised garden bed

- Tend your crop without straining your knees or back.
- Pick fresh herbs or veggies a few steps from your kitchen.
- Soil quality is easy to control; just fill your planter with a quality potting mix.
- Creeping weeds can't sneak into your plot.
- Fewer weed seeds blow in.
- Its height foils rabbits and other non-climbing critters.
- Placed near your house, it discourages shy wildlife.
- Plant diseases are less likely.
- When frost threatens, covering tender plants is easy.

Figure A
Patio Planter

Overall Dimensions:

**70-1/2" long x 30-3/4" wide x 33" tall
(72" tall with trellis)**

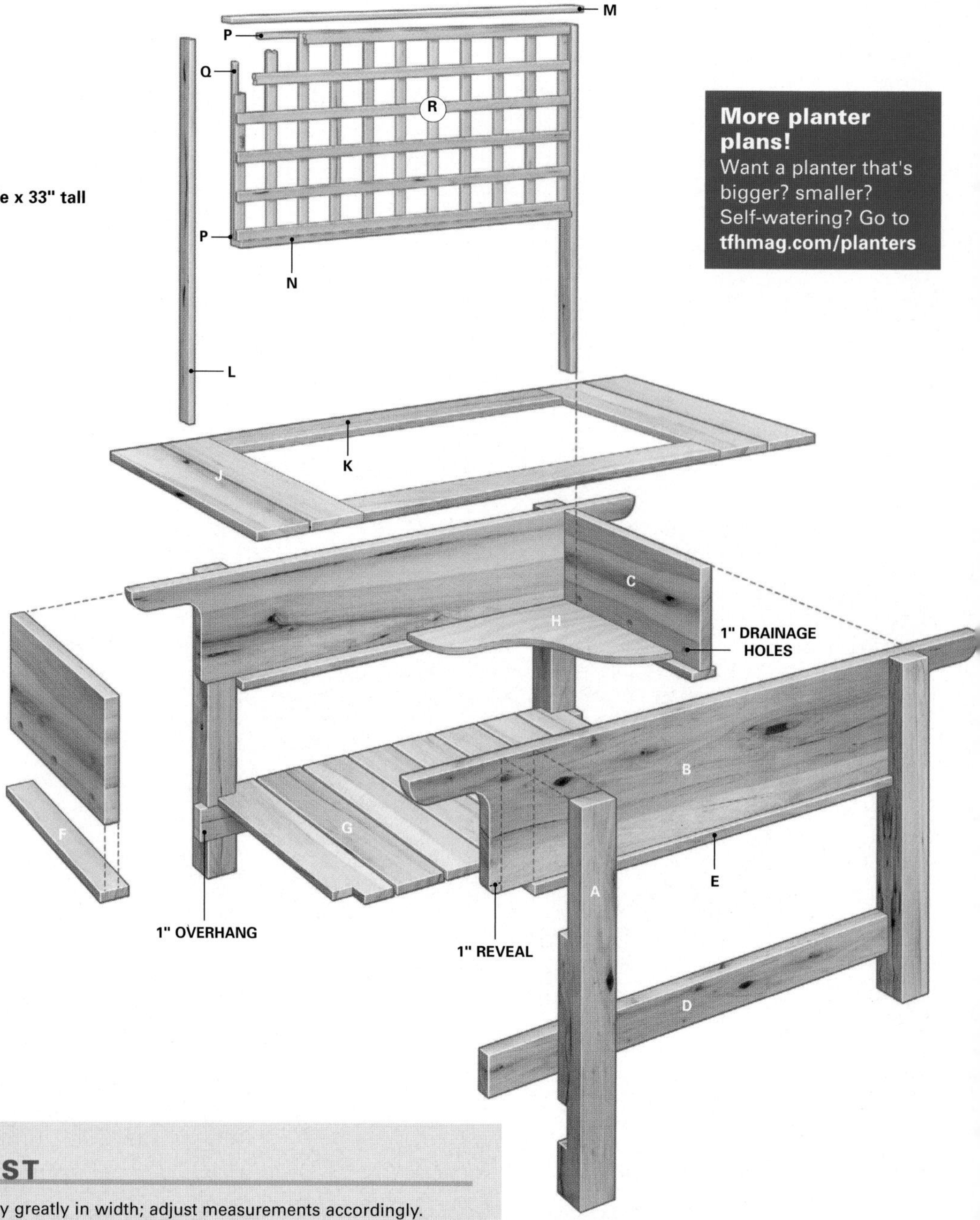

More planter plans!
Want a planter that's bigger? smaller? Self-watering? Go to **tfhmag.com/planters**

1" DRAINAGE HOLES

1" OVERHANG

1" REVEAL

CUTTING LIST

Treated lumber can vary greatly in width; adjust measurements accordingly.

KEY	QTY.	MATERIAL	DIMENSIONS	PART
A	4	4x4 treated pine	3-1/2" x 3-1/2" x 32"	Leg
B	2	2x12 treated pine	1-1/2" x 11-1/4" x 70"	Long box side
C	2	2x12 treated pine	1-1/2" x 11-1/4" x 24"	Short box side
D	2	1x4 treated pine	1-1/2" x 3-1/2" x 53"	Rungs
E	2	5/4 treated pine decking	1" x 3-1/2" x 44"	Long bottom supports
F	2	5/4 treated pine decking*	1" x 3-1/2" x 23"	Short bottom supports
G	8	5/4 treated pine decking	1" x 5-1/2" x 27-1/2"	Bottom shelf slats
H	1	Treated plywood	3/4" x 24" x 48"	Box bottom
J	4	5/4 treated pine decking	1" x 5-1/2" x 30-3/4"	Top shelf slats
K	2	5/4 treated pine decking*	1" x 3-1/2"x 48"	Long shelf slats
L	2	5/4 treated pine decking**	1" x 2-3/4" x 48"	Lattice panel sides
M	1	5/4 treated pine decking**	1" x 2-3/4" x 50"	Lattice panel top
N	1	5/4 treated pine decking**	1" x 2-3/4" x 46"	Lattice panel bottom
P	2	5/4 treated pine	1" x 1" x 46"	Long lattice stops
Q	2	5/4 treated pine***	1" x 1" x 22"	Short lattice stops
R	1	Treated pine lattice	1" x 24" x 46"	Lattice panel

* If 4"-wide material is unavailable, rip it from 6" material
** 5/4x6 material ripped in half
*** 5/4 material ripped into strips

Figure B
Side and Leg Details

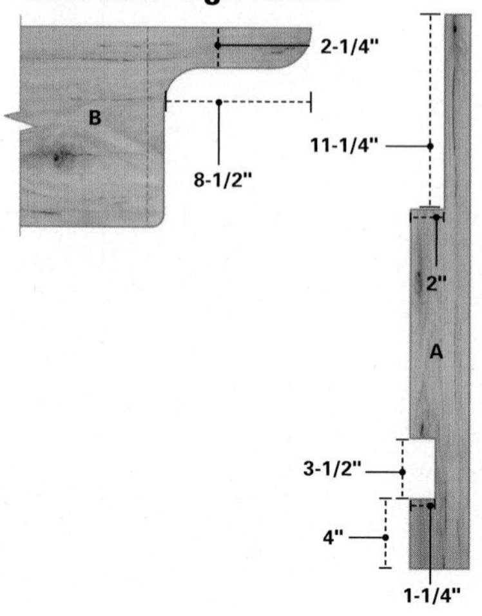

2-1/4"

11-1/4"

8-1/2"

2"

3-1/2"

4"

1-1/4"

1 Cut the lower leg notches. Set your saw depth to 1-1/4 in., then make a series of cuts no more than 1/2 in. apart. Drive a chisel into the cuts and pry; the little fingers will shear off. Flatten the remaining nubs with a chisel. Grab a 2x4 scrap and make sure it fits into the notch.

2 Cut the upper leg notches. Set your saw depth to 2 in. and make a series of cuts near the end of the notch. Break out the fingers as shown in Photo 1. To complete the notch, make the long cut. Your saw won't cut completely through the leg, so you'll have to flip the leg over and cut from the other side.

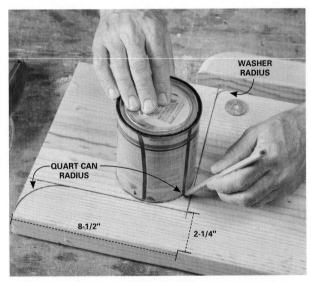

3 Mark the shelf supports. Cut the long box sides (B) to length, then use a square, a paint can and a washer to mark the shelf supports. Make the straight cuts with a circular saw and the curves with a jigsaw. Soften the cut edges with sandpaper or a router and round-over bit.

4 Assemble the box. Join the sides to the ends with 3-in. exterior screws. Drill pilot holes and drive the screws until the heads are slightly sunk into the wood. You can cover the heads with exterior wood filler or leave them exposed.

Skills and materials

All of the materials are available at any home center. The legs and planter box are made from treated dimensional lumber. The extension tables, bottom shelf and trim boards are made from what's commonly known as "5/4 decking material" or just "deck boards."

Take note: Treated lumber is more variable in width and thickness than standard dimensional lumber. We found 2x12s ranging from 11-1/8 in. to 11-3/4 in. wide at our home center. And we found two types and thicknesses

Is treated lumber safe for veggies?

Lots of articles online claim that it isn't safe to grow edible plants in containers made of treated lumber. But read closer, and you'll see that they're talking about wood treated with arsenic (CCA), which was banned for residential use back in 2003. The treated lumber you can buy today contains no arsenic and is considered safe for food contact and growing food. Some common types of treated lumber are ACQ, CA and MCQ.

5 **Add the legs.** Mark the leg locations 1 in. from the ends of the sides using a framing square. Position the legs and fasten them to the box side with 3-in. screws.

6 **Install the rungs and supports.** Place the rungs in the leg notches and secure them with 3-in. screws. Position the bottom supports (E, F) so they extend about 5/8 in. inside the box and screw them in place.

7 **Install the shelf slats and bottom.** Space the shelf slats (G) evenly and screw them into place. Notch the end slats to fit around the legs. Then install the planter bottom.

8 **Build the lattice panel trellis.** Build the panel support frame as shown, then install the stops and lattice panel. Secure the frame to the planter by driving screws through the panel legs into the planter box.

of treated decking material: The "premium" stuff was almost 1-1/4 in. thick while the standard was barely 1 in. Keep this in mind as you build—and adjust your measurements accordingly.

Let's build this thing

Cut the four legs (A) to length, then mark the positions of the upper and lower notches. Create the lower notches by making a series of 1-1/4-in.-deep cuts as shown in **Photo 1**, prying the fingers away with a chisel, then smoothing the bottoms with a chisel. Create the upper notches by making a series of 2-in.-deep kerf cuts (to create a square bottom) and long circular saw rips (to remove the bulk of the material) as shown in **Photo 2**. **Note:** Your notches should be as long as your 2x4s and 2x12s are wide.

ROUND-OVER BITS: THE KEY TO A PRO LOOK

A lot of the projects I build are of the quick and simple variety. But I've discovered one step that makes almost any project, including this one, look more polished: I eliminate all the sharp edges with a router and round-over bit. The softer edges look nicer, prevent splinters and hold finishes better. I used a 1/4-in. round-over bit on this project. A 1/2-in. bit is shown here.

9 **Cap off the planter.** Screw shelf boards to the shelf supports; the inner ones should extend just a little past the inside edge of the box. Install the side trim, letting those edges extend slightly inward, too.

Cut the box sides to length, then use a quart paint can and washer to create the curved corners (**Photo 3**). I used a 1-1/4-in. washer, but any large washer will do. Cut these out using a circular saw and jigsaw. Assemble the box as shown in **Photo 4**, then lay it on its side to install the legs (**Photo 5**). Install the 2x4 rungs in the lower notches, letting the ends extend an inch past the legs.

Flip the planter upside down and install the bottom support boards as shown in **Photo 6**. These support the plywood bottom and provide a decorative touch. The overhang should be the same on both sides.

Position the planter upright and install the slats for the bottom shelves (**Photo 7**). Space them about 1/4 in. apart and notch the corners of the outer slats as needed. Drill three or four 1-in. drainage holes about 1/2 in. up from the bottom of each end board. Plop the 3/4-in. plywood bottom into place and secure it with a few 1-1/4-in. screws.

Install the top shelf slats, letting the inner slats slightly extend over the lip of the planter box (**Photo 9**). Then install the long trim boards on each side.

The trellis and finishing touches

The lattice panel trellis is an optional but great feature for those wishing to grow plants requiring support.

Begin by ripping a 5/4x6 x 10-ft. board in two. Construct the panel frame (L, M, N) as shown in **Photo 8**, then rip 5/4 x 5/4 stops (P, Q) out of scrap material and secure them to the frame. Cut the lattice to size, set it into the frame and nail it to the stops using 3d nails. Secure the lattice panel to the back of the planter with screws.

I applied a coat of exterior stain to the planter. You can also leave the wood natural and let it mellow to a soft gray. To prevent soil from seeping out the drainage holes, line the bottom of the planter box with landscape fabric, letting it extend a few inches up each side. Fill the planter with soil or other growing medium and get digging.

MATERIALS LIST

ITEM	QTY.
4x4 x 6' treated lumber	2
2x12 x 8' treated lumber	2
2x4 x 10' treated lumber	1
5/4x4 x 8' treated decking	3
5/4x6 x 10' treated decking	5
3/4" x 2' x 4' treated plywood	1
1" x 2' x 4' treated lattice	1
3" deck screws	5 lbs.
1-1/4" screws	1 lb.
2-1/2" screws	1 lb.
3d galvanized nails	1 lb.
Exterior finish	1 gallon

Handy Hints®

PINECONE SCOOPER

My pine trees drop cones all summer long, and my old back doesn't like me bending over a lot to pick them all up. I don't have a dog, but a pooper scooper has turned out to be this man's best friend! Gently squeezing the handle opens its jaws, allowing me to pick up pinecones with no back pain.

— Don Greer

EXTENSION CORD TAMER

I was always struggling to keep the extension cord away from the blade of my electric hedge trimmer. So I attached a carabiner clip to a belt loop on the back of my pants and threaded the cord through it, which keeps the cord behind me and out of harm's way.

— Graham Daly

A BETTER WAY TO REPLANT

When I bring home new flowers or shrubs for my garden, I avoid yanking them out of their plastic pots by the stems because it can hurt the plants. Instead, I use a sharp knife to cut down two or more sides of each pot to free the plant, being careful not to tear the roots when separating the soil from the container.

— Leslie Poehler

SHREDDED PAPER

NO MORE SMELLY LAWN CLIPPINGS

After mowing, I dump all my lawn clippings into a "green refuse" bin. But after a day or so, the grass clippings turn into a slimy, smelly mess. To combat the stench, I raided my electric paper shredder and threw a few handfuls of shredded paper into the bottom of the barrel. The paper helps absorb the moisture and reduce the smell.

— Emil Machrone

MUD LADLE

No sooner did I finish digging footing holes for a new shed than it rained, filling all the holes with water. It looked like mud soup! I had to get rid of it quickly in order to pour concrete, so I fashioned a "mud ladle" out of a section of round ductwork, a piece of 3/4-in. plywood and a solid wood handle. Thanks to my invention, I was able to scoop out all the water in just a few minutes.

— Dave Choudek

Dream
Garage Storage

✓ **BASIC TOOLS**
You only need two
power tools

✓ **FAST**
Build it in a
weekend or less

✓ **BIG CAPACITY**
Turns the whole wall
into storage space

✓ **INEXPENSIVE**
Make it from low-cost
pegboard and lumber

SUPER STORAGE —
SIMPLIFIED

Simple and inexpensive, with huge storage capacity

by **Travis Larson, Senior Editor**

← BUILD A FLIP-UP
WORKBENCH!

What it takes

TIME: 1 to 3 days

COST: $80 *(per 4' x 8' bay)*

SKILL: Intermediate

TOOLS: Circular saw, screw
gun, chalk line, 4-ft. level

✓ *FLEXIBLE*
**Move shelves or
hooks instantly**

✓ *COMPACT*
**Leaves plenty of
parking space**

✓ *MODULAR*
**Build one section
or several**

Dream Garage Storage

RECONFIGURE AS YOUR NEEDS CHANGE

The items on your wall may come and go as your hobbies and storage requirements evolve. The beauty of this system is that you can rearrange shelves, add or substitute pegboard accessories, and even mount hanging systems that are designed for ordinary walls, so your wall will always suit your needs.

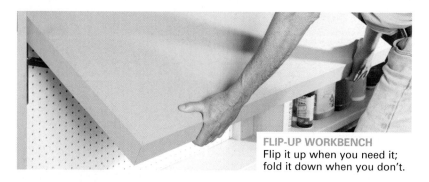

FLIP-UP WORKBENCH
Flip it up when you need it; fold it down when you don't.

PEGBOARD ACCESSORIES
Dozens of brackets are available to hang just about anything.

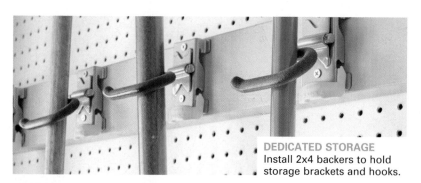

DEDICATED STORAGE
Install 2x4 backers to hold storage brackets and hooks.

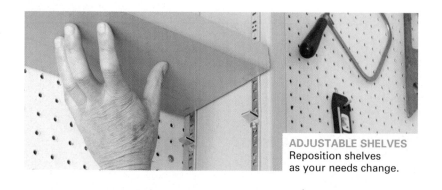

ADJUSTABLE SHELVES
Reposition shelves as your needs change.

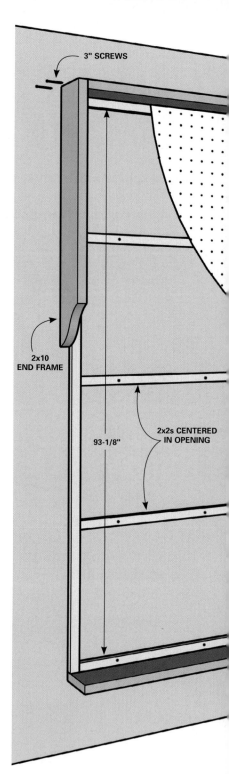

3" SCREWS

2x10 END FRAME

93-1/8"

2x2s CENTERED IN OPENING

It's mostly framing lumber and pegboard

Check out **Figure A** to get the gist of the construction. After you establish the 2x2 grid work (see **Figure B**), you frame the perimeter with 2x10s. Then you cut the pegboard to fit and screw or glue it to the grid work. If you choose glue, you'll have to tack it in place until the glue sets. Then add the 2x8 partitions directly over

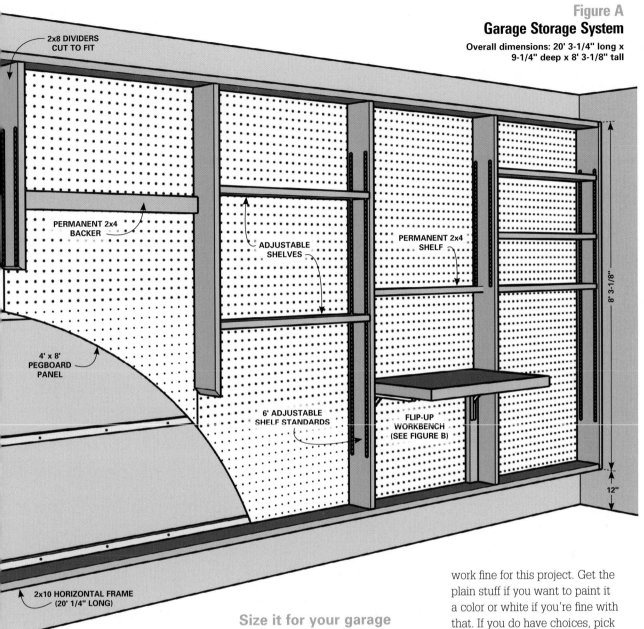

Figure A
Garage Storage System
**Overall dimensions: 20' 3-1/4" long x
9-1/4" deep x 8' 3-1/8" tall**

2x8 DIVIDERS
CUT TO FIT

PERMANENT 2x4
BACKER

ADJUSTABLE
SHELVES

PERMANENT 2x4
SHELF

4' x 8'
PEGBOARD
PANEL

6' ADJUSTABLE
SHELF STANDARDS

FLIP-UP
WORKBENCH
(SEE FIGURE B)

8' 3-1/8"

12"

2x10 HORIZONTAL FRAME
(20' 1/4" LONG)

the pegboard seams. Use a 4-ft. level to make sure those are plumb so your shelves will fit in any location within each bay.

Screw all the framing in place by end-screwing or toe-screwing as needed with 3-in. screws. We show this project on a finished wall. But there's no reason you can't install it over exposed studs or even a concrete or block wall. If you're installing it over masonry, anchor the 2x2s with 3-in. concrete screw anchors (Tapcon is one brand). If the concrete is frequently damp, use treated 2x2s and they'll last forever.

Size it for your garage and storage needs

Think of this project in terms of 4 x 8-ft. bays. They can be vertical like ours or horizontal if that better fits your needs. Do one bay or as many as you want; the construction is the same.

Now, about the pegboard

If you're willing to shop around, you can find a lot of pegboard choices: thick, thin, metal, custom colors, etc. But if you shop at home centers or lumberyards, you generally only find 3/16-in.-thick plain brown and pegboard coated on one side with white melamine (**Photo 5**). Either one will

work fine for this project. Get the plain stuff if you want to paint it a color or white if you're fine with that. If you do have choices, pick the thickest available with the larger (1/4-in.) holes.

While you're at the store, check out the pegboard accessories. You'll find all kinds of baskets, brackets, hooks, screwdriver holders, etc., designed to hang just about anything you can think of. Wait until the project is done and think it through before buying any at this point.

Pegboard is dusty and messy to cut. Do it outside if you can or your entire garage and everything in it will be covered with dust. Wear a dust mask. Make your cuts with the good side down to eliminate tear-out on the show side.

Dream Garage Storage

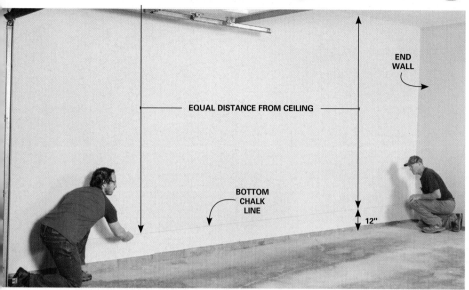

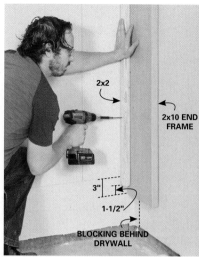

1 **Establish the bottom first.** Measure up from the floor 12 in., then measure down to get the distance from the ceiling. Transfer that measurement to the other end of the wall and snap the bottom line for the base of the pegboard wall. Measure up from the bottom chalk line 93-1/8 in. and snap the top chalk line. Then snap horizontal lines spaced every 2 ft. from the top. Use a level to mark the stud centers and the other end of the wall.

2 **Begin framing at the end wall.** Cut the two 2x10s to 99-1/8 in. long (one for each end). Center one above and below the top and bottom chalk lines and screw it to the corner blocking. There should be blocking extending at least 1 in. away from the corner. Center an 8-ft. 2x2 between the 2x10 ends, and screw it into place with 3-in. screws.

3 **Build the grid work.** Cut the horizontal 2x2s so they'll break in the middle of studs. Screw them to each stud with 3-in. screws using the chalk lines as a guide. Cut the last 2x2s 1-1/2 in. short of the end chalk line before fastening them to the studs. Then screw the last vertical 2x2 to the ends of each horizontal 2x2.

Write up a shopping list

It's impossible to give you a materials list for this project because your wall will be different from ours. But you won't have any trouble making your own. (See "Shopping tips," below.) After you establish how many bays you want, look at **Figure A** and count the parts. That'll give you a pretty accurate custom materials list for the project.

Choose the lengths of your 2x10s in multiples of 4 ft. That way, they'll join directly over the pegboard splices, and the horizontal 2x10 splices will be supported by the vertical 2x8s (**Photo 4**). That's why we used both 8- and 12-ft. 2x10s for the horizontal pieces. Joined together, they add up to our 20-ft. pegboard wall. Get one 8-ft. 2x8 for every two shelves you want (**Photo 7**). Here's a heads-up: 2x8s and 2x10s will be 1/8 to 1/2 in. over the stated lengths. So you'll have a little built-in fudge factor, but you may have to do a little trimming from time to time.

Place shelf standards in any bays where you want adjustable shelves. Choose 6-ft. standards if they're available, and space them 1 ft. up from the bottom 2x10.

Shopping tips

■ Buy 10-ft.-long 2x10s for the end frames. The final lengths are a few inches longer than 8-ft.
■ Pick horizontal frames in 4-ft. increments: 8 ft. for two bays, 12 ft. for three bays, etc.
■ Get one 4 x 8-ft. sheet of pegboard for each bay.
■ Buy four 8-ft. 2x2s for each bay.
■ When it comes to hardware, buy a 1-lb. box of 3-in. screws and a 1-lb. box of 1-1/2-in. washer-head screws. You'll have more than you need, but they'll come in handy someday.

4 Build the 2x10 frame. Center and screw the last vertical 2x10 to the end 2x2. Cut the horizontal 2x10s so any splices will fall over the 2x8 dividers. (Get a helper to support the boards for this part.) Then begin attaching the horizontal 2x10s to the end 2x10s and to the horizontal 2x2s with 3-in. screws.

5 Install the pegboard. Cut the pegboard to length if needed, then rest it on the bottom 2x10 and screw it to the 2x2s with 1-1/4-in. washer-head screws, four per 2x2. (You'll see the 2x2s through the pegboard holes.) If needed, cut the last pegboard panel to width.

Dream Garage Storage

6 **Add the dividers.** Cut the 2x8 dividers to length, then center them over the pegboard seams. Plumb them with a 4-ft. level and screw them to the top and bottom 2x10s. Then toe-screw them to the horizontal 2x2s.

7 **Screw in the shelf standards.** Mount the standards on the dividers. Then cut the 2x8 shelves 1/4 in. shorter than the space between the standards and rest them on shelf standard brackets.

Paint before assembly

You'll spend as much time painting as you do building this system. We primed all the lumber with Zinsser Bulls Eye 1-2-3, not only to provide a good base for the paint, but also to keep knots from eventually bleeding through the color coat. Then we rolled on two coats of latex wall paint, eggshell sheen.

A 3-in. roller frame with a 1/2-in.-nap sleeve works very well for all the painting. You can skip the paint tray and dip the sleeve right into the gallon paint can.

We used prefinished white pegboard—no painting needed. If you want to custom-paint unfinished pegboard, rough up the surface with 100-grit sandpaper, then prime and paint it the same way. But use a 1/4-in.-nap roller to ensure thin coats. If you use a thick-nap roller, the peg holes will likely become plugged with paint. It took nearly a full gallon of paint to roll two coats over all the framing members.

Lay out the 2x2 mounting grid

Study **Figure A** to help you digest the following layout directions. Measure from the floor to make a mark at 12 in. (**Photo 1**). Then mea-sure down from the ceiling to the mark and transfer it to the other end of the pegboard wall. (Garage floors are rarely level, but you can usually trust the ceiling.) Snap the bottom line. Measure up from the bottom line 93-1/8 in. to snap the top line. The 2x2s will go below the bottom line and above the top line to give you 96-1/8 in. outside to outside when they're in place.

If your pegboard will butt against a wall, install the 2x10 end frame first and measure from that to establish the 20-ft. 1/4-in. vertical grid line at the other end. (Or make the line to suit the number of bays you wish to have: 4 ft. 1/4 in., 8 ft. 1/4 in., etc.) Then snap horizontal lines spaced about every 2 ft. for the 2x2s that support the pegboard. Lastly, use a 4-ft. level to mark the end of the wall and the center of each stud (**Photo 2**).

Dealing with openings

Our expanse of plywood didn't include any windows, doors or electrical outlets or switches, but yours might. Surround windows with 2x10s just like you did with the perimeter. But beware of doors. Putting a 2x10 on the hinge side of a door means it'll open only 90 degrees. Experiment with the door swing to figure out which placement will work for you. If you have electrical boxes, you're required by code to install box extenders so the outlet or switch will be flush with the pegboard surface.

Sturdy, adjustable shelving

You can buy dedicated pegboard shelving brackets, but we wanted sturdy, adjustable 2x8 shelves, so we mounted 6-ft. shelf standards on most of the 2x8s (**Photo 7**). The 2x8s can span the full bay width without sagging. Unless you spend the time making all the bays exactly the same width, the shelf length will vary from one bay to the next.

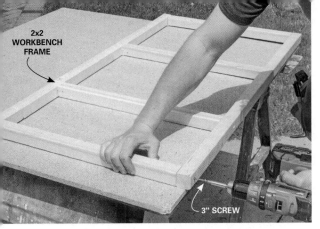

2x2 WORKBENCH FRAME

3" SCREW

8 Assemble the workbench frame. Build a 2x2 framework 24 in. deep and 2 in. narrower than the bay opening you intend to install it in.

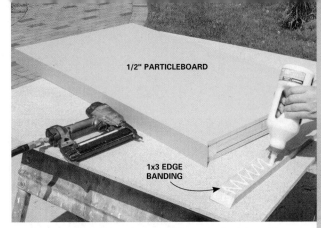

1/2" PARTICLEBOARD

1x3 EDGE BANDING

9 Sheathe the top and bottom. Cover both sides with 1/2-in. particleboard. Use it to square the ladder as you glue and nail it to the 2x2s. Then add 1x3 edge banding to the bench edges.

FOLDING SHELF BRACKET

27" 2x4 HINGE SUPPORT

10 Add the folding shelf brackets. Cut 27-in.-long 2x4 hinge supports and screw them through the pegboard into the 2x2s with 3-in. screws. Then attach the folding shelf brackets with 1-1/2-in. washer-head screws.

11 Attach the top from underneath. Rest the bench on the top, centered between the 2x8 uprights and 1/4 in. away from the pegboard, then screw it to the brackets from underneath with 1-1/2-in. washer-head screws.

Built-in, flip-up workbench

Our bench is 40 in. high and can be folded down into its own bay when you're not using it. The height is based on the pegboard wall base being located 1 ft. above the floor and the how-to steps shown in **Photos 8 – 11.** If you want a different height, you'll have to do some design work. But make sure to allow for a 1-1/2-in. gap between the bottom of the bench and the 2x10 when it's folded down. You'll need that gap for your fingers to safely open and close the bench.

You won't find these special folding shelf brackets in stores. Search online for "KV 16" Folding Shelf Bracket" and you'll find plenty of sources—and varying prices too! We paid about $65 with shipping for both. Make sure you get two. It's easy to misorder and only get one. It happened to us, folks!

Figure B
Flip-up workbench

To build a bench to match this one, you'll need a 4 x 4-ft. sheet of 1/2-in. particleboard, two 8-ft. 2x2s and two 8-ft. 1x3s for trim for the edges.

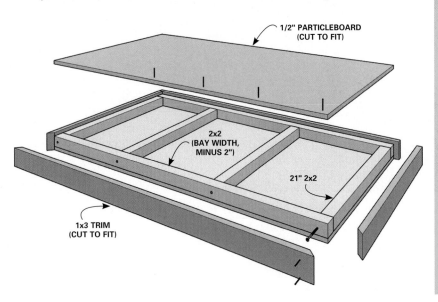

1/2" PARTICLEBOARD (CUT TO FIT)

2x2 (BAY WIDTH, MINUS 2")

21" 2x2

1x3 TRIM (CUT TO FIT)

SMART GARAGE STORAGE

7 great solutions for DIY mechanics

by **Rick Muscoplat, Contributing Editor**

1 **Keep your tools handy with a rolling cart**

In the old days you laid out the tools you needed on a fender pad. Try that on a late-model vehicle with a sloped fender and you'll find your tools on the floor. Buy a rolling cart (U.S. General No. 5107; $45 at harborfreight.com) and keep all your tools at your fingertips.

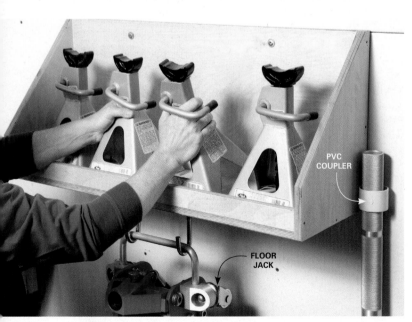

PVC COUPLER

FLOOR JACK

2 **Jack and jack-stand holder**

Haven't you tripped over your jack stands long enough? Build this simple storage rack and get them off the floor. If you have a lightweight floor jack, add mounting hooks under the holder. Screw a 2-in. PVC coupler to the side of the rack and a 2-in. cap on the wall near the floor for the handle.

SLIDING LOCK

3 **Hang 'em high**

Air tools don't come with hooks, they don't nest well in drawers, and on a workbench top they just add to the clutter. So plunk down 20 bucks for this locking air tool holder and your life will be complete. Your tools will be neatly organized on the wall, and you can snap on a padlock to keep them securely in place. The Lisle locking air tool holder (No. 49960) is available at auto parts stores and online.

4 Grab one glove at a time

To keep your box of nitrile gloves handy and make it easier to grab just one glove instead of a handful, add this magnetic glove box holder to your shop. It costs about $20 at auto parts stores. You could even put it on your toolbox or rolling cart and yank out new gloves wherever you need them. You can also find many styles of glove dispensers online.

5 PVC drawer organizers

When you're right in the middle of a project, you don't need to waste time pawing through drawers looking for tools. So use this handy setup to keep your tools neatly arranged in your workbench drawer.

Cut 1- or 2-in. PVC pipe to length. Glue on end caps and slice each pipe in half on a band saw. Screw them to the drawer bottoms and load them up!

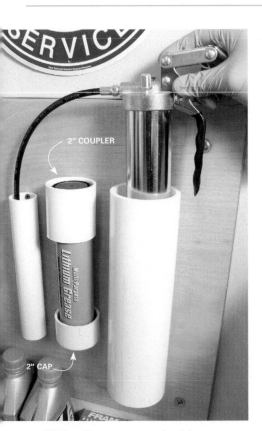

6 Grease gun holder

A grease gun is big and, uh, greasy. But you don't have to get it on your drawers or cabinets. Cut a few sections of 1-in. and 3-in. PVC pipe and screw them to a plywood backer to make this slick grease gun holder. Then attach a 2-in. coupler and cap to hold a backup tube of grease.

7 Sheet metal drawer liners

If you use old kitchen cabinets in your workshop, it's a bad idea to throw oily, greasy tools into those drawers, where the wood soaks up everything. So here's a tip for you:

Instead, take careful measurements of the width, depth and height to any HVAC shop. For about $20 per drawer, you can get a custom liner for each one. The interiors will look like new, and you'll be able to clean them as needed.

INDEX

A

ACQ nails, 79
Aerators, faucet, 136
Air conditioners, 134, 138
Air tool holders, 282
Alarms
    freeze alert, 112–113
    smoke and carbon
        monoxide, 5, 15
Aluminum wiring
    precautions, 5
Anchor bolts, 81
Anti-short bushings, 104
Ants, carpenter, 11
Asbestos, 5, 70–71, 74

B

Baby wipes, 94
Bags, plastic, 72, 139, 231,
    243
Balls, storing, 238
Barn door project, 21–27
Baseboards
    protecting, 96
    replacing heater covers
        for, 12
Basements, fixing wet,
    50–52
Bathroom projects
    medicine cabinet,
        122–128
    subway tile, 28–34
Batteries
    Bluetooth speaker, 110
    smoke detector, 5, 15
    thermostat, 106
    Wi-fi thermostat, 106
Beads, edge and corner, 43
Bench project, 152–157
Benchtop organizer
    project, 189-190
Bits, pattern, 165
Bluetooth wireless
    speakers, 110–111
Boards
    buying, 180–184
    distressing of, 22–26
    preventing warp of, 151
    See also Lumber; Wood

Brushes, purchasing, 20
Buckets, five-gallon, 5, 242
Bumpers, cabinet door, 67
Bungee cords, 237
Bushings, anti-short, 104
Butt joints, 149

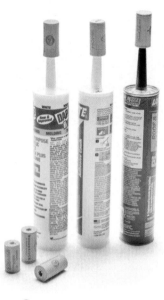

C

Cabinet projects
    benchtop organizer,
        190–191
    medicine cabinet,
        122–128
    under-cabinet drawer,
        35–38
Cabinets, Euro hinges for,
    63–68, 124, 127
Cables
    cutting metal-clad, 103
    fixing charger, 103
    purchasing coaxial, 106
Carabiners, 272
Carbon monoxide, 5, 211
Carburetors, buying, 247
Carpenter ants, 11
Carpeting
    preparing floor for, 60
    vacuuming, 15
Carts
    purchasing rolling, 282
    tool cart project,
        173–179

Caulk
    caddy, 237
    concrete, 211
    radon reduction and, 44
    sealing tubes of, 238
    self-sealing under-
        layment and, 83–84
    toilets and, 136
    wet basements and, 52
Ceilings
    paint mishap, 92
    textured, 5, 69–76
    tile, 120
Cellular PVC, 219–220
Cement, PVC plumbing,
    212
Chairs
    fixing, 196
    patio chair project,
        158–163
Charger cables, fixing, 103
Circuit breakers, resetting,
    100
Clamps, 93, 141, 237, 242
Cleaning work areas, 19
Coaxial cables,
    purchasing, 106
Coffee bag ties, 239
Composite wood, 219, 221
Concrete
    caulking, 211
    pouring, 232–236
    working with bagged,
        141, 228–231
Concrete-forming tubes,
    242
Cords
    extension, 141, 272
    window blind, 5
Corner beads, 43
Cup hinges, 63–68, 124,
    127
Curve tracers, 196
Cutting board project, 203

D

Dadoes, 164–167
Dead bolts, 12, 91

Decks
    board movement on,
        148
    cleaning and
        refinishing, 224
    replacing boards on, 226
    restoration coating, 225
    synthetic decking for,
        226
    tiles and exterior floor
        coverings for, 227
Dehumidifiers, 138
Dog spots, fixing yard, 246
Doors
    hands-free hack for, 244
    reinforcing, 81
    rustic barn door project,
        21–27
    sticking, 10, 151
Doorways, self-sealing
    underlayment and, 84
Downspouts, 50, 52
Drafts, air conditioner, 138
Drain lines, testing,
    135–136
Drawers
    organization for, 283
    tool cart project,
        173–179
    under-cabinet drawer
        project, 35–38
Drills
    bit savers for, 195
    corded vs. cordless, 67,
        208
    drill dock project,
        192–194
    hard soil and, 143
    mixing paint with, 97
Drying compound, 41
Drywall
    backing, 80
    basics, 39–43
    covering ceiling with,
        70
    hacks, 144
    screw guns, 16
    sheets, 40
Duct tape, 98, 233

E

Edge beads, 43
Electrical panel upgrades, 105
Electrical surges, 107–109
Engineered wood, 219, 221
Euro hinges, 63–68, 124, 127
Extension cords, 141, 272

F

Fasteners, drywall, 42
Fiber cement, 219, 222
File cabinets, 121
Fire-proof safes, 121
Fire-resistant drywall, 40
Fires, household, 101
Fire-stop collars, 48
Fire table project, 248–256
Flat pry bars, 144
Floors
    coverings for deck, 227
    primer for, 84
    protecting, 58
    self-leveling
        underlayment, 82–86
Flowerpot saucers, 138, 238
Foam, cutting, 143
Foil duct tape, 98
Foundations, wood, 13
Framing tips, 77–81
Freeze alert systems, 112–113
Furniture sliders, 59

G

Garage projects
    benchtop organizer, 190–191
    dream garage storage, 274–281
    drill dock, 192–194
    tool cart, 173–179
Garden bed project, raised, 266–271
Garment bags, 240
Generators, 210–211
Gift projects
    cutting board and serving tray, 203
    keepsake boxes, 202
    knife rack, 199
    tic-tac-toe board, 203
    tool tote, 198
    two-way serving tray, 200–201
    wine rack, 205–208
Glove dispensers, 283
Glue guns, hot, 185–188
Golf bags, 243
Golf tees, 98
Goofs, 87, 117, 139
Grab bars, 59
Grain, wood, 147
Grease gun holsters, 283
Greenboard, 40
Gutters, 52

H

Hearing protection, 5
Heaters
    covers for baseboard, 12
    space, 101
Hiding places, 118–128
Hinges
    Euro / cup, 63–68, 124, 127
    spring, 15
Hooks
    picture frame, 61
    plumbing, 243
Hose storage, 244
Humidity, high, 151

I

Insulation, vermiculite, 5
Ironing boards, 120

J

Jack stand holders, 282
Jack studs, 79
Jigsaw blades, 143
Joint compound, 41
Joints, wood, 148

K

Keepsake boxes project, 202
Key magnets, 119
Keypads, garage door, 120
Kitchen cabinet hiding places, 121
Kitchen projects
    cutting board, 203
    knife rack, 199
    under-cabinet drawer, 35–38
    wine rack, 205–208
Knockdown textured ceilings, 72

L

Ladders, transporting, 237
Lath, 83
Lawn clipping storage, 273
Lead paint, 5, 22
Leaks
    basement, 50–52
    carpenter ants and, 11
    detecting, 136
    wall, 83
Ledges project, picture, 168–172
Levels, 142
Light fixtures, 102
Lightning, 101, 107
Liquid tape, 106
Lumber
    buying rough-sawn, 180–184
    treated, 269
    See also Boards; Wood

M

Magnets, 119, 197
Mailbox storage, 241
Manometers, 49
Manufactured products, trim, 218–220
Masks, dust, 14
Masonite, 58
Medicine cabinet project, 122–128
Medium-density fiberboard (MDF), 14, 151
Melamine, 53–57
Metal-clad cables, 103
Mirrors, as message board, 62
Miter joints, 148
Mud ladles, 273

N

Nails, ACQ, 79
Nozzles, spray paint, 89–90

O

Organizers
    benchtop organizer project, 189-190
    PVC drawer, 283
Ornament holders, 240
Outlets, 106, 114–116

P

Paint
    bleed, 97
    brushes, 93, 96
    can lids, 96, 98
    mini-rollers, 142
    peeling, 149
    and primer, all-in-one, 92
    spray-, 88–91
    stirrers, 97
    touch-up, 95
Painting tips, 93–98
Password protection, 121
Patio chair project, 158–163
Patio doors, adjusting sticking, 10
Patio planter project, 266–271
Pegboard, 276–277, 279–280
Pet urine, 60, 246
Photo albums, 121
Picture frames, 61
Picture hangers, 189
Picture ledges project, 168–172
Pine boards, distressing, 22–26
Pinecones, picking up, 272
Plumbing
    final checks, 135–137
    pipe pump, 138
Plywood
    cutting, 60, 142
    grades, 60
    veneered, 151
Poly ash, 219, 222
Polyurethane, 20
Pooper scoopers, 272
Popcorn ceiling texture, 71–76
Power tools, factory-reconditioned, 196
Pressure washers, 224
Projects
    barn door, 21–27
    bench, 152–157
    benchtop organizer, 190–191
    cutting board, 203
    drill dock, 192–194
    fire table, 248–256
    garage storage, 274–281
    keepsake boxes, 202
    knife rack, 199
    medicine cabinet, 122–128
    patio chairs, 158–163
    patio planter, 266–271
    picture ledges, 168–172
    pub shed, 257–265
    serving tray, 200–201, 203
    subway tile, 28–34
    tic-tac-toe board, 203
    tool cart, 173–179
    tool tote, 198
    under-cabinet drawer, 35–38
    wine rack, 205–208
PVC
    cellular, 219–220
    drawer organizer, 283
    grease gun holster, 283
    hooks, 244
    plumbing cement, 212
    tool holder, 242

R

Rabbets, 164–165, 167
Racks
    tool, 242
    wheelbarrow, 243
    yard tool, 244
Radon reduction, 44–49
Rags, disposing, 20
Rakes, garden, 141, 229
Refinishing decks, 224
Refrigerator coils, 134
Remodeling
    floor protection during, 58
    layout planning, 62
Respirators, activated carbon, 91
Restoration coatings, deck, 225
Retaining walls, 213–217
Roller trays, paint, 98
Rolling carts
    purchasing, 282
    tool cart project, 173–179
Roofs
    hanging tools on, 141
    safety, 5
Rough-sawn lumber, purchasing, 180–184

S

Safety
    glasses, 5, 54
    hazards, 5
    and working with melamine, 54
Sanding sealers, 19
Sanding trim, 18–19
Sandpaper storage, 191
Saw blades, reciprocating, 195
Sawhorses, cardboard, 197
Saw storage, circular, 195
Screws
    drywall, 42
    extractor for, 12
    masonry, 59
    tricks involving, 59
Security systems, home, 113
Self-leveling underlayment, 82–86
Serving tray projects, 200–201, 203
Setting compound, 41
Shears, lopping, 144
Shed project, 257–265
Sheet metal drawer liners, 283
Shelves
    floating, 118
    melamine, 56–57
    project, 168–172
Showerheads, 137
Shutoff valves, 135
Siding hack, vinyl, 237
Sinks, 135–136
Smoke detectors, 5, 15
Sneakers as hiding place, 119

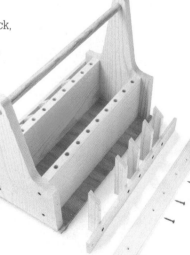

Socket safety, 197
Space heaters, 101
Speakers, Bluetooth
    wireless, 110–111
Spontaneous
    combustion, 5
Spray-painting, 88–91
Spring clamps, 93, 141, 242
Spring hinges, 15
Sprinkler head hiding
    place, 119
Staining trim, 18
Sticker stains on wood,
    182
Stir sticks, 94
Storage tips
    garage, 282–283
    spring, 241–244
    under-sink, 240
    workshop, 189-195
Storm windows, 212
Stretch wrap, 240
Stud sticks, 144
Subway tile, installing,
    28–34
Surge protection devices
    (SPD), 102, 107–109

T

Tabletops, wood, 149
Tape
    drywall, 42
    foil duct, 98
    liquid, 106
    self-sealing, 97
    tearing tricks, 61
Tape measure hangers,
    191
Tennis ball hideaway, 119
Textured ceilings
    covering, 69–71
    removing, 71–76
Thermostats, 106, 113
Tic-tac-toe board project,
    203
Tie-down straps, 141
Tile
    deck, 227
    installing subway,
    28–34
Tissue box holders, hiding
    place, 120
Toilets
    checking for leaks, 136
    fill valves and, 137

joists and, 81
    mishaps involving, 139
    quieting noisy, 130
    shopping for, 132–133
Tongue-in-groove planks,
    71, 150
Toolbelt tricks, 60
Tool organization projects
    tool cart, 173–179
    tool tote, 198
Tools
    bucket for, 242
    factory-reconditioned
    power, 196
    hacks, 140–144
    racks for, 242, 244
Topcoats, 20
Towel bars, magnetic, 138
Treated lumber, 269
Trim
    dry-brushing, 18
    finishing, 17–20
    MDF, 14
    painting, 95
    protecting, 96
    sanding and staining,
    18
Trimmers, 79
Type X drywall, 40

U

Under-cabinet drawer
    project, 35–38
Urine, pet, 60, 246
USB outlets, 114–116
Utilities, buried, 5

V

Vacuuming
    carpet, 15
    mishap, 87
    radon reduction and, 47
    refrigerator coils, 134
    before remodel, 58
    sawdust, 197
Varnish, 20
Veneered plywood, 151
Vinyl siding hack, 237
Vision protection, 5

W

Wall tile project, 28–34
Warping boards, 151
Wasps, 247
Water
    from dehumidifiers, 138
    heaters, 134
    for lawns, 246
    main valves, 139
    softeners, 130–131
Wet basements, fixing,
    50–52
Wet saw hacks, 61
Wheelbarrow racks, 243
Wi-Fi thermostats, 113
Wills, 119
Windows
    and cord blinds, 5
    storm, 212
Wine corks, 238
Wine racks
    project, 205–208
    as towel holder, 238
Wireless speakers,
    Bluetooth, 110–111
Wires
    connectors for, 102, 104
    masonry screws and, 59
Wood
    acclimating, 149
    composite, 219, 221
    engineered, 219, 221
    floors, 148, 151
    foundations, 13
    manufactured, 150,
    218–219
    movement, 146–151
    problems with using,
    218–219
    stoves, 101
    tongue-in-groove, 71,
    150
    See also Boards;
    Lumber
Workbench, flip-up,
    276–277, 281
Workshop storage hints,
    189

ACKNOWLEDGMENTS

FOR THE FAMILY HANDYMAN

Editor-in-Chief	Gary Wentz
Senior Editors	Travis Larson
	Mark Petersen
Associate Editors	Mary Flanagan
	Jeff Gorton
	Brad Holden
	Jason White
Managing Editor	Donna Bierbach
Art Director	Vern Johnson
Senior Designer	Marcia Roepke
Graphic Designer	Mariah Cates
Photographer	Tom Fenenga
Production Artist	Mary Schwender
Lead Carpenter	Josh Risberg
Editorial Services Associate	Peggy McDermott
Production Manager	Leslie Kogan

CONTRIBUTING EDITORS

Tom Caspar	David Munkittrick
Rick Muscoplat	David Radtke

CONTRIBUTING PHOTOGRAPHERS

Paul Nelson	Bill Zuehlke

ILLUSTRATORS

Steve Björkman	Mario Ferro
Jeff Gorton	Susan Jessen
David Radtke	Frank Rohrbach III

OTHER CONSULTANTS

Al Hildenbrand, electrical
Rune Eriksen, electrical
Tim Johnson, electrical
John Williamson, electrical
Les Zell, plumbing

For information about advertising in
The Family Handyman magazine, call (646) 518-4215

To subscribe to *The Family Handyman* magazine:
- By Internet: familyhandyman.com/customercare
- By email: customercare@familyhandyman.com
- By mail: The Family Handyman
  Customer Care
  P.O. Box 6099
  Harlan, IA 51593-1599

We welcome your ideas and opinions.
Write: The Editor, The Family Handyman
2915 Commers Drive, Suite 700
Eagan, MN 55121
Fax: (651) 994-2250
E-mail: feedback@familyhandyman.com